ÍNDICE

ARTÍCULOS

Verbal Aspect and Process Types in Ancient Greek from a Systemic Functional Linguistic Standpoint (Part Two)

STANLEY E. PORTER

This paper, the second of two parts, addresses further the question of process types in Systemic Functional Linguistics (SFL) as they relate to aspectually prominent languages, in particular the ancient Greek of the New Testament. Part one called the use of process types into question for aspectual languages and suggested a reformulation based upon grammatical/morphological verbal aspect. This paper provides further information on how to think of aspect instead of process types and provides examples to demonstrate how such a reformulation would work with the text of the New Testament.

Keywords: verbal aspect, process types, Greek New Testament, Systemic Functional Linguistics

Introduction

Part one of this paper examined M. A. K. Halliday's process types. These are widely accepted and used in Systemic Functional Linguistics (SFL) as the basis of describing functions of verbs (processes) in the transitivity system. The transitivity system is the heart of SFL's description of the ideational metafunction, that is, the function concerned with the "what" or subject matter of a text. In that first paper, I found that these process types are probably not serving the function for which they were developed, even in description of the English language, to say nothing of ancient and in particular New Testament Greek.[1] There are significant and readily apparent flaws in a variety of approaches, because they try to typify actions based upon lexical meanings, starting with Zeno Vendler and continuing through to Halliday and others (see below for references). This approach to verbal action may still have a place within description of the English language (I leave it to others to decide, although I am not

[1] See Stanley E. Porter, "Verbal Aspect and Process Types in Ancient Greek from a Systemic Functional Linguistic Standpoint (Part One)," *FilNeot* 36 (2023) 31-63. One major correction I need to make in that paper is to change "mental" to "material" on p. 36 paragraph two line one. This is correctly stated and developed on p. 52.

optimistic), but it seems unsatisfactory for an aspectual language such as Greek.

The Greek verbal system, and hence the transitivity system, is best conceived along different lines. Rather than examining lexical meaning as an attempt to describe verbal action, which is what Halliday and those who have used similar schemes have done, a better description of the language is provided by the morphologically based aspectual system. The aspectuality system is a system network (system networks are means of graphically displaying the meaning potential [choices] within the language) that reflects how users of the language choose to conceptualize a process that is then, in conjunction with the causality system, configured within the clause as part of the transitivity system and hence the ideational metafunction. This provides a suitable parallel to the attitude system (Halliday's mood system) as a correlate system within its own respective metafunction (the interpersonal, concerned with the question of who or relations of participants). More than that, use of verbal aspect rather than process types provides a systemic means of displaying semantic choice. There is the final benefit that such a systemic configuration fulfills the expressed original purpose of what appears to have been meant by the SFL notion of lexis as most delicate grammar to provide a means by which the lexicogrammar leads to its greatest delicacy in the choice of lexical items. The initial conclusions of this preliminary study indicate that this modeling of the Greek transitivity system without process types but with morphological/grammatical aspect provides the means for speaking in systemic ways about transitivity in the Greek of the New Testament. As stated at the end of part one of this article, I now demonstrate how this perspective would be realized in the Greek New Testament by examination of examples.

Reconfiguring Verbal Aspect Instead of Process Types

In his chapter on clause as representation, concerned with the experiential metafunction (as part of the ideational metafunction, here distinguishing the experiential from the logical), Halliday points out that the three metafunctions are united in the clause, with each having its own function. Halliday states that "experientially, the clause construes a quantum of change in the flow of events as a *figure*, or configuration of a process," along with participants and circumstances.[2] The major

[2] M. A. K. Halliday, *Halliday's Introduction to Functional Grammar* (IFG4), 4th ed., rev. Christian M. I. M. Matthiessen (London: Routledge, 2014), 212 (bold original). For Halliday the notion of "figure," which he several times defines as a configuration of process,

question—one that I raised in part one of this article—is *how* this process is configured. For Halliday, this configuration is by means of "one of a small number of different process types in the experiential grammar of the clause."[3] Halliday equates the process types and the limited number of choices (apparently a closed system) with the similar limited number of choices of mood.[4] However, as previously indicated, Halliday's equation does not work in his model, since his discussion of process types begins with lexical differentiations, not grammatical ones, as does his mood and modality system. This can be remedied by discussion of the process being grammaticalized rather than lexicalized, such as is the case with verbal aspect. Halliday devotes a major section of his introduction to functional grammar (fourth edition) to the discussion of process types, nearly one-hundred pages when one includes his treatment of their relationship to participants and circumstances, arguably the single largest subject of discussion in the entire, large book.[5] The definition and use of process types is clearly of importance to Halliday and to SFL as it has developed. As a result, he provides an initial justification and definition of process types.

For Halliday, process types represent a fundamental feature of the grammar of English. He describes the basis for process types as capturing the "flow of events" and segmenting them into units by means of clausal grammar. His process types—which we have already discussed in the previous part one—are differentiated lexically, not grammatically or even systemically. They are related to the process as it transpires in time (a temporal view of the verbal system of English).[6] This may be an adequate description of English (I have my doubts, as I have expressed in part one, especially with emphasis upon lexis in the description of processes, but I am not concerned with that here), but it is clearly inadequate for

participants, and circumstances (Halliday, IFG4, 44; cf. also 30), is "congruently realized by the clause" (Christian M. I. M. Matthiessen, Kazuhiro Teruya, and Marvin Lam, *Key Terms in Systemic Functional Linguistics* [London: Continuum, 2010], 97). I am focusing upon one component of this figure, the process, although other elements must enter into the discussion.

[3] Halliday, IFG4, 213.

[4] As I pointed out in part one of this article, I find Halliday's treatment of the mood/modality system inadequate for Greek. His system of mood is developed for English, and even then within some unnecessary restrictions. See Stanley E. Porter, "Systemic Functional Linguistics and the Greek Language: The Need for Further Modeling," in *Modeling Biblical Language: Selected Papers from the McMaster Divinity College Linguistics Circle*, ed. Stanley E. Porter, Gregory P. Fewster, and Christopher D. Land, LBS 13 (Leiden: Brill, 2016), 9–47. My result is that there is a significantly larger number of choices realized in the Greek attitude system based upon clause types.

[5] Halliday, IFG4, 211–310.

[6] Halliday, IFG4, 213 (bold original).

Greek, an aspectual rather than a temporal language.[7] For an aspectual language, one must use the aspectual system, a morphologically-based grammatical system that is realized in individual lexical items, not one that begins with such items (as does Halliday). Nevertheless, in light of my previous argument against lexically-based process types—whether Zeno Vendler, Beth Levin, or Halliday and his followers[8]—and the admitted weaknesses in SFL's conceptualization of aspect (and tense, for that matter),[9] I believe that what Halliday says about process types can and must be re-stated, not in terms of these process types but in terms of verbal aspect. I attempt to do that in this article.

[7] I have clearly expressed elsewhere my opinion on Greek being a non-temporal language. See, among others, Stanley E. Porter, *Linguistic Analysis of the Greek New Testament: Studies in Tools, Methods, and Practice* (Grand Rapids: Baker, 2015), 175–91. Even those who maintain that Greek is temporal generally only argue this for the indicative mood. Even if this is the case, and I do not believe that it is, temporality is clearly secondary to aspectuality, which is a semantic feature across the entire verbal system, with both indicative and non-indicative verbs including participles and infinitives being aspectual. Only a small group of aspectually vague verbs, and the future form, are not fully aspectual. See Stanley E. Porter, *Verbal Aspect in the Greek of the New Testament, with Reference to Tense and Mood*, SBG 1 (New York: Peter Lang, 1989), 403–39 and 442–47.

[8] For example, see Zeno Vendler, "Verbs and Time," *Philosophical Review* 66 (1957) 143–60; repr. in Vendler, *Linguistics in Philosophy* (Ithaca, NY: Cornell University Press, 1967), 97–121; Beth Levin, *English Verb Classes and Variations* (Chicago: University of Chicago Press, 1993); and Halliday, IFG4, noted above. Two New Testament Greek scholars who make use of Vendler's scheme, although to varying degrees, are Buist M. Fanning, *Verbal Aspect in New Testament Greek* (Oxford: Clarendon, 1990), 43–45 and 127–63; and Mari Jean Broman Olsen, *A Semantic and Pragmatic Model of Lexical and Grammatical Aspect* (PhD diss., Northwestern University, 1994; New York: Garland, 1997), 13 and elsewhere; cf. also but without reference to Vendler, Juan Mateos, *El Aspecto Verbal en el Nuevo Testamento* (Madrid: Ediciones Cristiandad, 1977), 20–22. For a thorough critique of Vendler, see Francis G. H. Pang, *Revisiting Aspect and Aktionsart: A Corpus Approach to Koine Greek Event Typology*, LBS 14 (Leiden: Brill, 2016), esp. 31–34, 57–62, and 92–112; and in shorter form in Pang, "*Aktionsart* as Epiphenomenon: A Stratal Approach to Process Typologies," in *Greeks, Jews, and Christians: Historical, Religious and Philological Studies in Honor of Jesús Peláez del Rosal*, ed. Lautaro Roig Lanzillotta and Israel Muñoz Gallarte, Estudios de Filología Neotestamentaria 10 (Córdoba: Ediciones El Almendro, 2013), 449–74; and Pang, "Aspect and *Aktionsart* Once Again," in *Modeling Biblical Language*, ed. Porter et al., 48–72. For use of Levin in New Testament studies, see Olsen, *Semantic and Pragmatic Model*, 195–200 (Levin was Olson's doctoral supervisor), and in SFL, see Christian M. I. M. Matthiessen, "Frequency Profiles of Some Basic Grammatical Systems: An Interim Report," in *System and Corpus: Exploring Connections*, ed. Geoff Thompson and Susan Hunston (London: Equinox, 2006), 103–42; Halliday, IFG4, bibliography; Matthiessen, "Extending the Description of Process Type within the System of Transitivity in Delicacy based on Levinian Verb Classes," *Functions of Language* 21 (2014) 139–75. I am not aware of another similar critique of Levin in New Testament studies than my own.

[9] See Carl Bache, *English Tense and Aspect in Halliday's Systemic Functional Grammar: A Critical Appraisal and an Alternative* (London: Equinox, 2008).

Before I do so and exemplify the results, allow me to include two sets of further comments, one on process types and then one on participant roles. These are not essential to my argument but help to establish the context in which such a discussion must occur. In part one of this article, I note many problems with process types, including their basis, determinations, definitions, systemic grounding, and utilization, especially in relation to participant roles. One further factor to consider that I introduced but did not previously develop more fully is Halliday's exposition of process types in relation to each other. Halliday contends that the material and relational processes constitute the most frequent according to his corpus analysis, along with a distant third, mental. However, he also notes three other process types that he places at the boundaries of the initial three, thus forming what I depict below as a triangle, even though Halliday represents it as a wheel or complex circle.[10] I choose to represent it in the following way for the sake of examination.

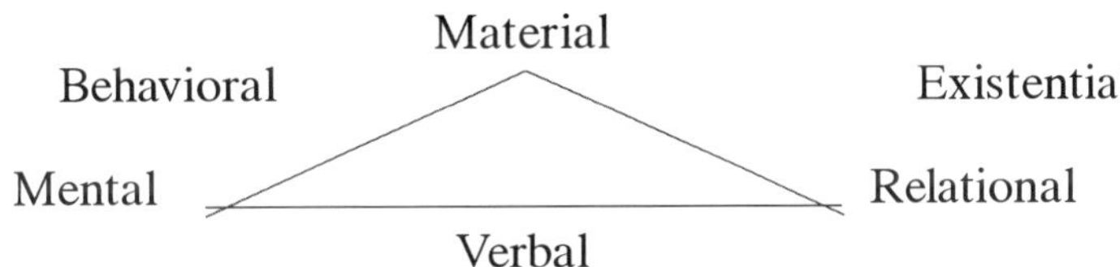

Figure 1. Process types arranged in relation to each other

The implications of this figure are that process types are both not entirely separate since they are related to others but also distinct in being situated either at the vertex or between others. Once one examines these relationships, however, one wonders about their configuration and whether such relationships are forced and even ad hoc. Whatever one thinks of process types, the justification for such relations demands further explanation. For example, Halliday places the existential process type between material and relational processes and thereby forges a relationship among them, in which existential is said in some way to mediate the other two. Material is concerned with processes such as creating and changing, while relational is concerned with identity, while existential with existing. One might argue that relational is the common element between the other two, rather than the existential, since the relational has a relation to material being not necessarily found in the existential. The mental process type is directly equated by Halliday with feeling, which seems to be thoroughly misconceived and mis-defined, as feeling is not

[10] Halliday, IFG4, 215.

mental but emotional, while mental concerns a variety of processes based in thinking. Thinking and feeling, therefore, should not be arranged on the Hallidayan process circle as next to each other, since they are not contiguous but arguably conceptual opposites. Similar comments can be made about the entire diagram.

More importantly, if we were to imagine the frequency of appearance of these various process types, we would imagine that material, mental, and relational would predominate, probably in roughly equal proportions, since they are the major types according to Halliday (certainly material and relational). However, the situation gets more complex, based upon Halliday's corpus of process types. First, mental process types are significantly fewer than material and relational, in fact, only slightly more frequent than verbal processes, which are much higher (to a factor of two and four) than behavioral and then existential process types. Based on Halliday's bar graph of his sample texts (and my extrapolation), the following percentages of process types are represented in his corpus of examples:[11]

Material processes	40%
Relational processes	36%
Mental processes	9%
Verbal processes	8%
Behavioral processes	4%
Existential processes	2%

Table 1. Halliday's percentages of process types

If I read correctly the graph that Halliday provides, over 75% of all processes are of only two types, material and relational. Two others appear similarly but in greatly reduced numbers (mental and verbal processes), and the final two (behavioral and existential processes) in somewhat similar and even more greatly reduced numbers. In other words, there is little in the corpus evidence to support from a probabilistic standpoint the kind of conceptual description that Halliday provides for the process types. I cannot see that a circle (or perhaps even a triangle) is the best way to represent their conceptual relationship. Rather than there being two sets of three process types, as Halliday wishes to describe them, instead one finds that Halliday's corpus statistics indicate that there are three sets of two process types each, with the first two disproportionately more highly represented and the final two greatly underrepresented. It seems

[11] Halliday, IFG4, 215.

to me that these statistics indicate the need to reconceptualize process types, certainly in English, with a reconfiguration of their relationships to each other at the least. I am not sure what geometrical figure might be appropriate to represent these process types and their relations. One might well argue that, on the one hand, the tool is too fine-grained with categories that only represent very small percentages of the instances, but, on the other hand, not granular enough if three-quarters of the instances fall in only two categories. It is no wonder that Halliday and Hasan had trouble systemizing the process types and conceiving of them in other than lexical terms. The result is that such process types provide little confidence for use in English, to say nothing of how they might be used in Greek.

The use of process types in study of New Testament Greek is not widespread. In fact, it is arguably only recently that some scholars have drawn upon process types from SFL in their descriptions of Greek. Therefore, the number of works to consult regarding Greek is still relatively small and still in its infancy in use of such process types. Nevertheless, a similar situation as has been described above is found in what is arguably one of the best uses of Hallidayan process types in New Testament studies. This monograph is not primarily a study of process types, but a study of three passages in Acts using linguistic stylistic analysis, in which process types are a part of the discussion of the ideational metafunction. According to the identification of the process types by the author, here are the percentages of the Hallidayan process types for the three passages in Acts that form the basis of that monograph:[12]

Material processes	52%
Verbal processes	20%
Mental processes	12%
Relational processes	8%
Behavioral processes	5%
Existential processes	2%

Table 2. Percentages of process types in Acts

[12] Zachary K. Dawson, *The Message of the Jerusalem Council in the Acts of the Apostles: A Linguistic Stylistic Analysis*, LBS 22 (Leiden: Brill, 2022), who studies these three passages in Acts: Acts 10:1–11:18; 15:1–29; and 21:17–25. The figures are my own, compiled from the appendixes that Dawson provides. The author presents detailed transitivity structure analyses of these three passages that are a model of this type of analysis. The appended transitivity structure charts provide much more information than just process types. My use of this work is in no way a criticism of the fine and convincing scholarship found in this book that has introduced many new and challenging methodological and textual findings for other scholars to consider.

For the vast majority of the identifications of process types, I would agree with the categories used in the monograph, although on the basis of what I have said above regarding process types there is always room for discussion. However, large-scale agreement would be expected since 40% of instances in Halliday's sample group are material, and when combined with relational are 76%. Nevertheless, these results raise some very interesting questions in and of themselves. I realize that Halliday's sample is itself relatively small (8425 instances) and that the Acts monograph's is even smaller (204 instances). One difference is that the percentages and their relationships have changed. Material and relational processes constituted 76% of Halliday's instances. In the small sample from Acts, material and relational processes are only 60%, even though material processes have grown from 40% to 52%, over half of all the process types. This raises a question regarding both identification of material process types and the value of such analysis with such overwhelming statistics. It is not just that the material processes are large, but that the others, as a whole, have decreased. One cannot speak of there being two or three prominent process types in the Acts sample, but only one prominent process type, the material. The next most frequent process type, verbal processes, is only 20%, less than half of the material processes. This is fourth on Halliday's frequency list, but not one of his major three process types. A further difference is that the verbal and relational processes have switched places, with relational moving from Halliday's second place to the Acts monograph's fourth place, but with similar percentages for the process in the fourth position. The mental process type is still the third most frequent, but less frequent than the first two as already noted above. The bottom three process categories, even though they are slightly different, are about equally represented. I am not sure what can be made of these last three results, since they are reasonably infrequently found within the corpus. Much more research needs to be done on both English and Greek. However, I suspect that this indicates that differences in register or genre may have something to do with the differing results, although how the categories are interpreted may also be a major factor. In particular, I think the question of how one identifies a material process, and even more importantly whether this is an appropriate category in light of its pervasive usage, may be an issue for both English and Greek studies. The representation of the other processes both numerically and relationally to the others is also an object of concern. To summarize, it would appear that at least in this instance there is rough parity with Halliday's conception of process types. But with this parity seems to come the similar problems that we have identified previously.

I turn now to participant roles, a topic that requires much further discussion that I cannot give to it here. Halliday's participant roles also are a source of possible confusion. Halliday includes them in his figure, which consists of processes, participants, and circumstances. However, Halliday's participant roles are different from participants. The participant roles are determined by his process types, not by the participants.

Process Type	*Category*	*Participants (directly involved)*	*Participants (indirectly involved)*
Material	Events/actions	Actor/goal	Recipient/client, scope/initiator
Behavioural	Behaving	Behaver	Behaviour
Mental	Sensing	Senser/phenomenon	Inducer
Verbal	Saying	Sayer/target	Receiver, verbiage
Relational	Being	Carrier/attribute, identified/identifier, token/value	Attributor, beneficiary Assigner Assigner
Existential	Existing	Existent	

Table 3. Process types and participant roles[13]

Thus, as I noted in part one of this article, a material process establishes participant roles as actor/goal for those directly involved and recipient/client or scope/initiator for those indirectly involved. A similar configuration can be given for all six of the process types, as table 3 indicates. In other words, in Halliday's scheme, the participant roles are dictated by identification of the process type. The participant roles are not based upon their own system or conceived independently of the process types. If the process types are called into question (as I believe that I have done), then the participant roles are also, as I have also shown. This means that participant roles must be established by other means, and I would contend that they need to be reconceived by other than lexical means, the basis of Halliday's process types.

Instead of lexical meaning, in a systemic grammar one must turn to a systemic network for describing the meaning potential. Indication of participant roles is the function that causality plays, at least in part, within the transitivity system in Greek. The CAUSALITY system, which also contains the ERGATIVITY system, is systemically displayed as follows in its relationship to the ASPECTUALITY system:[14]

[13] Halliday, IFG4, 311, adapted.

[14] Ergativity in the Greek causality system was first suggested in Stanley E. Porter and Matthew Brook O'Donnell, "The Greek Verbal Network Viewed from a Probabilistic

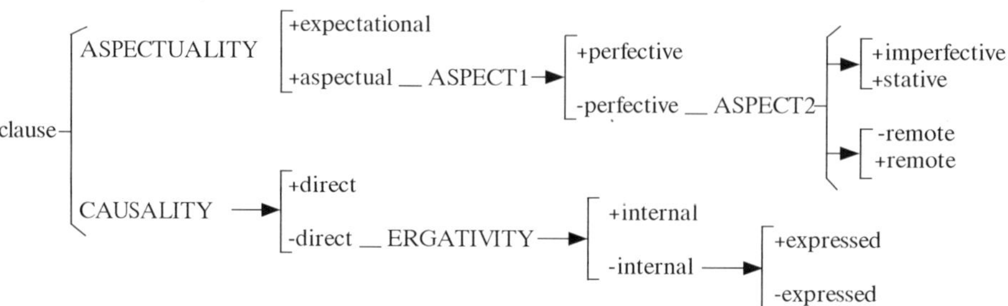

Figure 2. Transitivity in the Greek of the New Testament

I include more comments here than I did in part one so as to exemplify the causality system more fully. The participant roles are those of either [+direct] or [-direct] agency determined by the voice-form of the verb (with the Greek causality system and set of voice-forms synthetically, that is, morphologically and paradigmatically, determined within the voice system, rather than by means of analytic forms as in English, such as *was played*). [+direct] agency is realized by the active voice form, and [-direct] agency by the non-active or, better, ERGATIVITY system. These include the choice of [+internal] or [-internal] agency. [+internal] agency is realized by the middle voice form and [-internal] agency by the passive voice form, and this can be either [±expressed]. The ASPECTUALITY and CAUSALITY systems are—apart from a very small number of aspectually and causally vague verbs—simultaneous systems in the Greek verbal network and the major systems within Greek transitivity. It is this relationship of ASPECTUALITY and CAUSALITY that determines the nature of the process and the participant role. As an example, in Mark 1:2, γέγραπται realizes stative aspect and passive causality. Even though the verbal form is medio-passive, in this configuration there is expressed agency by means of the circumstantial adjunct ἐν τῷ Ἠσαΐᾳ τῷ προφήτῃ.

Some may object that this construal of participant roles is of a different type than that suggested by Halliday. Indeed they are different, and for a reason. Halliday's participant roles resemble those found in various case-based grammars where semantic roles are identified. These are referred to by different terminology, depending upon the grammati-

Standpoint: An Exercise in Hallidayan Linguistics," *FilNeot* 14 (2001) 3–41. See now also David L. Mathewson, *Voice and Mood: A Linguistic Approach*, Essentials of Biblical Greek Grammar (Grand Rapids: Baker, 2021), 56–72; and Stanley E. Porter, *The Pastoral Epistles: A Commentary on the Greek Text* (Grand Rapids: Baker, 2023), 11–12.

cal model, including valency, argument structure, and even theta roles.[15] They are an attempt to identify semantic roles played by what Halliday calls participants (others identify them with other terms) within the clause. Identification of such roles may have a major function to play in languages without robust morphologically-based case systems. Greek however has such a system. The question arises as to the relationship between grammatical case and semantic case. Cases developed in languages to represent semantic functions. I believe that there are strong indications that the grammatical cases in Greek retain semantic functions, and are used at the different ranks to do so. Halliday differentiates the interpersonal functions from the ideational functions, but I do not believe that that is necessary or wise for Greek. One clausal scheme is sufficient that combines the two around the basic clause components. Thus, the subject of an active voice verb reflects [+direct] agency as its primary semantic function and participant role, with the complement reflecting a different function as focus or recipient of the process, etc., determined by case, so that complements take different roles depending upon the case (case functions within the nominal group as well in a similar although differentiated way).[16] The subject of a middle voice verb reflects [-direct: +internal] agency, while the subject of a passive voice verb reflects [-direct: -internal] agency. There has been much discussion about the role of the subject in linguistics.[17] The grammatical subject, whether fully grammaticalized or implied, has an important role to play in causality as the exponent of the agency function, whether that is direct or indirect and internal or not. Greek seems to maintain this system for its participant roles.

[15] There are wide varieties of views on case. See Barry J. Blake, *Case*, Cambridge Textbooks in Linguistics (Cambridge: Cambridge University Press, 1994); Miriam Butt, *Theories of Case*, Cambridge Textbooks in Linguistics (Cambridge: Cambridge University Press, 2006); and some of the articles in Andrej Malchukov and Andrew Spencer, eds., *The Oxford Handbook of Case* (Oxford: Oxford University Press, 2009). I have explored the topic in relation to New Testament Greek in Stanley E. Porter, “The Case for Case Revisited,” *Jian Dao* 6 (1996) 13–28.

[16] On the Greek case system, see Stanley E. Porter, *Idioms of the Greek New Testament*, 2nd ed. (Sheffield: Sheffield Academic, 1994), 80–100, following J. P. Louw, “Linguistic Theory and the Greek Case System,” *Acta Classica* 9 (1966) 73–88. On the nominal group, see Porter, *Pastoral Epistles*, 14–15. On the use of cases within the nominal group, see Stanley E. Porter and Christopher D. Land, “The Ancient Greek Nominal Group, with Attention to the Greek New Testament,” *Word* 68 (1; 2022) 1–44.

[17] See, for example, F. R. Palmer, *Grammatical Roles and Relations*, Cambridge Textbooks in Linguistics (Cambridge: Cambridge University Press, 1994), for discussion of the issues. From a different angle, see some of the papers in Karl Simms, ed., *Language and the Subject*, Critical Studies (Amsterdam: Rodopi, 1997). The question of the subject and agency has been an important one in philosophy from the time of Plato and Aristotle to the present. The subject and agency have tended to be demoted in postmodern thought. For an assessment of such views, see Paul Smith, *Discerning the Subject*, Theory and History of Literature 55 (Minneapolis: University of Minnesota Press, 1988).

In light of these considerations, Halliday's justification and defense of process types offered above, if reconfigured appropriately in relationship to verbal aspect, applies equally well to verbal aspect (paraphrasing Halliday but with aspect in mind):[18] One's encounter with experience is that it is constituted by a flow or sequence of events or things that occur. This is how life is encountered and in response must be represented. This succession of events is divided into units of such events or changes by the grammar of the language through the clause. Each unit of such occurrences is construed as a figure, that is, a configuration of a process, participants, and circumstances. ASPECTUALITY, as a system within transitivity, is the grammatical category used in Greek to represent processes, while CAUSALITY is used to express participant roles. Rather than process types determining participant roles in Greek, these are two independent but simultaneous verbal systems within the transitivity system. The verbal aspects represent these events as perfective, imperfective, and stative, with sub-categories of imperfective/remote and stative/remote.[19] The imperfective and stative also have what might be called derived or minor aspects related to them (realized by the imperfect tense-form and the pluperfect tense-form). On the one hand, this configuration of the verbal aspects resembles the circular (or triangular) way that Halliday characterizes his process types, with three major ones and three minor ones. Greek has three verbal aspects, with two of them having the greatest frequency of usage, the perfective and imperfective, and the third, the stative, a distant third.[20] On the other hand, this configuration in some ways may serve as a useful corrective to Halliday's discussion of process types, because the Greek aspectual system, although it is tripartite, has two aspects that appear much more frequently than the third does. The perfective aspect (realized by the aorist tense-form) and the imperfective aspect (including present and imperfect tense-forms) occur around 11,650 and 10,775 times in the Greek New Testament (taking forms of εἰμί and other aspectually vague forms out of the equation, as they must be). The third, the stative aspect (realized by the perfect and pluperfect tense-forms), occurs around 1660 times. The future form occurs 1630 times and the imperfect around 1250 times (without forms of εἰμί and other aspectually vague verbs). The pluperfect occurs 86 times. The total number of verbs is approximately 25,705, used for these calculations. The

[18] Halliday, IFG4, 213, for what follows.

[19] One must also consider aspectually vague verbs, including the non-aspectual future form, as mentioned above. See Porter, *Verbal Aspect*, 403–39 and 442–47.

[20] My counts of the verbal forms may not be entirely accurate due to having to sift out forms of aspectually vague verbs in the imperfective aspectual category since available software does not reflect these categories. Nevertheless, the rough percentages should be accurate enough for this exercise.

statistical results indicate an arrangement in some ways like Halliday's process types, with two groups, the first with three members (perfective, imperfective, and stative aspects), and the second with three members (future form, imperfect form, and pluperfect form). Their relationships are also somewhat similar, in that the imperfect form grammaticalizes imperfective aspect and is thus closely related to the present tense-form that represents most instances within the imperfective aspect category; and in that the pluperfect is similarly positioned in relation to the perfect tense-form that represents the majority of instances within the stative aspect category. These results may be displayed in this way:

Perfective aspect	45%
Imperfective aspect (counting imperfect forms)	42%
Stative aspect (counting pluperfect forms)	6%
Future form	6%
Imperfect form	5%
Pluperfect form	.3%

Table 4. Percentages of verbal aspects and related tense-forms in New Testament Greek

The percentages of representation are higher for the perfective and imperfective, with 45% and 42% respectively, and thus represent about 87% of all the verbs in the New Testament. These results are somewhat higher than the two most frequent processes in Halliday's sample (and the corpus is about three times larger in size). In both the tripartite Hallidayan process types and aspectual systems, the third element is significantly less in frequency. The aspectual system, however, has some peculiarities that are not like the process types, in that two of the categories—the imperfect and pluperfect tense-forms—are subsumed in larger categories, even if they are broken out to indicate their own category, rather than being placed between or adjacent to other process types (although adjacency and subsumption may be similar, based on the Hallidayan circle of process types). There is a roughly similar representation of aspects in the last three categories that is commensurate with Halliday's process types.

Both Halliday's own statistics and those of the Greek verbal system seem to indicate that, while the aspectual and process systems may be tripartite, the percentages are similar but not commensurate. Nevertheless, as we have seen in both part one and now part two of this article, the process within a clause performs a valuable function within the grammar, parallel to that of the mood system as a grammatically based system, each within its respective metafunction. The ASPECTUALITY and CAUSALITY systems are both grammatically rather than lexically motivated in my construal of Greek and their purpose is that of "imposing linguistic order on our experience of the endless variation and flow of events." This is reflected in the transitivity system, which construes the change in events that occurs as what Halliday calls a figure—"as a configuration of elements centred on a process" at clause level.[21] These processes, rather than being construed by a set of Hallidayan process types, are construed by a set of verbal aspects.[22] As I wish to emphasize, but shifting Halliday's emphasis, each verbal aspect "constitutes a distinct model or scheme for construing a particular domain of experience as a figure of a particular kind."[23]

With this reconfiguration in mind, summarizing and augmenting my argument from part one, I now turn to some examples of use of verbal aspect and processes.

Examples of Verbal Aspect in Greek Transitivity

There are a few treatments of process types in descriptions of the Greek New Testament. These studies are to be commended for their use of SFL and their attempt to utilize them within the transitivity system. However, as seen in the comments made above, as well as in part one of this paper, I believe that verbal aspect should replace process types as a descriptive mechanism within the transitivity system for several good and sustainable reasons. In this section, I was at first tempted to do my own study of a text to illustrate the use of verbal aspect as a means of describing processes. Such a study might be beneficial. However, instead, I wish to introduce one recent work that, instead of drawing upon Hallidayan process types in its description of New Testament Greek, utilizes verbal aspect and provides a rationale for such usage. This is found in the recent monograph on Galatians by David I. Yoon.[24] I will first summarize Yoon's argument for the use of verbal aspect, then discuss some of the examples that he provides, and finally offer some further analysis to show how aspect provides a semantically robust means of textual description for an aspectual language.

[21] Halliday, IFG4, 213.
[22] Halliday, IFG4, 213.
[23] Halliday, IFG4, 213.
[24] David I. Yoon, *A Discourse Analysis of Galatians and the New Perspective on Paul*, LBS 17 (Leiden: Brill, 2019).

Summary of Yoon's Rationale

Yoon places his discussion of process types and verbal aspect within his treatment of the transitivity network as one of two components within the field of discourse (the other being lexis). After an appropriate outline of Halliday's view of process types, Yoon rightly recognizes problems that have been raised regarding the difficulty of defining the ideational metafunction and he proposes a way forward in his own method.[25] One of these is to eliminate discussion of process types (for Greek and for English). He argues for this on three grounds: (1) the use of process types requires too many fine distinctions to be drawn between them; (2) the differing process types require too many different participant roles be identified; and (3), most importantly, individual process types can be identified with too many process categories. He offers the example of the verb *grasp*, which may be mental, as in *I grasped the concept*, or material, as in *I grasped the wrench* (note the identical clausal configuration of Subject-Predicator-Complement).[26]

Yoon instead believes that "a taxonomy of types of Process can be realized through verbal aspect."[27] He argues for three verbal aspects, perfective, imperfective, and stative. He claims, "if aspect reflects the writer's subjective choice regardless of how the action takes place in reality, then aspect is a crucial part of understanding Process, especially in analyzing why a particular aspect was chosen over others."[28] In other words, "verbal aspect is important in understanding how the writer depicts the process as occurring."[29] The author does this by selecting a verbal aspect and by so doing identifies the Process type of the instance. Yoon discusses choice of aspect as indicating process type by differentiating two levels of analysis. The first level is the clause and clause complex, where the choice of aspect indicates the process type for the clause. The second level is the discourse level, where "the writer's consistent choice of a particular Process type (or aspect) is relevant."[30] More specifically within the Greek of the New Testament, narrative is distinguished by perfective aspect, and discursive texts by imperfective aspect.

Besides processes, however, Yoon addresses the question of participants, since these are closely related in Halliday's configuration of the clause (along with circumstances, to which Yoon gives less attention).

[25] Raised in particular in Porter, *Linguistic Analysis*, 148 and elsewhere.
[26] Yoon, *Discourse Analysis*, 92.
[27] Yoon, *Discourse Analysis*, 92.
[28] Yoon, *Discourse Analysis*, 93.
[29] Yoon, *Discourse Analysis*, 94.
[30] Yoon, *Discourse Analysis*, 94.

Rather than the causality system that I draw on above as establishing participant roles, although also in conjunction with the case system, Yoon draws entirely upon the case system to establish participants in the clause. Based upon the four cases, Yoon says that it "makes better sense in Greek . . . to identify Participants according to the case system as Primary Participants (nominative) and Secondary Participants (non-nominative). This terminology correlates to Halliday's Actor and Goal, etc."[31] Yoon brings the processes and participants together in his analysis at the discourse level through a system of tabulation based upon frequency of occurrence of the participants and processes as a means of describing "what the discourse might be about."[32] What that means is that the "field of each section [of a discourse], then, can be focused on the Primary Participants and the Processes that reflect the mainline of discourse [based on primary clauses]."[33] Yoon provides a table that shows his conception of the transitivity network of Hellenistic (and New Testament) Greek, in which the process is reflected in the three aspects (perfective, imperfective, and stative), the participant in primary (nominative) and secondary (accusative, genitive, and dative) participants, and circumstance by prepositional phrases, adverbs, and other elements.[34]

Use of Verbal Aspect in Transitivity

As mentioned above, Yoon analyzes all three metafunctions in Galatians, including transitivity in the ideational metafunction. This means that, for each textual unit that he identifies, roughly following the ancient Greek letter form, he discusses the use of verbal aspect within a given unit. He does so in relationship to the primary and secondary participants and notes their relationship.

As an example, I have chosen Gal 3:15–25, since this is a unit that contains instances of all three verbal aspects. I could have chosen any one or more of almost any of the other units to provide a similar examination. Yoon structures his description of verbal aspect in his transitivity analysis around four major discursive sections. First, Yoon notes the primary participants and then the secondary participants in this section. He bases these, as indicated above, on those participants that are found in the nominative case (primary) and those that are found in the other cases (secondary). As a result, the primary participants are "brothers,"

[31] Yoon, *Discourse Analysis*, 95.
[32] Yoon, *Discourse Analysis*, 96.
[33] Yoon, *Discourse Analysis*, 96.
[34] Yoon, *Discourse Analysis*, 97.

Paul, "no one," the promise, the pronoun "who," the law, God, mediator, righteousness, scripture, and "we/us."[35] Second, he turns to the verbal processes and categorizes them: "The Processes which depict perfective aspect (background) include: ἐρρέθησαν (λέγω), προσετέθη, μὴ γένοιτο, and συνέκλεισεν. Processes which depict imperfective aspect (mainline) include: λέγω (2x), ἀθετεῖ, ἐπιδιατάσσεται, οὐκ ἀκυροῖ, οὐ λέγει, and ἐφρουρούμεθα. Process[es] that depict stative aspect (supporting prominent material) include: κεχάρισται and γέγονεν."[36] He also rightly notes processes with aspectually vague verbs and does not include them in his aspectual description. Third, Yoon identifies the concepts that are associated with these processes: "The Processes which reflect mainline material are saying (and not saying), cancelling, rejecting, adding, and guarding. Processes which reflect supporting background material are saying (passive voice), adding (passive voice), not being (optative mood-form), and imprisoning. Processes reflecting supporting prominent material are giving and being."[37] Fourth, he relates the processes to the participants as a means of describing the field of the unit: "the field of this sub-section is primarily about the law and its relationship to the promise to Abraham given by God. Paul reiterates what he says and what the Scriptures do not say, that a ratified covenant is not rejected nor is anything added to it, that the law does not cancel the promise of God, and that the law guards them (as captives) until faith comes."[38] Similar kinds of explanations are found for the entirety of Galatians, including the sections that do not have any verbal processes in main clauses (e.g. Gal 1:1–5, but where this section does indeed have participants).

Yoon's example provides sufficient evidence to make several preliminary observations. The first is that he is focusing upon the transitivity system as a means of describing the field of the text. He does this by considering the major elements of transitivity, which include participants and, instead of processes, the verbal aspects. He devotes his attention exclusively to the clauses that are found in the mainline material, rather than dealing with secondary or offline material that is designed for development or support of the mainline.[39] The second observation is that his identification of the two separate elements, aspect of the processes

[35] For the most part Yoon uses the Greek terms that I have provided a gloss for. See Yoon, *Discourse Analysis*, 196.

[36] Yoon, *Discourse Analysis*, 196.

[37] Yoon, *Discourse Analysis*, 197.

[38] Yoon, *Discourse Analysis*, 197.

[39] For these categories and how they may be used in New Testament discourse analysis, see Stanley E. Porter and Matthew Brook O'Donnell, *Discourse Analysis and the Greek New Testament: Text-Generating Resources*, Library of New Testament Greek 2 (London: T&T Clark, 2024), 140–49 and esp. 155–62 for exemplification.

and participants, is a necessary basis for his discussion. There is some ambiguity in SFL based upon the concept of participants, since the term is used for entities that are actors at various levels in a text. These include the writer and addressee of a text as participants down to the participants in a clause. The focus of SFL is upon the clausal participants, sometimes called interactants to avoid the terminological confusion.[40] The third observation is that it is the interaction of the participants and the aspects that are the major focus of Yoon's determination of field, especially when he links the primary participants with their aspects, while also including the secondary participants in the clauses.

This summary reveals that there are some further considerations that perhaps should be brought into this discussion. It might appear that Yoon, rather than emphasizing the aspectual differences, is focusing upon the lexical meanings of the verbs. For instance, he uses English, a relatively low aspectual language, as his metalanguage, and so differences in the aspects do not emerge as readily as they might in his discursive description. However, it would be a mistake to think that Yoon's emphasis is upon lexical meaning or anything that could be construed as process types. Nevertheless, one might readily emphasize the semantic relationships among the aspects more fully. This might require special annotation or agreed translational conventions (such as perfective aspect in Greek is rendered with the simple form in English) to make clear the aspectual differences. These would be warranted, so that readers are able to appreciate that the choices of verbal aspect are means by which the processes are presented by the author, as perfective, imperfective, or stative, that is, the way that they are depicted by the author in relation to the other processes. A second consideration is that the causal relations could be emphasized more clearly. As noted above, Yoon does not rely upon causality in his analysis but differentiates participant roles based entirely upon the case system. The case system is important in clausal analysis, to be sure, but causality is the system that establishes the primary and secondary participant roles that are then grammaticalized in the case system. A way of including causality might be to use special notation or even simply labeling the causal relations within the English description.

As a possible example of what I am describing above, I re-examine Gal 3:15-25 and, using Yoon's language, reconfigure his field description in the following ways. In the first, I provide an abbreviated, annotated description of the clauses with aspectually labeled primary predicators that Yoon considers, with some slight modifications. I offset the verbless or aspectually vague predicator clauses and remove conjunctions for

[40] See Porter and O'Donnell, *Discourse Analysis*, 90 note 158.

clarity.[41] In the second, I provide glosses that attempt to bring out the annotated differences.[42]

1. Displayed Greek Text[43]

Primary Clauses Verbless and Aspectually Vague Clauses

Galatians 3:15

κατὰ ἄνθρωπον λέγω [IA, Paul SI, AC][44]

... *ἀνθρώπου* ...[45] *διαθήκην οὐδεὶς ἀθετεῖ ἢ ἐπιδιατάσσεται* [IA 2x, *οὐδεὶς* S 2x, AC + MC]

Galatians 3:16

τῷ ... Ἀβραὰμ ἐρρέθησαν αἱ ἐπαγγελίαι καὶ τῷ σπέρματι αὐτοῦ [*PA*, *αἱ ἐπαγγελίαι* S, PC]

οὐ λέγει [IA, promise SI, AVC][46]... ὡς ἐπὶ πολλῶν, ἀλλ' ὡς ἐφ' ἑνός

Galatians 3:17

τοῦτο ... λέγω [IA, Paul SI, AC]

[41] I realize that the content clauses in Gal 3:16 and 17 may be considered as secondary constructions but include them here because Yoon has included them in his description.

[42] One must always remember that glosses/translations are a very poor indicator of textual understanding. They are provided here only for the sake of drawing the contrasts indicated above.

[43] The key to the abbreviations used below are the following:

PA = perfective aspect
IA = imperfective aspect
SA = stative aspect
AC = active causality
MC = middle causality
PC = passive causality
S = subject
SI = implied subject

[44] I would not include *ἀδελφοί* as a participant, since it is a nominative of address. As a nominative of address it is syntactically independent of the main clausal structure. Nominatives of address function similarly to vocatives, on which see Stanley E. Porter and Matthew *Brook O'Donnell*, "The Vocative Case in Greek: Addressing the Case at Hand," in *Grammatica intellectio Scripturae: Saggi filologici di Greco biblico in onore di Lino Cignelli OFM*, ed. Rosario Pierri, Studium Biblicum Franciscanum Analecta 68 (Jerusalem: Franciscan Printing Press, 2006), 35–48.

[45] This ellipsis indicates deletion of a rank-shifted and embedded participle clause *κεκυρωμένην* functioning as a definer in the nominal group.

[46] I do not include *ὅς ἐστιν Χριστός*, since this is a secondary relative clause elaborating the "seed."

διαθήκην ...[47] *ὁ ...*[48] *νόμος οὐκ ἀκυροῖ* [IA, ὁ ... νόμος S, AC]

Galatians 3:18
εἰ ... ἐκ νόμου ἡ κληρονομία, οὐκέτι ἐξ ἐπαγγελίας
τῷ ... Ἀβραὰμ δι᾽ ἐπαγγελίας κεχάρισται ὁ θεός [SA, ὁ θεός S, MC]

Galatians 3:19
τί ... ὁ νόμος;
τῶν παραβάσεων χάριν προσετέθη [PA, law SI, PC]

Galatians 3:20
ὁ ... μεσίτης ἑνὸς οὐκ ἔστιν,
ὁ ... θεὸς εἷς ἐστιν

Galatians 3:21
ὁ ... νόμος κατὰ τῶν ἐπαγγελιῶν τοῦ θεοῦ;[49]
μὴ γένοιτο [PA, impersonal SI, MC]
ὄντως ἐκ νόμου ἂν ἦν ἡ δικαιοσύνη

Galatians 3:22
συνέκλεισεν ἡ γραφὴ τὰ πάντα ὑπὸ ἁμαρτίαν [PA, ἡ γραφὴ S, AC]

Galatians 3:23
ὑπὸ νόμον ἐφρουρούμεθα [IA, we SI, PC]

Galatians 3:24
ὁ νόμος παιδαγωγὸς ἡμῶν γέγονεν εἰς Χριστόν [SA, ὁ νόμος S, AC]

Galatians 3:25
οὐκέτι ὑπὸ παιδαγωγόν ἐσμεν

2. English Glosses Emphasizing Aspectual and Other Features

Primary clauses — Verbless and Aspectually Vague Clauses

[47] This ellipsis indicates deletion of the rank-shifted and embedded participle clause *προκεκυρωμένην ὑπὸ τοῦ θεοῦ* functioning as a definer in the nominal group.

[48] This ellipsis indicates deletion of a rank-shifted and embedded participle clause *μετὰ τετρακόσια καὶ τριάκοντα ἔτη γεγονὼς* functioning as a definer in the nominal group.

[49] I accept the reading *τοῦ θεοῦ*, since it is found in the major codexes (א A C D[gr]), minuscules, and the Byzantine tradition.

Galatians 3:15

I am speaking based on a human way ...
A human covenant no one is setting aside or is adding to ...

Galatians 3:16

To Abraham is given the promise and to his seed ...
It (the promise) is not saying . . . as upon many, but as upon one ...

Galatians 3:17

I am saying this ...
A covenant ... the law is not negating ...

Galatians 3:18

If from law is inheritance, it is no longer from promise ...
To Abraham through promise God is in the state of gracious provider ...

Galatians 3:19

What is the law?
On account of transgressions, it (the law) is added ...

Galatians 3:20

A mediator is not of one ...
God is one ...

Galatians 3:21

The law is opposed to the promises of God?
May it not be.[50]
Entirely from law would be righteousness

Galatians 3:22

The scripture closes up all things under sin ...

Galatians 3:23

We are being locked up under the law ...

Galatians 3:24

The law is in the state of having become our teacher of Christ ...

Galatians 3:25

We are no longer under a teacher ...

[50] On the reasons for this rendering, see Stanley E. Porter, "Μὴ γένοιτο in Paul: God Forbid? Possibly Not," *FilNeot* 35 (2022) 13–33.

Summary

We see from the display above that Yoon's description of the field is correct. To this description we may add the following further observations. The first is that a means of not just identifying but distinguishing the verbal aspects helps to understand the shape and flow of the text in the mainline of the discourse. Paul begins this section with several imperfective verbs that indicate the stance he will take to his material. On the one hand, the use of the imperfective aspect as constituting the backbone of a letter text is not unusual. In fact, it is often the case that the discursive material of a text, such as a letter, uses imperfective aspect in this way. Nevertheless, the focus, that is, foreground,[51] is upon Paul's human analogy that begins with his statement about human covenants. A human covenant is one that no one can set aside or even add to (with use of the ergative middle voice; it is not that no one is able to be added but that no one is able to add). Paul then shifts to perfective aspect to provide historical background to his discussion. In this context, one might well render such verbs with an English past-tense, although I have used the simple English present to distinguish it from the progressive English present used for imperfective aspect (admittedly awkwardly in some instances, but the emphasis is not on the translation). Paul continues his discursive exposition by means of imperfective aspect regarding the promise and covenant. At this point, he employs several clauses that are either verbless or with aspectually (and causally) vague verbs. I have indented these and rendered them with simple forms of the English verb *be* to illustrate an approximation of their function. The first is a truism about the law and promise. This is followed, however, by the first of two uses of the stative aspect in the mainline material of this textual unit. Paul recapitulates his position regarding Abraham and the promise by depicting this as reflecting a state of God's graciousness toward Abraham. In this context, the use of the stative aspect and middle voice causality as a means of depicting God's gracious act toward humanity is doubly frontgrounded, with God as the indirect but internal agent of such graciousness. This conception of the action through both aspect and especially causality may well raise some theological questions as a result. Paul then uses a verbless clause to ask what the law is, to which he replies that it, implying the law, is an added entity, using passive causality that does not specify agency. Paul interjects two statements about mediation and God's relation to it by means of aspectually vague εἰμί, and then a verbless clause to raise the question of whether the law is contrary to God's promises.

[51] On the grounding system of Greek discourse, see Porter and O'Donnell, *Discourse Analysis*, 140–49.

Paul answers with his negative statement, "May it not be," which retains the element of contingency in the Greek attitude system grammaticalized by the optative. Paul dismisses the idea of righteousness from the law by means of a clause with εἰμί. He concludes the unit with a crescendo in the mainline of the discourse, moving successively from perfective to imperfective to stative aspect, that is, from background to foreground to frontground. Paul's statement regarding scripture as a lock on all things under sin moves to a statement regarding humans before faith having been held captive under the law to a statement regarding the law being depicted as taking on the state of being our teacher or pedagogue that points to Christ.

There are, of course, many other elements to Gal 3:15–25 that I have not discussed here. These include the secondary clauses, along with embedded clauses, that provide offline or supporting material to the mainline. These too are important and can be analyzed in terms of their metafunctions, including field. However, the purpose here has been to show how a more graphically explicit identification of elements of the ideational metafunction may help to identify the field of a text more fully.

Conclusion

This paper has returned to the topic raised in my earlier paper on verbal aspect and process types in ancient, particularly New Testament, Greek, being examined from a SFL standpoint. In the first paper, I subjected various views of verbs as indicators of action types to analysis and found them all wanting. The use of process types in SFL was included in this analysis. I suggested there that Greek verbal aspect in conjunction with the system of causality in the Greek language provided a better way forward for describing the ideational function of processes. Rather than relying on discerning process types—which can be criticized along several different lines for their inconsistency and failure to provide criteria for identification—I have raised the prospect of using verbal aspect as a means of classifying and understanding predicators. I have focused upon predicators in primary clauses, based on previous work done in this area, although predicators in secondary and embedded clauses would benefit from such description as well. The configuration of verbal aspect is similar in many ways to that of process types within SFL, but it has the advantage of having been systemically established and it reflects formal features of the language. As a result, some of the inconsistencies of process types are mitigated and there is a morphologically and paradigmatically based means of aspectual identification. When aspect is combined with causality, one can link processes with participants in clausal structure and arrive at helpful descriptions of their use within texts.

STANLEY E. PORTER
McMaster Divinity College
1280 Main St. W.
Hamilton, ON L8S 4K1
CANADA
porters@mcmaster.ca

Linguistic Tools for Identifying the Structure of the Gospel of John[1]

JENNY READ-HEIMERDINGER

For the past 40 years or so, linguists have been working on aspects of Koine Greek that operate outside the domain of traditional sentence grammar. The overall purpose has been to identify principles of the language that function above the level of the sentence (discourse analysis). In this work, there is a focus on the cohesion of a text and, in recent applications of the approach, attention has been paid to analysing how authors structured their writings. By explaining and applying the tools that discourse analysis provides, this paper explores the structure of John's Gospel. The text of two manuscripts, Codex Vaticanus and Codex Bezae, is used for this study in preference to the familiar eclectic text which has been reconstructed without the application of discourse analysis tools. The narrative text of John's Gospel in the two manuscripts is analysed by paying exhaustive attention first, to the occurrence of connectives between sentences and secondly, to the word order of sentences in relation to the main verb. In this way, the organisation of the book is seen to emerge, from the overall macro-structure down through the hierarchical levels to the smallest units. The application of the resultant narrative framework to exegetical and theological study of John's Gospel is suggested as an avenue of study opened up by the analysis.

Keywords: John's Gospel – narrative structure – discourse analysis – sentence connectives – word order.

I. Introduction

The study of structure in the Gospel of John that is presented in this paper relates to a project carried out by a team of researchers composed of post-doctoral students and faculty members at the Institut Catholique de Toulouse, France. We worked first on the theoretical insights brought to the organisation of texts by recent advances in the study of Greek grammar, which have developed through the tools of discourse analysis.[2] We then went on to apply the theory to an exhaustive analysis of the Greek text of the Gospel of John, resulting in a body of data that was to

[1] The presentation of the theoretical aspects in this paper is adapted from my 'Discourse Analysis of the Book of Acts', in T. Scacewater (ed.), *Discourse Analysis of the New Testament Writings* (Dallas: Fortres Press,) 2020.

[2] There are many and varied approaches to discourse analysis, which have been developing over the last 50 years or so. With regard to the application of discourse analysis to NT Greek, the principal source used here for structural analysis is S.H. Levinsohn, *Discourse Features of New Testament Greek*, 2nd ed. (Dallas: Summer Institute of Linguistics, 2000).

provide the basis for identifying the structure as intended by the author. There followed many hours of discussion as to the interpretation and significance of our findings, a discussion that in some respects continues. It is the outcome of this work that is set out here. Throughout the project overall, we worked as a team, benefiting from the individual strengths of each member, constantly challenged by each other's questioning and always open to changing our ideas as we allowed the data to speak for itself. We consciously sought to avoid being guided by pre-existing structural analyses, or indeed prior exegetical analyses, in a desire to maintain the level of objectivity that would give the best chance to the text to reveal its structure rather than have one imposed on it.

In acknowledging the work of the team in presenting our work, I nevertheless accept responsibility for any and all shortcomings in this paper.

II. Linguistic markers of Structure

II.1 Ancient Manuscripts

In modern writing, the structure of a text is greatly assisted by the use of visual devices. Books are divided into chapters, with paragraphs to mark the grouping and separation of topics. Punctuation, too, plays a critical role in conveying the speaker's intentions by the grouping of material into phrases, clauses, sentences. In ancient Greek writing, on the other hand, there was not only no visual system in regular use for dividing the material into smaller units, there was no punctuation either. Furthermore, the extant NT manuscripts of the first centuries are written exclusively in capital letters, and usually without separation between sentences or even between words.

The familiar chapter divisions were introduced as late as the 13th c. and verses only in the 16th c., and cannot be relied upon in order to identify the author's intended organisation of a book. The problem with using other literary or rhetorical signposts – for example, changes in theme, location, time or protagonist, or the repetition of vocabulary or phrases – is that the high degree of subjectivity involved leads to not a little disagreement among exegetes as to where divisions occur. Contributing to the element of subjectivity is the difference in the expectations of readers who are vastly separated from the original 1st c. context, both in terms of time and of culture, as well as by language.

II.2 Discourse Analysis

Discourse analysis looks at the constraints and devices that operate in a language above the level of the sentence. As opposed to traditional grammar, which can be said to take the sentence (made up of words, phrases and clauses) as the basic unit, discourse analysis looks not only at the sentence and its components but also at the larger units which group sentences together in an organized structure, from the level of individual sentences up to the level of the whole discourse. From a study of the formal features of a language, its aim is to elucidate the principles that govern the way in which continuous discourse is constructed. Among its many concerns, it examines how the boundaries between the various units are signalled and what are the features that distinguish one level of unit from another. Discourse analysis is similarly concerned with the ways in which the units relate to each other, how they are ordered, and how they hold together to create a unified discourse. It seeks to identify the components that are central to the main idea of the discourse, and to establish how they are distinguished from the peripheral components.

That is not to say that the constituents of a sentence never form part of the studies of discourse analysts. On the contrary, components within the sentence are sometimes a central preoccupation, but they are considered within the context of larger spans of discourse, with the purpose of seeing how they are controlled by factors that operate on a level above the sentence or how, indeed, they influence portions of text beyond the sentence.

Because of the concern of discourse analysis with language above the level of the sentence, it opens up the way to consider how a writing is organised, specifically what are the inherent means available in a given language to group ideas or themes together, to create a framework that makes communication more intelligible and effective than would be a formless mass of utterances. All good speakers give shape to their discourse in a bid to get the audience's attention and keep them focused on what is being said. In the case of discourses intended to be read aloud rather than privately, communication is liable to be rendered ineffective if this condition is disregarded. The business of organising discourse is generally a natural and instinctive operation for a native speaker in everyday speech, though in formal communication it may necessitate more careful effort and skill, and implies a more arduous task for a non-native speaker. For it is important to recognize that each language has its own way of building discourses; the similarities that may exist between languages are unpredictable and by no means regular, which means that ancient Greek has to be examined as a distinct language, independent of any apparent overlap with English, for example.

II.3 Narrative Discourse

A primary consideration in thinking about the structure of the Gospel of John is that it is a narrative discourse. It is written as a story, with the typical features of a time frame, characters, locations, plot. As such, for discourse analysis purposes it is to be distinguished from writing that is overtly discursive, which presents an argument or seeks to persuade, for example. That is not to say that the author did not seek to inform or persuade his listeners but simply that whatever his purpose, he chose to express it as a narrative. It should be borne in mind that ancient conventions of recording factual reality allowed considerable licence with the organisation and selection of material, without the present-day demands that the details of reported events and characters correspond to literal reality of time and space. In biblical narrative, the historian's freedom to re-arrange the sequence of incidents or to change details – for example, dates or names of people and places – reflects at least in part the notion that reality is first and foremost spiritual in nature, existing outside the confines of time and space of the physical world. This is the truth that the biblical historian must seek to communicate, and in so doing may need to modify literal details in the interests of expressing it more clearly.[3]

The significance of this view of history for seeking for the structure of John's Gospel is that any indications of time or place that the author gives do not necessarily correspond to our contemporary notions of time and place, and any attempt to bring them into line with our familiar logic should be eschewed.

Direct speech within narrative

Within the narrative of John's Gospel are passages of direct speech placed in the mouths of characters in the story, notably Jesus. In some respects, the wording of these speeches is often closely tied to the wording of the surrounding narrative, so that on the basis of rhetorical or literary analysis there would be justification for considering their content as interlaced with the narrative content. From the point of view of discourse structure, in contrast, they are to be viewed as units that belong to the narrative episode in which they are found, forming a single segment with the surrounding narrative. With their own speaker, the portions of direct speech have their own internal structure which is independent of the unfolding narrative line. In the presentation of the structure of John's Gospel that follows, therefore, the internal structure of the speeches will

[3] For Jewish historians, including the authors of records collected in the NT, there is the further notion that the whole of the history of Israel is contained within the Torah, subsequent events being re-enactments of the earlier, paradigmatic ones. This perspective is a factor that needs to be taken into account for its contribution to the re-shaping of literal reality in the Gospels. For a discussion of the Jewish notion of history, see Bernard Barc, *Les arpenteurs du temps. Essai sur l'histoire de la Judée à la période héllenistique* (Lausanne: Éditions du Zèbre, 2000).

not be analysed; rather, they will be viewed as blocks embedded within the overall narrative framework.

II.4 Markers of Structure above the Level of the Sentence

Two principal features of *koine* Greek identified by discourse analysts as key to the organisation of narrative are:

a) word order within the sentence
b) connectives between sentences

While both of these clearly have a function within the sentence in which they are found, it is their contribution to the wider narrative that is of particular interest to discourse analysis. The notion of the sentence as a unit is, in itself, of importance. As the smallest building block of a narrative discourse, a sentence is defined as a group of words that has one main, finite verb, together with any dependent clauses that are subordinate to that verb. In our analysis of structure, we use the term 'elements' to refer to sentences according to this definition.

The two key structural features, word order and connectives, will now be considered in turn, before looking at how they function together as indications of structure.

II.4.a *Word Order*

Greek is often said to have a word order that is 'free' as opposed to 'fixed', and to differ in that respect from English. It is true that in a language that has case-markings, such as Greek has, word order plays a lesser role in indicating grammatical relations than in languages without case-markings. Aside from a few aspects (e.g., the second position of δέ and γάρ) that are determined by grammatical or syntactical considerations, the impression is often given in manuals of NT Greek that word order is largely a matter of a speaker's choice. Word order variation is commonly ascribed to personal custom or style, whether an unconscious habit on the part of the speaker or deliberately worked for rhetorical or stylistic effect.

In line with the interest of discourse analysis in looking at language in its real-life context, it is now recognized that there are, in fact, constraints operating on Greek word order but that these are of a semantic and pragmatic nature rather than a grammatical one. In other words, the constraints are connected with the function of the words and sentences within the discourse, not the grammatical relations that exist between the words or sentences. They operate on a deep level rather than a surface level. They have to do with such purposes as signaling which part of the sentence is the most important, introducing a new idea, indicating a contrast or conflict. Word order choice is thus not a matter of style, dependent on a writer's or scribe's preference or habit, but is a device that forms an integral part of the tools available to a writer for the communication of the message.

a.i) *Default word order*

Word order plays a particularly important role in structuring narrative, where its impact is not so much on the relationship among constituents within a sentence as on the relationship between sentences themselves. It has been observed[4] that sentences in a Greek narrative typically start with the verb, followed by the subject if it is expressed, then the object if there is one. This order, referred to as VSO, is as close to ordinary speech as can be determined in the NT (e.g., from the parables). The initial position of the verb in narrative reflects the fact that a story is about actions and events first of all - unlike hortatory discourse where people, a topic or a line of argument are more likely to be the prominent concern. Besides, in a continuous story in Greek, it is often unnecessary to specify the subject since this can be encoded in the verb ending and, furthermore, it can be understood to be the same as the subject of the previous main verb if no change is explicitly indicated.

It is usual to describe a typical pattern of word order as the 'unmarked' or 'default' order, and to go from there to identify the effects of modifying that unmarked order to produce patterns that are described as "marked". With regard to the initial position of the verb in a narrative sentence, this means that the word order is marked if the verb is *not* at the head of the sentence but some other constituent occupies that place. Placing any constituent before the verb at the start of a sentence in a narrative discourse ('fore-fronting') focuses special attention on it, because it disrupts the expected pattern.

a.ii) *Marked word order*

Two reasons have been identified for word order to be marked in this way.

- *Focus:* First of all, when a constituent is moved to any position further to the left than it would occupy by default, this can be a means to

[4] Levinsohn, *Discourse Features*, pp. 16-17.

underline it, to highlight it as being of particular importance at that point. For example, in a sentence where the subject is explicit, if the subject is placed before the verb, attention is being drawn to it for some reason such as contrast or surprise.

- *New point of departure:* In addition to focusing attention, there is another reason for placing a constituent before the verb at the start of a sentence, and it is this one that is relevant for the purpose of structure: a constituent may be fore-fronted in order to signal a new development in the narrative, one that forms a new basis for the next part of the story. This could be a change of place, time, protagonist, or topic, which acts a fresh 'point of departure' for the next part of the story.[5] Continuity is the norm in narrative, and so disrupting the expected order of words is a means to signal a change in direction of some kind. As such, these fore-fronted sentences serve as boundary markers, indications of structural breaks that the narrator intended for the narrative.

It is important to distinguish between the purpose of fore-fronting for focus and the purpose for establishing a new point of departure, because only the latter instances contribute to the structure of the narrative. A general rule is that if the fore-fronted constituent is already present in the narrative, even if not explicitly stated, then the purpose should be understood as focus. In such cases, the directing of attention is also liable to be localized and short-term, without serving to develop the story on a larger scale.

The narrator of John's Gospel employs a further device to mark a fresh point of departure, using the verb εἶμι (γίνομαι in the aorist) to introduce a new person into a scene that has already been set up (e.g. 5.5: ἦν δὲ ἄνθρωπος ἐκεῖ ...). In such sentences, the verb comes first but, by the presentative nature of the verb, the construction overall marks the importance of the new subject by setting it out in a separate sentence at the start of a new unit. The technique is a kind of fore-fronting *par excellence*.

Conversely, if there is a change in time, or place, protagonist or topic, but the verb is in first position in the sentence, then continuity of situation is indicated. Observing this principle may sometimes seem counter-intuitive, and it means that using the criteria of word order to discern the divisions of the narrative may conflict with the divisions identified by noting thematic or other changes, which commentators typically look for in order to locate boundaries. However, taking account of word order, specifically fore-fronting, provides an objective basis for identifying the shifts or developments in the narrative that the narrator apparently

[5] Levinsohn, *Discourse Features*, pp. 7-28.

intended. It reduces considerably the risk of anachronistically imposing on the text ways of understanding a story that derive from modern interpreters' expectations or preconceptions.

Word order, then, is a prime factor in signalling the start of a new unit. Exactly how the new unit relates to the previous one and, equally important, what the hierarchical status of the new unit is in relation to any others, are two specific matters that are considered by taking account of the connective used to join the new unit with the previous one.

II.4.b *Connectives*

Connectives is a term that refers to any means of joining together sentences where, as explained above, 'sentence' means a finite verb and any associated subordinate clauses or phrases. Unlike in English, for example, where it is common to make no explicit connection between sentences, in ancient Greek it is far more usual to make clear the connection, which the absence of punctuation renders all the more necessary. In his Gospel, John makes use of a variety of devices to express relationships between sentences, the explicit links usually being conjunctions; other explicit markers that he uses are adverbs or adverbial phrases, and pronouns, both demonstrative and relative. Exceptionally among NT writers, John also makes use of the distinctive feature of asyndeton, whereby there is no kind of word to link sentences. The absence of a connecting word is itself viewed as a particular type of connection, with a specific purpose of its own.

Indeed, not only does asyndeton have its own characteristic force, but so does each connective. Their very specificity allows connectives to indicate the nature of the relationship of a sentence with what has gone before, and even to anticipate what will follow. That much is generally recognized, with οὖν for example, understood to express the notion of consequence, unlike δέ which expresses a contrast of some kind. What is to be said, though, of John who, in comparison with the other evangelists, uses οὖν far more frequently and without necessarily any idea of consequence, and uses δέ relatively infrequently? Through detailed studies of connectives,[6] it becomes apparent that beyond their role in joining sentences together, connectives play a further critical function in deter-

[6] With reference specifically to Acts, see Levinsohn, *Textual Connections in Acts* (Scholars Press, 1987); see also his *Discourse Features of New Testament Greek*, where he extends his analysis to other New Testament writings. Levinsohn's work on connectives was reviewed, and largely confirmed, in an examination of variant readings by Read-Heimerdinger, *The Bezan Text of Acts: A Contribution of Discourse Analysis to Textual Criticism* (JSNTSup. 236; Sheffield: SAP, 2002), pp. 202–253.

mining the structure of narrative units, serving as signs of punctuation in place of capital letters, commas, semi-colons, full-stops, paragraph breaks and so on. In other words, they serve to mark boundaries between narrative units as well as to indicate the level of hierarchy a unit has within the wider structure of the book.

III. Methodology

With the theory set out, attention can now be turned to the practical outworking of it, as it emerged from the Toulouse project when we examined the Gospel of John to see what an analysis of the word order and connectives would reveal.

III.1 The Greek Text

In view of the linguistic significance of these two features, it is clear that it is the Greek text that has to be examined and not one in translation, for it is within the Greek itself that the author embeds the structure. At this point there arises the problem of knowing just what John wrote, for there is a fair amount of manuscript variation concerning both word order and connectives. While it is customary to ascribe this variation to scribal habit or preference, discourse analysis demonstrates that, given the significance of word order and sentence connectives as indications of organisation of the text, it would be more accurate to interpret the variation as arising from a different understanding of the structure of the narrative.

In preparing the current edition of the Greek New Testament[7], choice was made by the editors among variant readings without appealing to these criteria identified by discourse analysis, and the established text cannot therefore be relied on for an analysis of structure. Nor, however, is there any agreement among textual critics as to which manuscript is closer to the text that John wrote. In an attempt to be as objective as possible without bringing presuppositions to the study, the team in Toulouse decided to select the two early (pre-400)[8] manuscripts that are the most

[7] B. Aland, K. Aland, J. Karavidopoulos, C. M. Martini and B.M. Metzger (eds). *Novum Testamentum Graece* (Stuttgart: Deutsche Bibelgesellschaft/United Bible Societies, ^{28}2013) = N-A^{28}.

[8] It should be borne in mind that the date of a manuscript is not an indicator of the date of the text that it transmits and, indeed, the text of both of the manuscripts selected is attested by fragmentary documents as early as the 3rd c.

far apart in terms of their variant readings, namely Codex Bezae (D05) and Codex Vaticanus (B03), and to analyse both of them independently.[9]

A parallel text of D05 and B03 was constructed, indicating the variant readings according to four categories. A sample from John 5 is set out in Table 1 below.

Table 1
Sample of parallel texts of D05 and B03

Codex Bezae D05	Codex Vaticanus B03
5.5 Ἦν δὲ ↑ ἄνθρωπος ἐκεῖ τριάκοντα <u>καὶ</u> ὀκτὼ ἔτη ἔχων ἐν τῇ ἀσθενείᾳ αὐτοῦ· 6 τοῦτον ἰδὼν ὁ Ἰησοῦς κατακείμενον καὶ γνοὺς ὅτι πολὺν ἤδη χρόνον ἔχει, λέγει αὐτῷ· ... 7 λέγει αὐτῷ ὁ ἀσθενῶν· ... 8 λέγει αὐτῷ ὁ Ἰησοῦς· ... 9 καὶ ↑ ὑγιὴς ἐγένετο ὁ ἄνθρωπος καὶ <u>ἐγερθεὶς</u> ἦρεν τὸν κράβαττον αὐτοῦ καὶ περιεπάτει. ἦν δὲ σάββατον ↑.	5.5 Ἦν δέ <u>τις</u> ἄνθρωπος ἐκεῖ τριάκοντα ↑ ὀκτὼ ἔτη ἔχων ἐν τῇ ἀσθενείᾳ αὐτοῦ· 6 τοῦτον ἰδὼν ὁ Ἰησοῦς κατακείμενον καὶ γνοὺς ὅτι πολὺν ἤδη χρόνον ἔχει, λέγει αὐτῷ· ... 7 ἀπεκρίθη αὐτῷ ὁ ἀσθενῶν· ... 8 λέγει αὐτῷ ὁ Ἰησοῦς· ... 9 καὶ <u>εὐθέως</u> ἐγένετο ὑγιὴς ὁ ἄνθρωπος καὶ ↑ ἦρε τὸν κράβαττον αὐτοῦ καὶ περιεπάτει. ἦν δὲ σάββατον <u>ἐν ἐκείνῃ τῇ ἡμέρᾳ</u>.

Key: <u>underline</u>: words present in one manuscript only
arrow ↑: words absent from one manuscript
bold: **words in a different form**
italics: *words in a different order*

III.2 Identification of sentences connectives

In a first step, all the sentences of the Gospel were identified, that is, the main clauses with a finite verb together with any subordinate clauses clustered around them. The connectives (including conjunctions, pronouns, adverbs or adverbial phrases and asyndeton) between them were then marked up, each one assigned a different colour for ease of classification. The first benefit of this exercise was that it revealed at a glance the smallest units of structure, what we term the 'elements' – the complete sentences, each with one main, finite verb. Table 2 presents an example from John 5, though here without the different colours used to distinguish the connectives.

[9] The text of Codex Vaticanus (B03) is widely adopted for the N-A[28] edition. In Codex Bezae (D05), two quaternions (eight folios each) are missing from John's Gospel. The first would have had 1.16-3.16; for this section, Codex Sinaiticus (ℵ01), the early manuscript closest to D05 in the first part of John's Gospel, was used for the structural analysis, still in comparison with B03. The second quaternion had 18.14–20.13 and was lost some time before the 9th c. They were replaced with pages copied in Lyons (D05[s]).

Table 2

Identification of sentence connectives in narrative text

Codex Bezae D05
*5.5 ἦν δὲ ἄνθρωπος ἐκεῖ τριάκοντα καὶ ὀκτὼ ἔτη ἔχων ἐν τῇ ἀσθενείᾳ αὐτοῦ·
6 τοῦτον ἰδὼν ὁ Ἰησοῦς κατακείμενον καὶ γνοὺς ὅτι πολὺν ἤδη χρόνον ἔχει, λέγει αὐτῷ· ...
7 **λέγει** αὐτῷ ὁ ἀσθενῶν· ...
8 λέγει αὐτῷ ὁ Ἰησοῦς· ...
9 καὶ ὑγιὴς ἐγένετο ὁ ἄνθρωπος
καὶ ἐγερθεὶς ἦρεν τὸν κράβαττον αὐτοῦ
καὶ περιεπάτει.
ἦν δὲ σάββατον.
10 ἔλεγον οὖν οἱ Ἰουδαῖοι τῷ τεθεραπευμένω· ...
11 † ἀπεκρίθη αὐτοῖς· ...
12 ἠρώτησαν αὐτόν· ...
13 ὁ **ἀσθενὼν** οὐκ ᾔδει τίς **ἦν**,
ὁ γὰρ Ἰησοῦς **ἔνευσεν** ὄχλου ὄντος ἐν τῷ τόπῳ.
14 μετὰ ταῦτα εὑρίσκει αὐτὸν ὁ Ἰησοῦς ἐν τῷ ἱερῷ
καὶ εἶπεν αὐτῷ· ...

With the connectives thus noted, detailed examination of the function of each one was facilitated. The distinctive features of the particular kind of connection each made were observed and their specific purpose thus identified.

We found that approximately 10% of the several hundred connectives in John's Gospel are affected by variant readings, which in themselves provide valuable evidence of the ways in which different copyists understood sentences or passages to be linked together. It was interesting to discover that out of the 36 connectives at the level of the structural divisions, only three were variant (4.45, 46b; 7.1). More remarkable still was the finding that both forms of text agreed on the placing of the structural divisions (i.e., fore-fronted sentences that are not for focus), with neither of them indicating a boundary where the other one did not.

From this analysis, it was possible to get a much clearer idea than previously of the particular significance that John – and the early copyists – accorded to each connective. However, the detailed results of this analysis of connectives in general are not relevant to the discussion of structure and so are not reported here. What is of specific interest for a study of structure is the connectives that John's Gospel uses at places of disrupted (marked) word order, where a constituent is placed before the verb (see Table 3).

III.3 Identification of fore-fronted sentences

Having identified the sentences together with their connective, a second step was to single out the occurrences of marked word-order, where a constituent is placed before the verb. These were then categorised according to whether the fore-fronting was for the purpose of focus or, conversely, was to signal a point of departure. Those in the latter category were listed in their order of appearance in the narrative, together with the connective introducing them. Presentative sentences, which have the verb εἶμι or γίνομαι as first component followed by a person, were included as a special type of fore-fronted sentence (see #II.4.a.ii) above). Table 3 below sets out the results. The middle column of Table 3 sets out every instance of fore-fronted sentences marking points of departure, together with the connective; the left-hand column identifies the context for the new unit.

Table 3
Points of departure in the Gospel of John

Circumstance	**Points of departure**	**Reference**
Prologue	ἐν ἀρχῇ	1.1-18
Hinge prologue to narrative	καὶ αὕτη ἐστὶν ἡ μαρτυρία τοῦ Ἰωάννου, κτλ	1.19-28
the next day	τῇ ἐπαύριον	1.29-34
the next day	τῇ ἐπαύριον	1.35-42
the next day	τῇ ἐπαύριον	1.43-51
time	καὶ τῇ ἡμέρᾳ τῇ τρίτῃ γάμος ἐγένετο	2.1-11
After this	μετὰ τοῦτο	2.12-22
when	ὡς δὲ ἦν ... ἐπίστευσαν	2.23-25
presentative	ἦν δὲ ἄνθρωπος	3.1-21
After these things	μετὰ ταῦτα	3.22-36
when	ὡς οὖν ἔγνω... ἀφῆκεν	4.1-38
place	ἐκ δὲ τῆς πόλεως ἐκείνης πολλοὶ ἐπίστευσαν	4.39-44
when	ὡς [ὅτε N-A[28]] οὖν ἦλθεν ... ἐξεδέξαντο	4.45-46a
presentative	ἦν δέ [καὶ N-A[28]] τις βασιλίσκος	4.46b-54
After these things	μετὰ ταῦτα	5.1-3[4]
presentative	ἦν δὲ ἄνθρωπος	5.5-47
After these things	μετὰ ταῦτα	6.1-15
when	ὡς δὲ ὀψία ἐγένετο κατέβησαν...	6.16-21
the next day	τῇ ἐπαύριον	6.22-71

After these things	[+ καὶ N-A[28]] μετὰ ταῦτα	7.1-13
time	ἤδη δὲ τῆς ἑορτῆς μεσαζούσης ἀνέβη	7.14-36
time	ἐν δὲ τῇ ἡμέρᾳ τῇ μεγάλῃ	7.37-42
schism	σχίσμα οὖν ἐγένετο	7.43-52
again	πάλιν οὖν ἐλάλησεν	8.12-59
location	καὶ παραγῶν εἶδεν	9.1-10.18
schism	σχίσμα οὖν [πάλιν N-A[28]] ἐγένετο	10.19-42
presentative	ἦν δέ τις ἀσθενῶν	11.1-52
From that day	ἀπ' ἐκείνης οὖν τῆς ἡμέρας ἐβουλεύσαντο	11.53-57
time	ὁ οὖν Ἰησοῦς πρὸ ἓξ ἡμερῶν τοῦ πάσχα ἦλθεν	12.1-11
the next day	τῇ ἐπαύριον	12.12-19
presentative	ἦσαν δὲ καὶ Ἕλληνές τινες	12.20-50
Before Passover	πρὸ δὲ τῆς ἑορτῆς τοῦ πάσχα...ἠγάπησεν	13.1-17.26
speech	ταῦτα εἰπὼν ὁ Ἰησοῦς ἐξῆλθεν	18.1-19.27
after this	μετὰ τοῦτο	19.28-37
After these things	μετὰ δὲ ταῦτα	19.38-42
the first day	τῇ δὲ μιᾷ τῶν σαββάτων...ἔρχεται	20.1-18
time	οὔσης οὖν ὀψίας...ἦλθεν	20.19-29
Conclusion	πολλὰ μὲν οὖν... δέ	20.30-31
After these things	μετὰ ταῦτα	21.1-14
Time	ὅτε οὖν ἠρίστησαν λέγει	21.15-24
Conclusion	ἔστιν δὲ καὶ ἄλλα πολλά	21.25

IV. Results

IV.1 Observations

A number of features emerge from the analysis of the boundary sentences:

- All the instances of sentences where the word order indicates a new point of departure include an overt form of connective, whether a conjunction, or an adverb or an adverbial phrase.
- There is a preponderance of connections on the basis of time. This suggests that John conceived of his narrative as unfolding chronologically. That by no means signifies a literal time frame, but it

does denote a linear development, punctuated or prompted by the passage of time.

- The adverbial phrase μετὰ ταῦτα is used five times (3.22; 5.1; 6.1; 7.1; 19.38), with the final one including the conjunction δέ. That of 7.1 is accompanied by καί in B03, but not in D05 with wide and varied support including that of Codcx Sinaiticus (ℵ01). The opening sentence of ch. 21, commonly viewed as added at some point after the Gospel had already been concluded in ch. 20, is also linked to the previous material with μετὰ ταῦτα.
- μετὰ τοῦτο appears twice (2.12; 19.28).
- The boundary markers sometimes, but not always, coincide with chapter divisions which, being a medieval feature, are by no means a reliable guide to the author's intended structure.

IV.2 Structure Resulting from Analysis of Connectives

By noting the occurrences of fore-fronted word order, the structural framework emerges. The next task was to see if different levels could be established and, if so, what these were. In other words, the work consisted in seeing if some boundaries were stronger than others, and how the units between them related to each other.

IV.2.i Structural Hierarchy

Structural analysis of other NT narratives (notably the Gospel of Luke and Acts) reveals that they are highly organised in a hierarchical structure, with major (high-level) boundaries and, within those, lesser (low-level) ones. Figure 1 illustrates the decreasing extent of the units at descending levels. We have called the largest divisions 'sections', to which we assign Roman numerals. In the Gospel of John, they seem to subdivide into smaller units, on one or two further levels, labelled 'sequences' (with capital letters), and episodes (with lower-case letters) respectively. Making up the lowest level are the smallest units of discourse, the sentences or 'elements'.

Figure 1
Hierarchical Arrangement of Structural Units in John's Gospel

SECTIONS I, II
Sequences A, B
Episodes a, b...
Elements

IV.2.ii Internal arrangements of units within levels

Within each level, it can be observed that the units are arranged in patterns that are familiar not only from classical rhetorical literature but also the writings in the Hebrew Scriptures. Typical arrangements are:

- *linear*: units follow on from each other and are labelled successively. If they are discrete units, each is assigned a new letter (e.g. A B C D). If, on the other hand, they are two parts of the same event, they are given the same letter, with $_1$ added to the letter for the second part (e.g. A A_1).
- *concentric*: sometimes, the units are organised in a mirror arrangement, whereby the first units of a section or sequence are reflected or echoed in the later ones. In a concentric arrangement, there is a single centre and the mirrored units are numbered with $_1$ subscript (e.g. A B C B_1 A_1).
- *symmetrical*: in a symmetrical arrangement, there is a double centre and the mirrored units are again numbered with $_1$ subscript (e.g. A B B_1 A_1).
- *linear and symmetrical combined*: this type of pattern occurs when one opening unit stands alone and is followed by a cluster of units arranged either symmetrically or concentrically (e.g. A B B_1 B).

It is important to note that the length of the units at any level is by no means necessarily uniform. While such irregularity may jar with modern expectations of style, it can lead the analysis of structure astray if consistency is expected or sought. It should also be remembered that because direct speech is treated as integral to the narrative in which it occurs and is not analysed separately, a unit often appears long because of the extent of direct speech within it. This has a notable effect on Section VIII in Table 3 below, which extends from 13.1 to 19.37.

Not only can the length of comparable units vary, but so can the complexity. So, whereas one section may be made up of just two sequences (e.g., Section IV in Table 4 below), another may be made up of an intricate arrangement of sequences and episodes (e.g., Section VI in Table 4).

IV.2.iii Considerations in identifying the levels of the boundaries in John's Gospel

In seeking to classify into a hierarchy the structural boundaries noted in the analysis of fore-fronted sentences, the following observations were made:

- Each occurrence of μετὰ ταῦτα is located at the point of a major change in the direction of the narrative, following a group of units of which the action is cohesive – or, at least, seems to be viewed in that way by the author. This is indicative of a high-level boundary, which looks both back to the previous events (ταῦτα) and forward to what follows them (μετά).
- The two occurrences of μετὰ τοῦτο are found at two distinct levels. At 2.12, the demonstrative summarises as one event (τοῦτο) the series of incidents that has occurred over successive days culminating in 'the third day' (however that time frame may be interpreted). The sentence marks a high-level break from that time frame as it initiates a new direction of activity. At 19.28, in contrast, τοῦτο refers to the one particular event that has just occurred (the entrusting of the beloved disciple and his mother to each other), and introduces the final event of the crucifixion before a new series of activity opens at 19.38 with μετὰ δὲ ταῦτα (19.35-37 being a narrative aside that is assigned here to the second redaction). μετὰ τοῦτο at 19.28 is thus a low-level boundary marker.
- In addition to the high-level boundaries marked by μετὰ ταῦτα or μετὰ τοῦτο, at two further places (11.53; 13.1) there is a forceful change in the time-frame and in the unfolding development of the narrative. 11.53 marks a turning point in the drama of the Gospel overall. The expression ἀπ' ἐκείνης τῆς ἡμέρας, like μετὰ ταῦτα, looks both backwards and forwards; the conjunction οὖν, which is found in John to express the notion of an event developing from the previous one, links the definitive change in the intentions of the Jewish leaders to their fear of national destruction (12.50). 13.1 likewise marks a major development in the perspective of the narrative, setting Jesus' awareness of his impending death in relation to the Passover feast, to which the following events build up.
- The two examples of fore-fronted participles (9.1; 18.1) are connected to the narrative with καί and the demonstrative pronoun ταῦτα respectively. Both are exceptional and not repeated in the list of fore-fronted sentences in D05, although καί is found at 4.46b and 7.1 in B03. Analysis of occurrences of these two connectives elsewhere indicates that they both signal a strong connection with the previous material. This suggests that when they are are used in combination with fore-fronting, the link with the previous material is a strong one and that the boundary they mark is at a low level.
- The first three presentative components (3.1-11; 4.46b-54; 5.5-47) come immediately before a μετὰ ταῦτα boundary and relate to the preceding scenes as a retrospective comment on them in some way.

The remaining two presentative sentences (11.1-50; 12.20-50) are likewise a backward-looking reflection before a major change in direction in the narrative.

IV.2.iv Proposed Hierarchical Arrangement of the Gospel of John

Bearing in mind all of the above points, the Toulouse team detected nine narrative sections in John's Gospel with an introductory prologue and a colophon in conclusion. These were followed by a tenth section in ch. 21. It is striking that the structural divisions are not affected by variant readings, with the possible exception of 7.1 where B03 (retained by N-A^{28}) reads καί; its absence has considerable, and mixed, support including 𝔓^{66} and ℵ01^{*2}. D05. The only other variant readings within the structural boundaries, both adopted by N-A^{28}, are at 4.45, where B03 reads ὅτε while D05 supported by ℵ01 reads ὡς; and 4.46b where B03 introduces a presentative sentence with καί for which D05, again with mixed support including ℵ01, has the more usual δέ.

Table 4

Structural Units in the Gospel of John

Circumstance		**Points of departure**	**Reference**
Prologue	Introduction		1.1-18
Hinge to narrative	I [A_1]	καὶ αὕτη ἐστὶν ἡ μαρτυρία τοῦ Ἰωάννου ὅτε...	1.19-28
the next day	I [A_2]	τῇ ἐπαύριον	1.29-34
the next day	I [A_3]	τῇ ἐπαύριον	1.35-42
the next day	I [A_4]	τῇ ἐπαύριον	1.43-51
time	I [B]	καὶ τῇ ἡμέρᾳ τῇ τρίτῃ γάμος ἐγένετο	2.1-11
After this	II [A]	μετὰ τοῦτο	2.12-22
when	II [A_1]	ὡς δὲ ἦν ... ἐπίστευσαν	2.23-25
presentative	II [B]	ἦν δὲ ἄνθρωπος	3.1-21
After these things	III [A]	μετὰ ταῦτα	3.22-36
when	III [Ba]	ὡς οὖν ἔγνω... ἀφῆκεν	4.1-38
place	III [Bb]	ἐκ δὲ τῆς πόλεως ἐκείνης πολλοὶ ἐπίστευσαν	4.39-44
when	III [Ba_1]	ὡς [ὅτε] οὖν ἦλθεν ... ἐξεδέξαντο	4.45-46a
presentative	III [C]	ἦν δέ [καὶ] τις βασιλίσκος	4.46b-54

After these things	IV [A]	μετὰ ταῦτα	5.1-3[4]
presentative	IV [B]	ἦν δὲ ἄνθρωπος	5.5-47
After these things	V [A]	μετὰ ταῦτα	6.1-15
when	V [B]	ὡς δὲ ὀψία ἐγένετο κατέβησαν...	6.16-21
the next day	V [A_1]	τῇ ἐπαύριον	6.22-71
After these things	VI [Aa]	[+ καὶ] μετὰ ταῦτα	7.1-13
time	VI [Ab]	ἤδη δὲ τῆς ἑορτῆς μεσαζούσης ἀνέβη	7.14-36
time	VI [Ab_1]	ἐν δὲ τῇ ἡμέρᾳ τῇ μεγάλῃ	7.37-42
schism	VI [Ba]	σχίσμα οὖν ἐγένετο	7.43-52
again	VI [Bb]	πάλιν οὖν ἐλάλησεν	8.12-59
location	VI [Bb_1]	καὶ παραγῶν εἶδεν	9.1-10.18
schism	VI [Ba_1]	σχίσμα οὖν [πάλιν] ἐγένετο	10.19-42
presentative	VI [C]	ἦν δέ τις ἀσθενῶν	11.1-52
From that day	VII [A]	ἀπ' ἐκείνης οὖν τῆς ἡμέρας ἐβουλεύσαντο	11.53-57
time	VII [B]	ὁ οὖν Ἰησοῦς πρὸ ἓξ ἡμερῶν τοῦ πάσχα ἦλθεν	12.1-11
the next day	VII [B_1]	τῇ ἐπαύριον	12.12-19
presentative	VII [C]	ἦσαν δὲ καὶ Ἕλληνές τινες	12.20-50
Before Passover	VIII [A]	πρὸ δὲ τῆς ἑορτῆς τοῦ πάσχα...ἠγάπησεν	13.1-17.26
speech	VIII [B]	ταῦτα εἰπὼν ὁ Ἰησοῦς ἐξῆλθεν	18.1-19.27
after this	VIII [B_1]	μετὰ τοῦτο	19.28-37
After these things	IX [A]	μετὰ δὲ ταῦτα	19.38-42
the first day	IX [B]	τῇ δὲ μιᾷ τῶν σαββάτων...ἔρχεται	20.1-18
time	IX [B_1]	οὔσης οὖν ὀψίας...ἦλθεν	20.19-29
Conclusion	Colophon	πολλὰ μὲν οὖν... δε	20.30-31
After these things	X[A]	μετὰ ταῦτα	21.1-14
time	X[B]	ὅτε οὖν ἠρίστησαν λέγει	21.15-24
Conclusion	Colophon	ἔστιν δὲ καὶ ἄλλα πολλά	21.25

V. Discussion

There would be a great deal to say about the structure that emerges in Table 4. It is of particular relevance for exegetical discussion, which will constitute a later stage of the Toulouse project. While we are confident as a research team in the location of the boundaries, the precise relationship of the units between them is still considered to be provisional at this stage. Points that have generated both surprise and interest include:

- The series of the adverbial connective τῇ ἐπαύριον in Section I, culminating in τῇ ἡμέρᾳ τῇ τρίτῃ, highlights the close association between these sequences despite the apparent disparity of their content. It suggests intertextuality with the Torah narrative of the people's preparation to hear the commandments of God, culminating in their acknowledgement of Moses' authority to transmit them (Exodus 19).
- The cluster of episodes around the 'schism' underlines the significance for the author of the disagreement among the Jewish leaders.
- The simplicity of Section VIII is striking, and is surprising in view of its length, even without the direct speech The absence of any fore-fronted sentence after Jesus' command to his disciples to get up and move on at 14.31b until the fronted participial clause at 18.1, may perhaps indicate that the intervening direct speech passages have been added during a later redaction, by the same or a different author.
- The fact that Section X begins with μετὰ ταῦτα in the same way as Sections III, IV, V, VI and IX, would seem to confirm that this connective is indeed intended by John as a section boundary marker.

VI. Conclusion

At this stage, no further conclusions are drawn other than to say that the use of formal linguistic features to identify the structure of a narrative promises, on the one hand, to bring much-needed objectivity to the discussion concerning the intentions of the narrator of John's Gospel. On the other hand, it also promises interesting and intriguing insights into how the writer viewed the material he was presenting, the associations he made between events and the significance he accorded them. For both exegetical studies and studies in the theology of John's Gospel, the narrative framework can thus serve as an objective basis.

Following this stage of linguistic research, our current activity is focused on producing an annotated translation in French of the text of John's Gospel, comparing the Greek of Codex Bezae with that of the eclectic text generally adopted for translation and exegesis.[10]

Jenny READ HEIMERDINGER
Hurworth House
Front St
Appleton Wiske
Northallerton
North Yorkshire
DL6 2AA
ENGLAND
jgheimerdinger@gmail.com

[10] Jenny Read-Heimerdinger and Béatrice Papasoglou (eds), *Lire l'évangile en contexte primitif. Une traduction de l'Évangile de Jean selon le Codex de Bèze* (forthcoming).

Words that Do not Mean what They Say

CHRYS C. CARAGOUNIS

In particular contexts, the New Testament uses certain words with a meaning that is neither connected with their etymology nor with meanings that could normally fall within their semantic range. It is rather a case of using a word with a meaning that properly belongs to another word altogether.

This is not a New Testament phenomenon. It occurs already in classical authors. The present article establishes this usage by means of a large number of examples from a large number of Platōn's works. For this purpose the verb λέγειν is utilized, which, for example, in questions put to Sōkratēs, τί λέγεις; does not carry the sense of "What are you saying?" but "What do you mean (by what you are saying)?" We find this pregnant usage, for example, in Jn 2:21–22, where ἐκεῖνος δὲ ἔλεγεν and ὅτι τοῦτο ἔλεγεν do not mean "But he was speaking of" and "that this was what he had said" but "but He meant (by what he was saying)" and "That this was what he meant" respectively. In general, Bible translations and commentators have missed the real import of such New Testament sayings translating λέγειν by rote by the verb "to say."

The study presents three more verbs, μισεῖν = 'not to love more than' (e.g. Lk 14:26), γράφειν = 'to mean (by what we write)' (2 Cor 1:13), and εἰσφέρειν (εἰσενέγκῃς) = 'to hinder from', 'not to allow' (Mt 6:13). The usual, etymological translation of the last verb in the Lord's Prayer in Bible versions and commentators leads to an understanding of the nature of God that is contrary to the spirit of the New Testament.

Keywords: New Testament, translation, meaning, λέγειν, μισεῖν, γράφειν, εἰσφέρειν.

Speaking here strictly of the Hellenic language, there are some words in certain contexs that do not carry their usual meaning but a meaning that does not fall either etymologically or customarily within the semantic field of the particular word. The meaning that is expressed in such cases is a meaning that is demanded by the context, while the actual word functions only as the vehicle by which this meaning is conveyed.[1] This contextual meaning does not become one of the meanings of the particular word. It is rather the case that a particular word is used improperly, conveying a meaning it has not and will not acquire. Thus,

[1] This is the case in other languages as well, e.g. English. For example, if one of two persons speaking about their respective weight, told the other "I weigh 78 kilos," and you? The other might reply: "I am eighty kilos." In this context, the meaning of 'I am' clearly means 'I weigh,' although the verb 'to be' does not include the meaning of 'to weigh.'

the word employed is used instead of another word, which would more properly express the meaning required by the context.

In this study I intend to take up four New Testament words that exhibit this usage. Before I take up for discussion these words, I shall proceed to establish this usage by means of a few classical texts. This circumstance will show that the usage is quite old and that in this respect the New Testament authors only follow the example of earlier generations of Hellēnes.

Such examples occur in many classical authors,[2] but in order to economize space I shall concentrate on one of the most representative authors of classical antiquity: one who treated the Hellenic language – in particular, the Attic dialect – with unusual dexterity and sensitiveness and made one of the greatest contributions to beautifying and perfecting this fine instrument of expression of the human mind. This author is none other than the greatest philosopher of antiquity and a supreme *litteratus*: Platōn.[3]

I shall exemplify the procedure I outlined briefly above by concentrating on one single verb. I shall present a large number of passages from a large number of works by Platōn, to show how well-established this usage was and that the few examples that we meet in the New Testament are in full accord with classical usage. The verb on which my discussion of Platōn's texts will concentrate is the verb λέγω = 'I say,' 'I speak.'

In *Euthyphrōn* 10 a, Sōkratēs asks Euthyphrōn the question: ἐννόησον γὰρ τὸ τοιόνδε· ἆρα τὸ ὅσιον ὅτι ὅσιον ἐστιν φιλεῖται ὑπὸ τῶν θεῶν, ἢ ὅτι φιλεῖται ὅσιον ἔστιν; "Now, try to understand this: Is the holy loved by the gods because it is holy, or is it holy because it is loved by the gods?"[4] To this Euthyphrōn replies: οὐκ οἶδ' ὅτι *λέγεις*, ὦ Σώκρατες. Literally translated, the text says: "I do not know what you *are saying*, Sōkratēs." It is quite obvious here, however, that the translation "what you are saying" is thoroughly unsatisfactory. Euthyphrōn certainly knew the ordinary denotation of all the words that Sōkratēs had uttered. So, he could not possibly have meant that he did not understand Sōkratēs' words as such. Here, as very often, Platōn (and the main character of his works, Sōkratēs) is concerned with *meaning* in the communication, not with that of mere words. What Euthyphrōn did not understand was the *meaning* that Sōkratēs put into his words; that is, the *content* and *import* of what

[2] Sophoklēs, Aristophanēs, Xenophōn and others.

[3] The quotations are from the edition of Platōn by I. Burnet: *Platonis opera*, 5 Vols. (OCT) (Oxonii: E Typographeo Clarendoniano, 1900–1907, rp 1988).

[4] The word ὅσιος, often translated by 'holy' (e.g. LXX: Ps 15:10 (cf. Acts 2:27); 36:28; 85:2; 85:2; Prov 22:11), actually means "That which is in harmony with the will or laws of the gods, which they have determined/prescribed for humans."

he had said. Thus, the verb λέγεις carries a pregnant meaning. The word λέγεις functions as the instrument or vehicle for the real meaning that Platōn intends through it. Therefore, the translation ought to be: “I do not know what you *mean* (by what you are saying), Sōkratēs.” That this is the import of the verb is shown also by Sōkratēs’ initial exhortation to Euthyphrōn “try to *understand* this” as well as by Sōkratēs’ immediately following words: ἀλλὰ ἐγὼ πειράσομαι σαφέστερον φράσαι “But I shall try to put it *more clearly*.”[5]

This pregnant usage of λέγω is used in Platōn’s works almost times without number.[6] Often it occurs with the interrogative adverb, that expresses manner: πῶς; ‘how?,’ ‘in what way?’ A few examples of this are the following: in Platōn, *Phaidōn* 73 d, Phaidōn relates for Echekratēs the conversation Sōkratēs had with some of his disciples on the day of his death. At one point we read: ἆρα οὐχὶ τοῦτο δικαίως λέγομεν ὅτι ἀνεμνήσθη, οὗ τὴν ἔννοιαν ἔλαβεν; “Are we not right in saying: ‘when one grasps the meaning of something, he remembers it?’ to which the interlocutor replies: Πῶς λέγεις; “How/what do you *mean*?” In answer to this question, the first speaker proceeds to explain: οἷον τὰ τοιάδε “Such as these,” “Like, for example, the following,” and then he proceeds to give explanatory examples.

In Platōn’s various works, we meet with such formulations as *Phaidōn* 104 d: Πῶς λέγεις; “how/what do you mean”;[7] *Theaitētos*, 174 a: Πῶς τοῦτο λέγεις, ὦ Σάκρατες; “How do you *mean* this, O Sōkratēs?”;[8] *Politikos*, 262 c: πῶς, ὦ ξένε, λέγεις τοῦτο; “How do you *mean* this, O stranger?”;[9] *Symposion* 201 e: καὶ ἐγὼ, Πῶς λέγεις, ἔφην, ὦ Διότιμα; “And I said: what do you *mean*, O Diotima?”;[10] *Prōtagoras*, 333 e: πότερον, ἦν δ᾽ ἐγώ,

[5] Cf. also Platōn, *Euthyphrōn* 13 b: ἡ δὲ δὴ ὁσιότης καὶ εὐσέβεια θεῶν, ὦ Εὐθύφρων; οὕτω λέγεις; “And holiness is fear of the gods, O Euthyphrōn? *would you say so*?” In other words: “Is this your *meaning*?”

[6] Strangely enough, F. Montanari, in his commendable lexicon, *The Brill Dictionary of Ancient Greek* (Brill: Leiden-Boston, 2015), does not discuss this use of λέγω. The reason is probably that this meaning is not one of the proper meanings of λέγω, but a special usage, whereby an author intends another meaning than the normal meanings of the verb, which, in the context, is perceivable.

[7] See also Platōn, *Theaitētos*, 188d: Πῶς λέγεις; *Sophistēs*, 222 b: Πῶς λέγεις; *Gorgias*, 447 d: Πῶς λέγεις; 491 d: Πῶς λέγεις; *Politeia* 375 d: Πῶς λέγεις; *Philebos*, 13 b: Πῶς λέγεις, ὦ Σώκρατες; *Phaidros*, 227 d: πῶς λέγεις, ὦ βέλτιστε Σώκρατες; “What do you mean, most excellent Sōkratēs?”

[8] See also *Kratylos*, 393 d: Πῶς τοῦτο λέγεις; *Alkibiadēs*, 132 d: πῶς τοῦτο λέγεις; *Menōn* 96 e: πῶς τοῦτο λέγεις, ὦ Σώκρατες; *Politeia* 347 a: πῶς τοῦτο λέγεις, ὦ Σώκρατες;

[9] See further: Platōn, *Laws*, 696 b: πῶς τοῦτο, ὦ ξένε, λέγεις; “How do you mean this, O stranger?” *Alkibiadēs*, 117 d. πῶς αὖ λέγεις τοῦτο; “Now, how do you mean this (again)?”

[10] Platōn, *Charmidēs*, 170 a: πῶς λέγεις, ἔφη; *Euthydēmos*, 279 d: πῶς, ἔφη, τοῦτο λέγεις;

λέγεις ὦ Πρωτάγορα; “what is your opinion (= what do you mean), O Prōtagoras, I said?”; *Hippias*, 284 d: Νόμον δὲ λέγεις, ὦ Ἱππία; “Do you mean the law, O Hippias?”; *Parmenides*, 133 d: πῶς λέγεις, φάναι, τὸν Σωκράτην; “What do you mean? said Sōkratēs;”[11] *Lachēs* 199 d: ἢ πῶς λέγεις, ὦ Νικία; “Or how/what do you mean, O Nikias?” *Phaidōn*, 90 a: Πῶς λέγεις; ἔφην ἐγώ “What do you mean, said I.”[12]

The above plethora of Platonic examples, in which the author uses the verb λέγειν quite improperly by giving it a meaning that the verb as such does not possess, but which is demanded by the context, are sufficient evidence for ascribing to λέγειν in such contexts the sense of ‘to mean.’ Having established the sense of ‘to mean’ for λέγειν, by means of Platōn’s works, I shall now proceed to argue that this is the meaning of λέγειν in a number of places in the New Testament.

1. **Λέγειν (to say, to speak) = ‘to mean’**

An obvious example of this usage is Jn 2:21. In his argument against the Jews, Jesus had said Λύσατε τὸν ναὸν τοῦτον καὶ ἐν τρισὶν ἡμέραις ἐγερῶ αὐτόν (Jn 2:19).[13] To this, the Jews replied: τεσσαράκοντα καὶ ἓξ ἔτεσιν οἰκοδομήθη ὁ ναὸς οὗτος καὶ σὺ ἐν τρισὶν ἡμέραις ἐγερεῖς αὐτόν; (Jn 2:20) And now the evangelist takes over to explain what Jesus meant: ἐκεῖνος δὲ ἔλεγεν περὶ τοῦ ναοῦ τοῦ σώματος αὐτοῦ. ὅτε οὖν ἠγέρθη ἐκ νεκρῶν, ἐμνήσθησαν οἱ μαθηταὶ αὐτοῦ ὅτι τοῦτο ἔλεγεν, καὶ ἐπίστευσαν τῇ γραφῇ καὶ τῷ λόγῳ ὃν εἶπεν ὁ Ἰησοῦς (Jn 2:21–22).

How is John’s comment to be translated? In general translators of John have kept to the literal meaning of λέγειν = ‘to say’/‘to speak.’ Thus, *NRSV*[14]: “But he was *speaking of* the temple of his body ... his disciples remembered that he had *said* this.” This translation is most unsatisfactory, particularly in its second part. To the same effect, though varying in

[11] See also Platōn, *Parmenidēs* 127 e: πῶς, φάναι, ὦ Ζήνων, τοῦτο λέγεις; “Saying, How do you mean this, O Zenōn?”

[12] See further: Platōn, *Kratylos*, 400 b: Τὸ σῶμα λέγεις; “Do you mean the body?”; *Sophistēs*, 234 a: παιδιὰν λέγεις τινά; “You mean/intend some sort of joke?”; *Symposion*, 200 d: εἰ ἄλλο τι λέγεις ἢ τόδε; “Do you mean something else or this?”; *Lysis*, 207 e: Πῶς λέγεις, ἦν δ’ ἐγώ “What do you mean, said I”; *Gorgias*, 461 d: Τί τοῦτο λέγεις; “What do you mean by this?”

[13] The New Testamnent quotations are from *Novum Testamentum Graece*, eds. Barbara et Kurt Aland, Johannes Karavidopoulos, Carlo M. Martini, Bruce M. Metzger, 28 revidierte Auflage (Stuttgart: Deutsche Bibelgeselleschaft, 2012, korr. Druck 2015).

[14] *NRSV* = *New Revised Standard Version* (London: SPCK, 2015).

actual wording, *Tyndale*[15], *Rheims*[16], *KJV*[17], *RV*[18], *RSV*[19], *NEB*[20], *JerB*[21], *NAB*[22], *NASB*[23], *NIV*[24] *and Amplified Bible*[25]. Of non-English translations, *Die Bibel* (M. Luther Revised)[26] has: "Er aber redete von dem Tempel seines Leibes ... dachten seiner Jünger daran, daß er dies gesagt hatte." Similarly the *Elberfelder Bibeln* (revidierte)[27]. This is the rendering adopted also by the Dutch *Bijbel* (1951, rp. 1996)[28]: "Maar Hij sprak van de tempel zijnes lichaams ... herinnerden sijn discipelen zich, dat Hij dit gezegd had" ("But he spoke about the temple of his body ... his disciples remembered that he had said this"). The Dutch Bijbel (2004)[29] and the *Naardense Bijbel*[30] follow suit. The French *La Sainte Bible* (*Segond*)[31] similarly has: "Mais il parlait du temple de son corps ... ses disciples se souvinrent qu'il avait dit cela," followed by *La Bible en français courant*. The Swedish *Bibel 2000*[32] has "Men det tempel han talade om var hans kropp ... kom hans lärjungar ihåg att han hade sagt detta" ("But the temple he spoke of was his body ... his disciples remebered that he had said this"); the same wording is shared by the *Folkbibeln*[33]. In similar manner

[15] *Tyndale = Tyndale's New Testament*, Tr. by William Tyndale. Modern-spelling Edition by D. Daniel (New Haven: YUP 1995).

[16] *Rheims = New Testament* (of 1582, in *The Precise Parallel New Testament*. Greek Text with *King James Version, Rheims New Testament, Amplified Bible, New International Version, New Revised Standard Version, New American Bible, New American Standard Bible*, ed. J.R. Kohlenberger III (Oxford: Oxford University Press, 1995).

[17] *KJV = King James Version* (of 1611, innumerable editions).

[18] *RV = Revised Version* (Oxford: OUP, no date).

[19] *RSV = Revised Standard Version* (New York - Glasgow: Collins, 1952).

[20] *NEB = New English Bible* (Oxford: OUP 1970).

[21] *JerB = The Jerusalem Bible* (London: Darton, Longman & Todd, 1974).

[22] *NAB = New American Bible* (see under *The Precise Parallel New Testament*).

[23] *NASB = New American Standard Bible* (London: SPCK 2015).

[24] *NIV = The Holy Bible. New International Version* (London etc.: Hodder & Stoughton, 1986).

[25] *Amplified Bible = Amplified New Testament*, 1958 (1987) (see under *The Precise Parallel New Testament*).

[26] *Die Bibel = Die Bibel* Nach der Übersetzung Martin Luthers. Mit Apokryphen Stuttgart: (Deutsche Bibelgesellschaft, Revidierten Fassung 1984).

[27] *Elberfelder Bibel = Die Bibel Aus dem Grundtext übersetzt*. Revidierte Elberfelder Bibel (Wuppertal: Brockhaus 1986).

[28] *Bijbel* (1952, 1996) = *Bijbel. Vertaling 1951 in opdracht van het Nederlandsch Bijbelgenootschap bewerkt door de daartoe benoemde commissie* (Leeuwarden: Jongbloed b.v. 1996).

[29] *Bijbel (2004) = Bijbel met deuterokanonieke boeken* 's-Hertogenbosch: Uitgeverei NBG (Heerenveen, 2004).

[30] *De Naardense Bijbel = Die Naardense Bijbel*. De vollendige tekst van de Hebreeuwse Bijbel en het Nieuwe Testament, vertaald door Pieter Oussoren (Vught; Skandalon, 2007).

[31] *La Sainte Bible = La Sainte Bible* par Louis Segond, Nouvelle edition de Geneve (Société Biblique de Genève, 1979).

[32] *Bibeln 2000 = Bibeln* (Bibelkommissionens översättning) (Stockholm, 2000).

[33] *Folkbibeln = Bibeln. Den Heliga Skrift* (Svenska Folkbibeln, Stockholm: XP Media, 1998).

the Spanish *Santa Biblia* (1992)[34] has: "Pero el templo al que Jesús se refería era su proprio cuerpo ... sus discípulos se acordaron de lo que habia dicho" ("But the temple Jesus was referring to was his own body ... his disciples remembered what he had said") and the Italian *La Sacra Bibbia*[35] likewise has "Ma egli parlava del tempio del suo corpo ... i suoi discepoli si ricordarono ch'egli avea detta questo." ("But he was speaking of the temple of his body ... his disciples rembered that he has said this").

All of the above translations render λέγειν literally by the verb "to speak."[36] Because of the contrast to the previous statement of the Jews that is signalled by the contrastive conjuction δέ = "but," all of these translations essentially – though only implicitly – express the idea that Jesus meant his words in a different way than the Jews had understood them. Nevertheless, the difference intended here, is, to put it simply and directly, that John is using ἔλεγεν with the force of "he *meant* (by what he said)," which is missed by the above translations. Therefore, verses 21–22, should be translated: "But he *meant* [by what he was saying] the temple that consisted in his body. When, therefore, he arose from the dead, his disciples remembered that this was what he *meant*, and they believed the scripture and the word that Jesus had spoken."[37]

[34] *Santa Biblia* = *Santa Biblia. La Biblia en versión popular. Traducción directa de los textos originales: hebreo, aramaico y griego* (Madrid: Sociedad Biblica, 1992).

[35] *La Sacra Bibbia* = *Ossia l'Antico e il nuovo Testamento*, Versione riveduta (Roma: BFBS, no date).

[36] Of commentators, Alford, *The Greek Testament*, With a Critically Revised Text: A Digest of Various Readings: Marginal References to Verbal and Idiomatic Usage: Prolegomena: and a Critical and Exegetical Commentary, 4 Vols. (London etc.: Rivingtons), Vol. I, 6th ed. (1868); Vol. II, 5th ed. (1865); Vol. III, 4th ed. (1865); Vol. IV, 3rd ed. (1866), Vol. I., 711, makes no comment. Barrett, *The Gospel according to St. John, An Introduction with Commentary and Notes on the Greek Text*, 2nd ed. (Philadelphia 1978), 200–201, has nothing to say on the matter. Neither does Morris, *The Gospel according to John, The English Text with Introduction, Exposition and Notes* (NICNT) (Grand Rapids: Eerdmans 1971), 196 and 201 ff. have anything to say. Brown, *The Gospel according to John* (AB), 2 Vols., Vol. I, (London: Geoffrey Chapman 1966, rp. 1971); Vol. II (Garden City, NY: Doubleday & Co. 1970, rp. 1977); Vol. I. 116 and 124 f., is also silent. Bernard, too, *A Critical and Exegetical Commentary on the Gospel according to St. John*, 2 Vols. (Edinburgh: T & T Clark 1928, rp. 1963);Vol. I, 96 f., does not explain the ἔλεγεν of Jn 2:21 other than "was speaking" and this is the case with Beasley-Murray, *John (WBC)* (Waco, Texas 1987), 41 and Lindars, *The Gospel of John*, (NCBC), 1972, rp. (Grand Rapids: Eerdmans, 1986), 143 f. These authors concentrate, instead on speculations about which temple Jesus was speaking, disregarding John's own explanation.

[37] It is of interest that of all the translations that I have consulted, only two have rendered the text – though partly – in strict accordance with its meaning: the *Einheitsübersetzung: Das Neue Testament.* Einheitsübersetzung der Heiligen Schrift, Ökumenischer Text, Katolische Bibelanstalt (Stuttgart 1996), has "Er aber *meinte* den Tempel seines Leibes ... erinnerten sich seine Jünger, daß er dies gesagt hatte" and the *Bijbel in Gewone Taal* (Nederlands Bijbelgenootschap: Haarlem 2014): "Maar med de tempel *bedoolde* Jezus zijn eigen lichaam ... herinnerden de leerlingen zich wat Jezus gezegd had" – in both these translations

During the interrogation of Jesus by the High Priest, related by Matthew (26:59–68), Peter was approached by a servant girl who identified him as one of Jesus' followers (Mt 26:69). Peter's immediate reaction was: Οὐκ οἶδα τί λέγεις, literally: "I do not know what you are saying." Peter knew very well the meaning of the words the girl had used. What he was pretending not to understand was what she *meant* by what she was saying. This time the *NASB, NAB, NIV* and *NRSV* all have rendered with "what you are talking about," which give a tolerable sense, with the *Amplified Bible* coming out clearly: "what you *mean.*" In Luke's Gospel (22:60) it is one of the men servants who confronts Peter, to whom he gives the same basic reply: Ἄνθρωπε, οὐκ οἶδα ὃ λέγεις, "Man, I do not know/understand what you are saying," i.e. "what you *mean!*" Mark (14:68), like Matthew, has a servant girl reveal Peter's connection to Jesus, to which Peter gives the emphatically negative reply: Οὔτε οἶδα οὔτε ἐπίσταμαι σὺ τί λέγεις, "I neither know nor understand what you are saying (i.e. what you *mean*)."

According to Jn 6:70–71, when many of Jesus' loose followers left him while his disciples affirmed their commitment to him, Jesus said: οὐκ ἐγὼ ὑμᾶς τοὺς δώδεκα ἐξελεξάμην; καὶ ἐξ ὑμῶν εἷς διάβολος ἐστιν. ἔλεγεν δὲ Ἰούδαν Σίμωνος Ἰσκαριώτου· οὗτος γὰρ ἤμελεν παραδιδόναι αὐτόν, "Was it not I who chose you twelve? And yet (in spite of that) one of you is a Devil. (Thereby) he *meant* Judas, son of Simon Iskariot; for it was he who would betray him."[38]

In a dispute with the Jews, Jesus made the point that his teaching was in accordance with what he had heard from Him who had sent him (meaning the Father) (Jn 8:26). At this point (Jn 8:27), John, as his habit was, makes the comment: οὐκ ἔγνωσαν ὅτι τὸν πατέρα αὐτοῖς ἔλεγεν, "they did not understand that he *meant/intended* the Father" – not merely "said [this of] the Father."[39]

During the last supper and following the giving of the piece of bread to Judas, Jesus said to him: "What you are about to do, do quickly." Thereupon John comments: τινὲς γὰρ ἐδόκουν, ἐπεὶ τὸ γλωσσόκομον εἶχεν Ἰούδας, ὅτι λέγει αὐτῷ [ὁ] Ἰησοῦς· ἀγόρασον ὧν χρείαν ἔχομεν εἰς τὴν ἑορτήν (Jn 13:29), "Some (of the disciples) thought that because Judas had the purse, Jesus said (i.e. *meant*): Buy what we need for the Feast."

the second part is wrongly translated "gesagt hatte" and "gezegd had." It ought to have been "he *meant!*"

[38] Typically, Barrett, *The Gospel of St. John*, 307-308, like other commentators, has nothing to say on the meaning of ἔλεγεν, which is conveniently understood as "he spoke about." Alford, too, in his *The Greek Testament*, Vol. I., 771, refrains from commenting on ἔλεγεν.

[39] Barrett, *The Gospel of St. John*, 343, seems to recognize this. Brown, *The Gospel according to John*, Vol. I, 350 f. offers no comment, nor does Beasley-Murray, *John*, 97.

Again, the verb λέγει is usually rendered in our translations incorrectly by 'to say' or 'to tell.'[40]

John, writing for non-Jewish readers, is in the habit of translating the meaning of Semitic words into Hellenic. This is the case, for example, at Jn 20:16. At Jesus' calling Maria Magdalene by her name, outside the grave, she turned around and exclaimed: Ραββουνι. Since this was a non-Hellenic word, John proceeds to translate its meaning into Hellenic. He writes: ὃ λέγεται Διδάσκαλε, literally "which is *said* Teacher."[41] Obviously, this is not what John meant. The word λέγεται is here used in the sense of 'it means,' i.e. "which *means* Teacher." Here, finally, *NASB, NAB, NIV, NRSV* and *Amplified Bibl*e render with the verb 'to mean.'[42] The same is the case with Acts 9:36. Luke finds it necessary to interpret the Semitic name *Tabitha* by writing: ἣ διερμηνευομένη λέγεται Δορκάς "which, when translated, *means Dorkas.*"

In addition to the above examples, there are some texts in which the verb λέγειν carries a particular sense. For example, Mk 12:18: Καὶ ἔρχονται Σαδδουκαῖοι πρὸς αὐτόν, οἵτινες λέγουσιν ἀνάστασιν μὴ εἶναι, "And (certain) Sadducees came to him who say there is no resurrection." This strictly literal translation is quite flat. The verb λέγουσιν, in the context, does not mean 'they say,' as *Rheims, KJV, NAB, NASB, NIV, NRSV* and the *Amplified Bible* render it but 'they hold as a tenet,' 'they teach,' in other words, "it is their belief or their opinion".[43] Thus, the sense of "they *mean*" underlies the use of λέγουσιν.

In Lk 9:20 Jesus, having heard of the opinion of the Jewish people about himself, asks his disciples: Ὑμεῖς δὲ τίνα με λέγετε εἶναι; "But as for you/but you yourselves, who do you say that I am?" Here, again, it is obvious that Jesus is not merely asking about what the disciples *say* about Jesus' identity but about their crystalized opinion of him; "Who do you *think* I am?" in other words, "What is your *opinion* of me?" The question is one of *meaning*! The same is the case with Jn 9:17: Τί σὺ λέγεις περὶ αὐτοῦ; "What do you *think* of him?" – not the over-literal translation of *Rheims, KJV, NAB, NASB, NIV, NRSV* and the *Amplified Bible.*

1 Cor 1:10: Παρακαλῶ δὲ ὑμᾶς, ἀδελφοί, διὰ τοῦ ὀνόματος τοῦ κυρίου ἡμῶν Ἰησοῦ Χριστοῦ, ἵνα τὸ αὐτὸ λέγητε πάντες has been translated literally by *Rheims* and *KJV.* The versions of *NAB, NASB, NIV, NRSV* and the *Amplified Bible* have perceived the special force of

[40] Lindars, *The Gospel of John*, 460, speaks only indirectly: "the beloved Disciple, who does not know the meaning of Jesus words."

[41] Bernard, *The Gospel according to St John*, Vol. II, 667, does not translate λέγεται.

[42] Brown, *The Gospel according to John*, Vol. II, 1010, bypasses it without comment.

[43] Voelz, *Mark*, 2 Vols. Concordia Commentary (Saint Louis: Concordia Publishing House, 2019), Vol. II, does not comment on the meaning of λέγουσιν (894), though he speaks of the Sadducees' rejection of the resurrection (892), i.e. he recognizes their tenet.

λέγητε and rendered it more semantically by some such verb as 'agree,' 'be in agreement,' and 'be in perfect harmony.' However, in 1 Cor 1:12: λέγω δὲ τοῦτο, ὅτι ἕκαστος ὑμῶν λέγει, it is quite obvious that what Paul means is: "This is what I *mean*!" And this translation is adopted by the more modern translations: *NAB, NASB, NIV, NRSV* and the *Amplified Bible.*[44]

Finally, 1 Cor 14:16: ἐπεὶ ἐὰν εὐλογῇς ἐν πνεύματι, ὁ ἀναπληρῶν τὸν τόπον τοῦ ἰδιώτου πῶς ἐρεῖ τὸ 'Αμήν ἐπὶ τῇ σῇ εὐχαριστίᾳ, ἐπειδὴ τί λέγεις οὐκ οἶδεν; Does λέγεις refer to the actual glossolalia sounds that the ἰδιώτης hears but does not understand or to their *import*, that is, the *message* they convey? Translations such as *Rheims, KJV, NEB, NAB, NASB, NIV, NRSV, Amplified Bible, JerB, TEV*[45], have opted for the former.[46] Commentators, too, seem to understand λέγεις of the actual sounds.[47] In the context, such a reference must be certainly included. Glossolalia was not understood by anyone except (probably) by the speaker. But the question is whether Paul's meaning ends here or that it also means that the message is not understood – if it is not interpreted.

2. Μισεῖν (= to hate) = 'not to love more than'

The above finding about the semantic usage of λέγειν in certain contexts as 'to mean' rather than 'to say,' applies to other verbs as well. This is the case with the verb μισεῖν.

In Lk 14:26 we read the unsettling statement of Jesus: Εἴ τις ἔρχεται πρός με καὶ οὐ μισεῖ τὸν πατέρα ἑαυτοῦ καὶ τὴν μητέρα καὶ τὴν γυναῖκα καὶ τὰ τέκνα καὶ τοὺς ἀδελφοὺς καὶ τὰς ἀδελφάς, ἔτι τε καὶ τὴν ψυχὴν ἑαυτοῦ, οὐ δύναται εἶναί μου μαθητής, literally: "If anyone comes to me and does not *hate* his father and mother and wife and children and brothers and sisters, and in addition, his own soul, he cannot be my disciple."

This statement from the founder of Christianity gives the impression that Christianity is a religion of hate. Jesus is demanding of his disciples to hate their closest relatives! This, not only stands in conflict with the many statements in the New Testament about love towards other people (e.g. Mt 22:39; Rm 13:8 f.) and even toward enemies (Mt 5:44; Rm 12:20) but also with the explicit commandment "Honour thy father and thy

[44] The *Rheims* and *KJV* adopt their usual literal renderings even here.

[45] *TEV* = *Today's English Version* (New York: American Bible Society, 1966).

[46] Similarly, *Die Bibel* (Luther revised), *Einheitsübersetzung*, the *Bibeln 2000* and *Folkbibeln*, *La Sainte Bible*, the *Bijbel* (1951, 1996), the *Santa Biblia* and the *La Sacra Bibbia*.

[47] E.g. Fee, *The First Epistle to the Corinthians*, (NICNT) (Grand Rapids: Eerdmans 1993), 673.

mother" (Ex 20:12; Deut 5:16. Cf. also Ex 21:17), which is repeated and confirmed by Jesus, according to Mt 15:4.

It is obvious here that μισεῖ cannot possibly mean 'hate.'[48] The verb μισεῖ is used improperly with another meaning, a meaning that is not connected with it etymologically nor is it one of the recognized meanings associated with this verb. The meaning demanded here is found in the parallel wording of Mt 10:37: Ὁ φιλῶν πατέρα ἢ μητέρα ὑπὲρ ἐμὲ οὐκ ἔστιν μου ἄξιος· καὶ ὁ φιλῶν υἱὸν ἢ θυγατέρα ὑπὲρ ἐμὲ οὐκ ἔστιν μου ἄξιος, "He who *loves* father or mother *more than me* is not worthy of me; he who *loves* son or daughter *more than me* is not worthy of me." Luke's radical wording here is not unique (cf. Lk 12:49–53).[49]

We have the same Semitic understanding of 'hate' in Mt 6:24 (= Lk 16:13): Οὐδεὶς δύναται δυσὶ κυρίοις δουλεύειν· ἢ γὰρ τὸν ἕνα μισήσει καὶ τὸν ἕτερον ἀγαπήσει ... "No one can serve two masters: for either he will hate the one and love the other ..." Here, love and hatred are juxtaposed as inevitable, as if being fond of one master inexorably leads to hatred of another master. But this is not so in ordinary human relations. Surely, what Jesus means by μισήσει is that a servant who finds one master lovable and devotes himself entirely to him will most probably not be able to give the same devotion and service to another master.[50] In other words, it is a question of degrees of dedication to two masters.

In Rm 9:13 Paul quotes somewhat freely Mal 1:2–3: οὐκ ἀδελφὸς ἦν Ἠσαῦ τοῦ Ἰακώβ; λέγει Κύριος· καὶ ἠγάπησα τὸν Ἰακώβ, τὸν δὲ Ἠσαῦ ἐμίσησα, "Was not Esau the brother of Jacob? says the Lord; yet I loved Jacob but Esau I hated." Sanday and Headlam, following Alford,[51] warn that "There is no need to soften these words as some have attempted, translating "loved more" and "loved less."[52] This may be so. However, 'hate' can hardly mean hate in this context. The Malachi passage is depended on Genesis 27. In that story there is nothing that speaks of God's hatred of Esau. Rather the gist of the story is that God chose Jacob but rejected Esau.[53] In the Romans context Paul is arguing for the sovereignty

[48] Alford, *The Greek Testament*, Vol. I., 585, understands it as "the hate is the general, not personal, feeling of alienation in the inmost heart." This sounds like special pleading.

[49] Plummer's comments in his *The Gospel according to S. Luke* (ICC) (Edinburgh: T. & T. Clark. 1896, 8th ed. 1964), 364, does not address the present issue. Marshall, *The Gospel of Luke. A Commentary on the Greek Text* (NIGTC) (Exeter: Paternoster Press, 1978), 592, is more to the point, recognizing Hebrew influence in the use of the verb.

[50] See also Marshall, *The Gospel of Luke*, 624.

[51] Alford, *The Greek Testament*, Vol. II., 408.

[52] Sanday and Headlam, *The Epistle to the Romans* (ICC) (Edinburgh: T. & T. Clark, 1900), 247. This is the case with the relation of Jacob with Rachel and Leah (one is loved more than the other – but not hated! – Gen 29:29–31. See also Deut 21:15).

[53] Similarly Dunn, *Romans* (WBC), 2 Vols. (Dallas, TX., 1988), Vol. II, 545 and Cranfield, *A Critical and Exegetical Commentary on the Epistle to the Romans*, 2 Vols., (ICC),

of God in electing and rejecting. And this is precisely what suits Paul's quotation: Τὸν Ἰακὼβ ἠγάπησα, τὸν δὲ Ἠσαῦ ἐμίσησα "Jacob I loved, but Esau I *rejected*."[54]

Mt 5:43 states: Ἠκούσατε ὅτι ἐρρέθη, Ἀγαπήσεις τὸν πλησίον σου καὶ μισήσεις τὸν ἐχθρόν σου. There is no such explicit command in the Old Testament. The second part of the statement, μισήσεις τὸν ἐχθρόν σου, represents the gist of various Old Testament commandments and especially the actual facts of negative attitude toward enemies by the Israelites (e.g. Ps 3:7; 6:10; 9:3, 6; 17:9–13; 18:37, 40; 21:8–10; 26:5; 31:6; 68:1–2; 71:10–13; 86:14–17; 139:21–22). Against this barrage of negative attitudes toward enemies comes Jesus' radical statement: ἀγαπᾶτε τοὺς ἐχθροὺς ὑμῶν (Mt 5:44; Lk 6:27).[55]

3. Γράφειν (to write) = 'to mean'

In 2 Cor 1:13 Paul writes: οὐ γὰρ ἄλλα γράφομεν ὑμῖν ἀλλ' ἢ ἃ ἀναγινώσκετε ἢ καὶ ἐπιγινώσκετε. This statement of Paul's is normally translated "For we write you nothing other than you can read and also understand" (NRSV, reflecting the same basic rendering in other translations: e.g. *Rheims, KJV, NAB, NASB, NIV, NEB, TEV, Die Bibel* (Luther revised), *La Sainte Bible*, *Santa Biblia,* and *Bibeln 2000*). The *Einheitsübersetzung* hints at the correct force of the original: "Und wenn wir euch schreiben, *meinen wir* nichts anderes, als was ihr lest und versteht."[56]

Indeed, one may wonder, what can γράφομεν here mean? Is this an elliptic way of saying οὐ γὰρ ἄλλα γράφομεν ὑμῖν *καὶ ἄλλα ἐννοοῦμεν*, "For we do not write to you one thing but mean another?" This would, indeed, be the natural way of completing the thought of the first part. But in Paul's writing the second member of a statement with such a import is supplied by ἀλλ' ἢ ἃ ἀναγινώσκετε. This second part, however, combined with the first part, is not an acceptable sentence; it does not give

(Edinburgh: T. & T. Clark, 1975–1979), Vol. II., 480. Barrett's explanation is "The Hebrew idiom means, 'I preferred Jacob to Esau'," in *The Epistle to the Romans* (BNTC) (London: Adan & Charles Black, rp. 1967), 182.

[54] Cf. Cranfield, *Romans*, Vol. II, 480: "'love' and 'hate' are rather to be understood as denoting election and rejection respectively."

[55] See also the interesting information supplied by Davies, W. D. - Allison, D.C., *The Gospel according to Matthew* (ICC), 3 Vols. (Edinburgh: T & T Clark 1988-97), Vol. I, 549 f.

[56] The *JerB* also seem to perceive the force of the verb, although its rendering is not quite felicitous.

a full or logical sense.[57] It is simply the case that γράφ ομεν, 'we write,' does not represent the thought of Paul, when using this verb. Paul is using this verb to convey a thought that is coveyed by the process of writing but which is not part of the meaning of 'write.' What Paul means is: "We do not *mean* (by what we write) anything other than what you read or understand/perceive."

4. Εἰσφέρειν (to bring in, to lead in) = 'to hinder from,' 'not to allow,' 'to prevent'

Mt 6:13: καὶ μὴ εἰσενέγκῃς ἡμᾶς εἰς πειρασμόν, ἀλλὰ ῥῦσαι ἡμᾶς ἀπὸ τοῦ πονηροῦ, literally: "And do not *lead us into temptation*, but deliver us from evil/the Evil One." The verb εἰσενέγκῃς has caused great problems in Bible translations. The classical rendering of the *KJV* "and lead us not into temptation but deliver us from evil" reflects the translation of many versions, English and non-English.[58] Some translations have tried to soften the objectionable character of the saying by rendering with "do not expose us to temptation;"[59] others prefer to render πειρασμόν with "testing;"[60] while one translation adopts a peculiar rendering.[61] Strangely Allen,[62] in his commentary, has nothing to say about this particular verse and this is the case with Johannes Chrysostomos' Commentary, too,[63] as

[57] Margaret Thrall's comments in *The Second Epistle to the Corinthians* (ICC), 2 Vols. (Edinburgh: T. & T. Clark 1994-2000), Vol. I, 133 f., are not relevant in this connection. Nor does Alford, *The Greek Testament*, Vol. II., 632, have anything to say.

[58] *Tyndale, Rheims, RV, RSV, NASB, NIV, Die Bibel* (Luther revised): "Und führe uns nicht in Versuchung", *Elberfelder Bibel, Einheitsübersezung, La Sainte Bible*: "ne nous induis pas en tentation", the *Bijbel* (1951, 1996): "en leid ons niet in verzoeking"; *Bijbel* (2004); the *Folkbibeln.* The older Neohellenic translations keep to the verb of the original (e.g. Ἡ Καινὴ Διαθήκη. Τὸ πρώτυπο κείμενον μὲ νεοελληνικὴν μετάφρασιν (*Βιβλικὴ Ἑταιρεία, Ἀθῆναι*, 1967), but the latest one renders: "Καὶ μὴ μᾶς ἀφήσεις νὰ πέσουμε σὲ πειρασμό" ("And do not let/allow us (to) fall into temptation" (Ἡ Ἁγία Γραφὴ (Παλαιὰ καὶ Καινὴ Διαθήκη), (*Ἀθῆνα· Ἑλληνικὴ Βιβλικὴ Ἑταιρεία, 1997*). It is of interest that Hellenic sensitivity here avoided rendering into Neohellenic the verb εἰσενέγκῃς literally.

[59] E.g. *La Bible = Ancient et Nouveau Testament en français courant* (Bruxelles: Alliance Biblique Universelle, 1997): "Et ne nous expose pas à la tentation"; *La Sacra Bibbia*: "non ci esporre alla tentazione;" *Santa Biblia*: "Y no nos expongas a la tentación."

[60] *NRSV*: "And do not brings us to the time of trial;" *TEV*: "Do not bring us to hard testing." Similarly *JerB* "Do not put us to the test;" *NEB, Bibel 2000* and *De Naardense Bijbel.*

[61] *Bijbel in Gewone Taal*: "help ons on nooit tegen u te kiezen" (= "Help us never to choose against You").

[62] Allen, W.C., *A Critical and Exegetical Commentary on the Gospel according to S. Matthew* (ICC) (Edinburgh: T.& T. Clark, rp.), 60.

[63] Johannes Chrysostomos, *Ὑπόμνημα εἰς τὸ κατὰ Ματθαῖον Εὐαγγέλιον, 3 τόμοι, (Ἕλληνες Πατέρες τῆς Ἐκκλησίας)* (Θεσσαλονίκη 1978, 1990), Vol. I, 680.

well as with others.

What is problamatic with such a translation is that it gives the impression that God is in the habit of leading His people into temptations. For this reason, Jesus instructs his disciples to beg God not to do so. Such a view of God is hardly in harmony with the character of God as revealed in the various New Testament documents, nor with the statement of Jas 1:13 that God ἀπείραστος ἐστιν κακῶν, "cannot be tempted by evil."

The verb form εἰσενέγκῃς (< εἰσφέρειν) does, as a matter of fact, mean 'to bring in,' 'to lead in.' But some commentators[64] think that a hypothetical causative form of a Hebrew verb with a "permissive force" might lie behind it.[65] Although Delitzsch[66] does use the *hiphil* of the verb בוא, 'to come,' 'to enter,' in order to translate this sentence,[67] this indicates literal dependence on the Hellenic verb used here. The fact is that we do not know the actual Hebrew or Aramaic word behind the Hellenic verb. The question, then, must be decided on the level of the Hellenic text, and this has to do with whether Matthew is using the Hellenic verb in its proper sense or has attributed to it a sense that is not normal for this verb.[68] The attempts to soften the meaning of the verse include the understanding of πειρασμόν as 'trial.'

The meaning of πειρασμός is determined by the meaning of the cognate verb πειράζειν. The meanings of this verb in the New Testament vary among 'to test,' 'to tempt' and 'to joke' or 'to tease.' The difference between 'test' and 'tempt' is that in the former case somebody tests somebody in order to (a) either find out how he will react or (b) in order to bring out his stable, solid and worthy character. The idea of tempting, on the other hand, is always evil, trying to cause someone to fall, to be damaged or to be destroyed. When God is the tester, the purpose of testing is not to find out something that God does not know but to bring out the acceptable or commendable character of the person who is tested, as in the case of Abraham: ἐπείραζεν τὸν Ἀβραάμ (Gen 22:1). Since God knew how Abraham would react, it was a case of bringing out Abraham's faith and obedience.[69] The possibility of tempting Abraham

[64] E.g. Davies and Allison, *The Gospel according to St Mathew*, Vol. I, 613. Marshall, *The Gospel of Luke*, 461 f., on Lk 11:4, who, too, shares the Hebrew causative view, adopts J. Carmignac's understanding that the text should mean not "do not cause us to succumb to temptation" but "cause us not to succumb to temptation."

[65] E.g. Hill, D., *The Gospel of Matthew* (NCB) (London: Oliphants 1977), 138.

[66] *Delitzsch's Hebrew tr. of the NT*, The Bible Society in Israel (no date): הברית ההדשה נעתקים מלשו יון ללשון עברית. על ידי פרופ׳ פרנץ דליץ.

[67] In his translation of the New Testament into Hebrew: וְאַל תְּבִיאֵנוּ לִידֵי נִסָּיוֹן.

[68] Alford, *The Greek Testament*, Vol. II, 62, is of the opinion that "The leading into temptation must be understood in its plain literal sense."

[69] This is underlined also by the fact of God's provision of a ram to take Isaac's place.

is here utterly excluded. The negative meaning of 'to tempt' is exemplified by the temptation of Jesus, when Satan tried in various ways to bring about Jesus' fall.

In the New Testament we have a third use of the verb πειράζειν. According to Jn 6:5 Jesus asked Philippos: πόθεν ἀγοράσωμεν ἄρτους ἵνα φάγωσιν οὗτοι; τοῦτο δὲ ἔλεγεν πειράζων αὐτόν. With onc or two exceptions,[70] all of the translations that I have consulted, render the second part in some such way as: "This he said in order to *test* him."[71] The same is the case with commentators.[72]

How much this sentence has been misunderstood, is illustrated by Bernard's irrelevant comments: "John thinks it necessary to explain *why* Jesus asked Philip ... because he hesitates to represent Him as asking a question which would suggest His ignorance of the answer."[73] If Bernard had known of the meaning of 'teasing,' he would not have made this comment.

If in our discipline we had approached the Hellenic language holistically and diachronically[74] rather than circumscribing our interest to the so-called "New Testament Greek," – a bare two-three centuries of its more than twenty-eight centuries history and development – we would have become aware that for example, πειράζειν can also express the sense of 'to tease' or 'to joke,' a sense that fits this particular context admirably. Clearly then, here it is not a question of tempting Philippos or even of testing him either to find out how he would react or to bring out his faith in Jesus – since Jesus knew it all. Rather, "Jesus was teasing Philippos ... in asmuch as he knew what he was going to do."

However, in Mt 6:13 πειρασμός means neither 'testing' nor 'teasing' but 'tempting.' The problem with the interpretation of this sentence is not πειρασμόν but εἰσενέγκῃς. We saw, above, that translating μὴ εἰσενέγκῃς with "do not lead," gives an intolerable sense. Exactly as we saw in the cases of λέγειν, μισεῖν and γράφειν, that these verbs in their several contexts had acquired a meaning other than their natural meanings, so, too,

[70] *Santa Biblia*: "Pero lo dijo por ver qué contestaria Felipe" ("But he said this in order to see what Philippos would answer").

[71] E.g. *Rheims, KJV, JerB, NAB, NASB, NIV, NRSV, Amplified Bible, La Sainte Bible; Die Bibel* (Luther revised), *La Sacra Bibbia*; *Bibeln 2000.*

[72] Morris, *The Gospel according to John*, 343; Beasley-Murray, *John*, 82. Lindars, *Commentary on the Gospel of John*, 241, bypasses the issue. Barrett, *John*, 274, similarly, understands it of testing.

[73] Bernard, *The Gospel according to St. John*, Vol. I, 175.

[74] As the present author has argued in at least three of his books, i.e., Caragounis, C.C., *The Development of Greek and the New Testament. Morphology, Syntax, Phonology, and Textual Transmission* (WUNT 167) (Tübingen: Mohr, 2004); *New Testament Language and Exegesis, A Diachronic Approach* (WUNT 323) (Tübingen: Mohr, 2014) and *New Testament Investigations. A Diachronic Perspective* (WUNT 487) (Tübingen: Mohr, 2022).

the verb εἰσενέγκῃς is here used with a meaning that is not encompassed by its semantic range. The meaning contemplated by μὴ εἰσενέγκῃς ἡμᾶς εἰς πειρασμόν is "hinder us from falling into temptation"/"Do not allow us to fall into temptation"/"See to it that we do not fall into temptation." As James (1:14) expresses it, Ἕκαστος δὲ πειράζεται ὑπὸ τῆς ἰδίας ἐπιθυμίας ἐξελκόμενος καὶ δελεαζόμενος. The prayer of Mt 6.13, therefore, is for God to hinder/to prevent such an eventuality.

CHRYS C. CARAGOUNIS
Repslagarevägen 6
SE-245 35 Staffanstorp (Lund)
SWEDEN
mail@chrys-caragounis.com

An Ingenious Greek Construction in the Septuagint and the New Testament

JOHN A. L. LEE

The subject of this paper is a special construction used intermittently by writers of ancient Greek. It appears in relative clauses containing both a participle and a main verb structured in a particular way. The structure achieves a significant stylistic effect. Specimens of the construction in Classical Greek are presented first, then post-Classical evidence up to the second century BCE. The post-Classical evidence indicates that it was a higher-register feature showing skill in writing quality Greek. The discussion then turns to the LXX and the NT, and the noteworthy fact that the construction occurs there. It is found twice in LXX Leviticus and elsewhere only in the literary books. The NT shows similar phenomena, with one instance in Matthew's Gospel and several in Acts and the Epistles.

Keywords: Greek syntax, relative pronoun, register, style, Septuagint, New Testament.

1. Introduction

Greek syntax, aided by its most flexible instruments the article, relative pronoun, and participle, can be used to create sentences of appealing skill and ingenuity. They may be long and complex, or they may be short, even just an idiomatic phrase. To understand how it is done may require careful analysis. This paper[1] is concerned with one such construction that originates in the Classical period and continues to be used intermittently for the next two millenia. My focus here is on the instances in the Septuagint and the NT rather than a survey of the whole phenomenon. The background in the main stream of Greek will however be covered to set the scene for the biblical texts.

Let us consider a specimen in the *prooemion* of a speech of the great exponent of Greek oratory Demosthenes:

(1) Demosthenes 19.1
δεήσομαι δὲ πάντων ὑμῶν ... μηδεμίαν μήτε χάριν μήτ᾽ ἄνδρα ποιεῖσθαι περὶ πλείονος ἢ τὸ δίκαιον καὶ τὸν ὅρκον ὃν εἰσελήλυθεν ὑμῶν ἕκαστος ὀμωμοκώς.

[1] An expanded form of a paper presented at the Australasian Society for Classical Studies annual conference in February, 2021.

I ask you all ... to consider neither any favour nor any man more important than justice and the oath which each of you came in having sworn.

The relative clause (ὃν ... ὀμωμοκώς), translated literally above, has this structure: the relative pronoun in the accusative (ὅν) is governed by the participle (ὀμωμοκώς), which agrees with the subject of the main verb of the clause (εἰσελήλυθεν), here expressed by another word (ἕκαστος) as well as by the third person ending (-εν). The main verb, however, has no connection to the relative pronoun except through agreement with the participle. One might say it 'hangs' from the participle. For this reason a possible term to describe it is 'the hanging verb construction.'[2]

2. Further Classical evidence

The evidence for the Classical period is not easily found. The reference books do not identify the construction as such and only notice examples incidentally in other connections.[3] Their data combined with the results of my own enquiries suggest that it was used only intermittently, in oratory and in prose. By its nature it is unlikely to be suitable to verse. In addition to the ordinary relative pronoun, the construction extends to the relatives ὅσος and οἷος. The historians are the main source of examples so far. The following is a selection, beginning with one in the famous funeral speech of Pericles, at a famous *locus*.

(2) Thucydides 2.43.3–4
ἀνδρῶν γὰρ ἐπιφανῶν πᾶσα γῆ τάφος ... οὓς νῦν ὑμεῖς ζηλώσαντες καὶ τὸ εὔδαιμον τὸ ἐλεύθερον, τὸ δ' ἐλεύθερον τὸ εὔψυχον κρίναντες μὴ περιορᾶσθε τοὺς πολεμικοὺς κινδύνους.
Every land is the tomb of famous men ... whom now you imitating, and judging freedom to be prosperity and courage to be freedom, do not shrink from the dangers of war.[4]

[2] The collection of 56 *prooemia* in the Demosthenic corpus yields only one other example, at D., *Prooem.* 42.2.

[3] R. Kühner and B. Gerth, *Ausführliche Grammatik der griechischen Sprache*, II *Satzlehre* (Hannover and Leipzig: Hahnsche Buchhandlung, 1898, 1904), II.2, 100–101; E. Schwyzer and A. Debrunner, *Griechische Grammatik*, II *Syntax und syntaktische Stilistik* (Munich: C. H. Beck, 1950), 405; H. W. Smyth, rev. G. M. Messing, *Greek Grammar* (Cambridge, Mass.: Harvard University Press, 1956), §§2147d, 2543; E. van Emde Boas, A. Rijksbaron, L. Huitink, and M. de Bakker, *The Cambridge Grammar of Classical Greek* (Cambridge: CUP, 2019), §50.16 [*CGCG*].

[4] Noted as an example of 'relative connection' in *CGCG* §50.16, without comment on the participle. OCT Thucydides puts a stop at ἐνδιαιτᾶται preceding οὕς. I have not found any other 'hanging verb' in this speech, except possibly at 2.44.2.

(3) Thucydides 3.105.1[5]
καταλαμβάνουσιν Ὄλπας, τεῖχος ἐπὶ λόφου ἰσχυρὸν πρὸς τῇ θαλάσσῃ, ὅ ποτε Ἀκαρνᾶνες τειχισάμενοι κοινῷ δικαστηρίῳ ἐχρῶντο.
... they seized Olpae, a strong fortress on a hill near the sea which once the Akarnanians fortifying had used as a common court.

(4) Xenophon, *An.* 3.4.13
εἰς τοῦτον δὲ σταθμὸν Τισσαφέρνης ἐπεφάνη, οὕς τε αὐτὸς ἱππέας ἦλθεν ἔχων καὶ τὴν Ὀρόντα δύναμιν ... καὶ οὓς Κῦρος ἔχων ἀνέβη βαρβάρους καὶ οὓς ὁ βασιλέως ἀδελφὸς ἔχων βασιλεῖ ἐβοήθει.
At this stage Tissaphernes appeared, the cavalry that he himself came having, and the force of Orontas... and the *barbaroi* whom Kyros went up having, and those whom the king's brother aided the king having.

(5) Xenophon, *An.* 6.6.4
ἔπεμπον δὲ καὶ οἱ πολέμιοι ἤδη οἳ πλησίον ᾤκουν πρὸς Ξενοφῶντα ἐρωτῶντες ... ὅ τι δέοι ποιοῦντας φίλους εἶναι.
The enemy peoples who lived nearby also sent word now to Xenophon asking ... what it was necessary (them) doing to be friends.

(6) Herodotus 3.42.4[6]
τὸν δὲ ὡς ἐσῆλθε θεῖον εἶναι τὸ πρῆγμα, γράφει ἐς βυβλίον πάντα τὰ (= ἃ) ποιήσαντά μιν οἷα καταλελάβηκε.
Since the event struck him as of divine origin, he wrote in a letter all the things which having done what (οἷα) had befallen him.

(7) Demosthenes 18.98[7]
... οὐ φοβηθέντες τὴν τότε Θηβαίοις ῥώμην καὶ δόξαν ὑπάρχουσαν, οὐδ' ὑπὲρ οἷα πεποιηκότων ἀνθρώπων κινδυνεύσετε διαλογισάμενοι.
... not fearing the power and reputation the Thebans then possessed, nor considering on behalf of men having done what kind of things you would be taking risks.

The subtlety and flexibility of the construction can be seen. In example (2), a second participle (κρίναντες) is inserted with its own objects and floating free of the relative (οὕς), further delaying the arrival of the main verb (μὴ περιορᾶσθε). In example (3), while the object (ὅ) of the partici-

[5] Noted in Smyth, *Greek Grammar*, §2543. Smyth mistakes the construction and explains the case of the relative as due to an 'omitted pronoun' (αὐτό).

[6] Kühner-Gerth, *Grammatik*, II.2, 101.

[7] Kühner-Gerth, *Grammatik*, II.2, 101; Schwyzer-Debrunner, *Grammatik*, II 405; Smyth, *Grammar*, §2147d.

ple (τειχισάμενοι), which is the true object of the main verb (ἐχρῶντο), is accusative to suit the participle, the 'predicate noun' (δικαστηρίῳ) is dative to suit the verb.[8] In (4) the antecedents are incorporated (ἱππέας, βαρβάρους) and in (5) an impersonal verb (δέοι, optative in an indirect question in past sequence) is the main verb; notice also the complement of the infinitive in the accusative (φίλους) to agree with its subject. In the Herodotean example (6) the relative clause is made more complex by another relative clause (οἷα καταλελάβηκε) inside it; the verb of this clause is connected to the relative (τά) only through its object (μιν) with which the participle (ποιήσαντα) agrees. Example (7) is one of a number of examples in which the relative pronoun is ὅσος or οἷος, enabling even more complexities; the relative (οἷα) is governed by the participle (πεποιηκότων, gen. after ὑπέρ), leaving the verb of the clause (κινδυνεύσετε) 'hanging.'[9]

It takes intimacy with Greek idiom and skill to write Greek in this manner. Xenophon, somewhat unexpectedly, seems to have more examples than other Classical authors, though some are the set use of ἔχων almost equivalent to 'with,' as in (4) above.[10] The extent of its use in other Classical authors could be a useful subject for investigation.

Also to be taken into account is the use of the construction in interrogative clauses. That is, the clause begins with an interrogative pronoun governed by a participle while the verb of the clause is connected to the interrogative word only through the participle. This type is fairly standard, especially in the idiomatic expressions τί μαθὼν ...; and τί παθὼν ...; meaning 'what happened that you ...?,' 'why on earth did you ...?'[11] Two examples:

(8) Aristophanes, *Clouds* 1506
τί γὰρ μαθόντες τοὺς θεοὺς ὑβρίζετε;
(Lit.:) What learning the gods you insulted?
= What made you insult the gods?

(9) Xenophon, *Mem.* 1.3.10[12]
καὶ τί δή, ἔφη ὁ Ξενοφῶν, ἰδὼν ποιοῦντα τοιαῦτα κατέγνωκας αὐτοῦ;

[8] 'Predicate noun': Smyth, *Grammar*, §§910, 1509.

[9] Sophocles, *Electra* 751 (Kühner-Gerth, *Grammatik*, II.2, 101) is not an example, though it shows the same virtuoso use of οἷα: στρατὸς . . . ἀνωλόλυξε τὸν νεανίαν, οἷ' ἔργα δράσας οἷα λαγχάνει κακά, 'the army mourned the young man, as such deeds having done such misfortune he gained.'

[10] With ἔχων: X., *An.* 6.4.16. Others: X., *An.* 2.5.22; 4.2.3; 4.7.6; 7.2.10.

[11] Kühner-Gerth, *Grammatik*, II.2, 519; LSJ, s.v. μανθάνω V; s.v. πάσχω III.4; Schwyzer-Debrunner, *Grammatik*, II, 391; Smyth, *Grammar*, §§2064, 2147d.

[12] Schwyzer-Debrunner, *Grammatik*, II 405.

> And seeing him doing what, said Xenophon, did you form such a bad opinion of him?

The expression with τί παθὼν ...; goes back as far as Homer; τί μαθὼν ...; appears not to be attested before the fifth century BC.[13] Perhaps this older type was the model for the type with the relative pronoun and participle.

3. Post-Classical evidence

The construction continues to be used by writers of the Koine Greek period. In this section a small sample will be noticed, sufficient to establish that fact, without going into an exhaustive study or reaching beyond the second century AD. One would expect to find it in writers of moderately literary Greek rather than in popular documents. That has proved to be the case, but there is also an instance in a papyrus document of the third century BC. It is less surprising than might have been thought. Register variation is a feature of all the documents, and writers sometimes reveal a quite high level of education. My examples are presented chronologically beginning with the documentary text.

> (10) PLond 7.2017.5 (241/240 BC)
> ... ἀποδ[οῦναί μοι αὐτὸ ἢ ἕτε|ρομ] μὴ χεῖρον δοῦ|ναί μοι ἐν ὧι μελετῶν ἀγωνιοῦμ[αι ἵνα μὴ] π̣ο̣λ̣[λ]ῶν κα[θ]υ̣σ̣[τερῶ π]αρὰ τὸ ἀμελέ|τητος εἶναι.
> [I ask you] to hand it [the lyre] over to me or give me another no worse, with which practising I will compete, so that I may not fall behind many [of the contestants] on account of being unpractised.

The writer is in dispute with his guardians about an instrument that was bequeathed to him by his teacher but is now missing and which he needs for a coming competition. It is clear from further passages in the text that he refers to needing the lyre for practice, not for use in the contest itself.[14] The words ἐν ὧι μελετῶν thus go together and ἀγωνιοῦμαι is a 'hanging' verb. The competition has been announced by the King himself (l. 28). This young man Heracleotes, aiming at a career as a musician, clearly came from a higher level of society and had had a good education.

[13] Eupolis Comicus, *Frag.* 9.193.4 καίτοι τί μαθὼν ἂν εἶδεν, εἰ μὴ προυδίδου; 'Yet why on earth would he have seen him unless he was engaged in treason? (Found by TLG search.)

[14] See lines 8–9, 21–2. He would of course need the lyre for the competition, but that is not the point he is pressing in his letter.

(11) Polybius 4.75.6
... ἅμα δὲ καὶ συνδεδραμηκότος ὄχλου συρφετώδους, ταχέως παρέδοσαν αὑτούς· ἐν οἷς ἦσαν καὶ μισθοφόροι διακόσιοι μιγάδες, οὓς ἧκεν ἔχων Ἀμφίδαμος ὁ στρατηγὸς τῶν Ἠλείων.
... and also being a mixed rabble run together, they quickly handed themselves over; among whom were also two hundred mercenaries of mixed origins, whom having had come Amphidamos the general of the Eleans.

The construction is found many times in Polybius, but most instances are similar to the Latin 'connective (or connecting) relative' or 'relatif de liaison,' probably reflecting Latin influence on Polybius's Greek.[15] There are however clear cases of the 'hanging verb' construction, as in example (11), which illustrates both types.[16]

(12) Dionysius of Halicarnassus, *De Lysia* 10
πολλὰ καὶ καλὰ λέγειν ἔχων περὶ τῆς Λυσίου λέξεως, ἣν λαμβάνων καὶ μιμούμενος ἄν τις ἀμείνων γένοιτο τὴν ἑρμηνείαν, τὰ μὲν ἄλλα τοῦ χρόνου στοχαζόμενος ἐάσω, μίαν δὲ ἀρετὴν ἔτι τοῦ ῥήτορος ἀποδείξομαι.

Though I could mention many other fine features of Lysias's diction, which taking and imitating one might become better in style, I will pass over the rest, having an eye to the time, and demonstrate one further virtue of this orator.

This Dionysius, writing in the first-century BC, is the famed advocate of a return to Attic style. It is no surprise that he often introduces the construction into his elaborate sentences.[17]

(13) Philo, *De virtutibus* 111
ἐπικουφιεῖς δὲ τὰς μὲν τῆς κεφαλῆς τρίχας ἀποκείρας, περιελὼν δὲ ὄνυχας, ἀπαμφιάσας δὲ τὴν ἐσθῆτα ἣν ἔχουσα ἐζωγρήθη, ...
And you shall alleviate (her calamity) by cutting off the hair of her head, and removing her (long) nails and stripping off the clothing which having she was captured ...

[15] J.-A. de Foucault, *Recherches sur la langue et le style de Polybe* (Paris: Le Belles Lettres, 1972), 88–89. Also sometimes in Greek: *CGCG*, §50.16, citing ex. (2) above; another is at Th. 2.36.4. The question often turns on the punctuation, which, as de Foucault points out, is 'un artifice moderne' (89).

[16] Another example: Plb. 3.76.5. Latinate type: 2.29.9; 3.19.8; 4.5.1; 5.7.3; 8.34.4, 5.

[17] Others: D.H., *Antiq. Rom.* 1.86.4; 2.18.1; 4.60.2.

This is just one of the examples readily found in Philo's works. The Latinate use of the relative also appears.[18]

(14) Epictetus 2.24.2
Δοκεῖ σοι, ἔφη, καθάπερ ἄλλου τινὸς εἶναι τέχνη οὕτως δὲ καὶ τοῦ λέγειν, ἣν ὁ μὲν ἔχων ἐμπείρως ἐρεῖ, ὁ δὲ μὴ ἔχων ἀπείρως;
Do you think, he said, that just as (there is) of anything else there is a technical skill also of speaking, which one person having will speak in a skilled way and another not having (will speak) in an unskilled way?

There do not appear to be many examples in Epictetus but one is sufficient to show the persistence of the construction, even in didactic and conversational discourse as in Epictetus.[19]

(15) Plutarch, *Sulla* 21.2
τούτους τε δὴ τὸ ῥηθὲν ἐπέστρεψε, καὶ τῶν ἐπὶ τοῦ δεξιοῦ κέρως σπειρῶν δύο προσεβοήθησαν, ἃς ἐπαγαγὼν τρέπεται τοὺς πολεμίους.
His words turned these troops around, and two of the cohorts on the right wing came to their aid, which leading against (them) he turned the enemy to flight.

This example in Plutarch, in whose works others can be found,[20] takes us to the second century AD and as far as we need to go. Later writers of Classicising Greek, such as the Church Fathers, are very likely to have used it. At any rate, an instance as late as 1514 can be cited in the Greek preface to volume 5 of the Complutensian Polyglot.[21]

Let us sum up so far. The 'hanging verb' construction originated in the Classical period, when it was used intermittently in literary prose and oratory. It was not a feature of colloquial language except in the idiomatic use with an interrogative. It continued to be used in a similar way in post-Classical Greek, where it appears in literary writings of the first to third centuries BC, and then up to at least the second century. Its use in this period was probably based on Classical models that were

[18] Further exx. of both types: *De ebrietate* 156; *De vita Mosis* 2.171; 2.259; *De spec. leg.* 2.194; *In Flaccum* 157.

[19] Another: Epict. 4.5.16.

[20] E.g., Plut., *Sertorius* 3.7; *Pericles* 6.1.

[21] Lines 57–62: ἃ δὴ ... ὁ μέγιστος ἀρχιερεὺς λέων δέκατος ... ἔπεμψε πρὸς αἰδεσιμώτατον κύριον τῆς ἱσπανίας καρδηνάλιον, οὗ χορηγοῦντος καὶ κελεύσαντος τὸ παρὸν βιβλίον ἐτυπώσαμεν. See J. A. L. Lee, 'Dimitrios Doukas and the Accentuation of the New Testament Text of the Complutensian Polyglot,' *NovT* 47 (2005), 250–290 at 263, 265 for translation and comment. The author was Demetrios Doukas, an educated Cretan and experienced editor of Greek texts.

read in the course of an education. It may have been taught as a stylistic device in itself. It conveyed a tone of higher-register Greek, at the same time displaying a high level of competence in Greek.

4. The Septuagint

4.1 The Pentateuch

One would not expect this construction to occur in the Septuagint, unless perhaps in the more literary translations or free compositions. The example above (10) in a third-century BC document alerts us, however, to the possibility that the well-educated translators of the LXX-Pentateuch, as they undoubtedly were, might know it and use it, even if their translation generally follows the Hebrew original fairly closely. There are two clear instances in the Pentateuch, in Leviticus:

(16) Lev 18:5
καὶ φυλάξεσθε πάντα τὰ προστάγματά μου καὶ πάντα τὰ κρίματά μου καὶ ποιήσετε αὐτά, ἃ ποιήσας ἄνθρωπος ζήσεται ἐν αὐτοῖς.
And you shall keep all my commands and do them, which doing a man will live by them.

(17) Lev 5:3
ἢ ψυχή, ἥτις ἂν ἅψηται παντὸς πράγματος ἀκαθάρτου ... (3) ἢ ἅψηται ἀπὸ ἀκαθαρσίας ἀνθρώπου, ἀπὸ πάσης ἀκαθαρσίας αὐτοῦ, ἧς ἂν ἁψάμενος μιανθῇ, καὶ ἔλαθεν αὐτόν.
Or a soul [= a person] who touches any unclean thing ... or touches of the uncleanness of a person, of any uncleanness of his, which touching he might be defiled, and it escaped his notice.

The first of these (16) is a straightforward example like others we have seen. The relative (ἃ) is governed by the participle (ποιήσας), while the verb (ζήσεται) is connected to the participle through the subject (ἄνθρωπος). The Hebrew structure is different, with two coordinated clauses, literally 'which will do them the/a man and will live by them' (*'asher ya'aseh 'otham ha'adam w'khay bahem*).[22] Both the Hebrew and the Greek amount to the same in meaning.

[22] Transliteration of Hebrew follows *SBL Handbook of Style* (2 ed., 2014), 58-59, 'General-Purpose Style.' In Lev 18:5 Muraoka sees only 'a striking syntactic restructuring': T. Muraoka, *A Syntax of Septuagint Greek* (Leuven: Peeters, 2016), 87 n. 5. The words are semi-quoted in Rom 10:5, Gal 3:12 with the construction changed.

The second (17) is much more artful. The Hebrew relative clause says only '(... uncleanness) which he becomes unclean by it' (*'asher yitmah bah*). In the Greek version the participle (ἁψάμενος) is introduced, governing the relative (ἧς, gen. with ἅπτομαι), and the 'hanging' verb has the indefinite construction (ἂν μιανθῇ) appropriate to a general prescription, as in the preceding verbs (ἥτις ἂν ἅψηται ... ἢ ἅψηται). The rendering gives the Hebrew meaning accurately in good Greek style.[23]

It is interesting enough that the construction appears in the LXX-Pentateuch, but that it is used in Leviticus is remarkable. This translator's competence as a translator and even his knowledge of Greek have been impugned by some.[24] These examples demonstrate the opposite.

There is a third instance in the Pentateuch that is possible but not certain:

(18) Gen 49:23
υἱὸς ηὐξημένος Ἰωσήφ, υἱὸς ηὐξημένος ζηλωτός, υἱός μου νεώτατος· πρός με ἀνάστρεψον. (23) εἰς ὃν διαβουλευόμενοι ἐλοιδόρουν, καὶ ἐνεῖχον αὐτῷ κύριοι τοξευμάτων.
Joseph is a son increased, a son increased (and) envied, my youngest son, return to me; about whom deliberating they spoke abuse and had a grudge against him, the lords of arrows.
Or: ... of whom they spoke abuse while deliberating ...

The Greek is to be read in the light of the narrative of Joseph's seizure and sale by his brothers (Gen 37:18). Then it makes good sense on the whole. Whether the participle (διαβουλευόμενοι) or the verb (ἐλοιδόρουν) belongs with the relative (εἰς ὅν) turns on the use of εἰς. It is workable with either verb. Perhaps the translator had not chosen between them but intended the ideas to be combined: 'they disparaged him as they debated what to do with him.' The compound <u>δια</u>βουλεύομαι (only here in LXX) implies 'debate back and forth.' The meaning 'have a grudge against' for ἐνέχω fits the story perfectly.[25] The reference of 'the

[23] This ex. is also discussed in J. A. L. Lee, 'The Rendering of the Hebrew Preposition b- in the Septuagint Pentateuch,' *JSCS* 57 (2024) [forthcoming].

[24] Cf. J. W. Wevers, *Notes on the Greek Text of Leviticus* (SCS 44; Atlanta, Ga., 1997), ix: 'he simply was not a careful grammarian'; 'Lev is more of an isolate [i.e., word-for word] type of translation than a contextual one'; and D. L. Büchner in A. Pietersma and B. G. Wright (eds.), *A New English Translation of the Septuagint and other Greek Translations Traditionally Included under that Title* (OUP: New York/Oxford, 2007), 84.

[25] So T. Muraoka, *A Greek-English Lexicon of the Septuagint* (Louvain: Peeters, 2009), s.v.; LSJ, s.v. I.

lords of arrows' is obscure. The Hebrew of the MT does not help: it bears almost no resemblance to the Greek and is obscure in itself.[26]

4.2 Other books of the LXX

Given the results for the Pentateuch, one might expect to find the construction in other Septuagint books, especially the literary books. The spread is actually rather limited. I have found it only in Wisdom, Daniel (LXX), Bel, and 2–4 Maccabees, all books classified as literary.[27] Other books especially known for their literary features, Proverbs, Job, and Sirach, have none.[28]

Two examples will suffice:

(19) Wis 2:3
... καὶ ὁ λόγος σπινθὴρ ἐν κινήσει καρδίας ἡμῶν, (3) οὗ σβεσθέντος τέφρα ἀποβήσεται τὸ σῶμα.
... and reason is a spark in the beating of our hearts, which being extinguished our body will turn into ashes.

(20) 2 Macc 10:17
... ἐπὶ τὰ τῶν Ἰδουμαίων ὀχυρώματα ὥρμησαν· (17) οἷς καὶ προσβαλόντες εὐρώστως ἐγκρατεῖς ἐγένοντο τῶν τόπων.
... they rushed at the strongholds of the Idumaeans, which attacking strongly they gained control of the places.

4.3 Construction with interrogative

The LXX also has some instances of the construction where the participle governs an interrogative, of the kind noticed above (8, 9). They are few but interesting. The first is:

(21) Gen 20:10
τί ἐνιδὼν ἐποίησας τοῦτο;
What seeing [in this place] did you do this?

[26] See J. W. Wevers, *Notes on the Greek Text of Genesis* (SCS 35; Atlanta, Ga., 1993), 831–832; J. Skinner, *Genesis* (ICC; 2nd ed.; Edinburgh, 1930), 529–530. Wevers almost wholly misunderstands the Greek of vs. 23. *NETS* makes the imperfects refer to habitual action.

[27] List of exx.: 2 Macc 4:33 (Lat.); 8:21 (Lat.); 10:17; 3 Macc 3:1 (Lat.); 5:16 (Lat.), 17(Lat.); 7:20 (Lat.); 4 Macc 1:29; 2:23; 4:21 (Lat.); 5:7; 8:4 (Lat.); 9:13; 11:10a, b, 18; 12:2 (Lat.); 16:16; Wis 2:3; 5:10(?); 7:14; 11:15; 13:3; Dan (LXX) 3:14; Bel 21. In 2 Esdr 19:29 (Neh 9:29), Lev 18:5 is reused but the insertion of αὐτά confuses the construction.

[28] For a list of the books see J. A. L. Lee, *The Greek of the Pentateuch: Grinfield Lectures on the Septuagint 2011–2012* (Oxford: OUP, 2018), 90.

Abimelech asks Abraam what made him say that his wife Sarra was his sister. The structure of the question in the Hebrew is very simple: 'what did you see that you did this thing?' (*mah ra'itha ki 'asitha 'et-hadabar hazeh*). The Genesis translator not only converts it into idiomatic Greek but chooses a nuanced verb found only here in the LXX instead of a plain one for 'see': ἐνεῖδον implies *see in* (a place, situation, person). Abraam answers that he could see no θεοσέβεια in this place and he thought they would kill him for his wife.[29]

The other instances of the interrogative with participle are in literary books, except for one in 4 Kgdms, which occurs in words of the King of Assyria, hardly by accident.[30] All this adds up to a picture of a higher-register feature, just like the participle with the relative.

5. The New Testament

A fair number of instances of the 'hanging verb' construction occur in the New Testament but it is infrequent and not spread generally. It is located in the more literary books, confirming that the feature continued to be associated with higher-level Greek. One example is in Matthew's Gospel, four are in Acts, and twelve are in the Epistles, with noticeable clusters in Timothy, Peter, and John.[31] Most instances are straightforward and clear in meaning, but one or two are rather awkward, as if the writer knew the construction but was not fully in control of it. I give a selection of four examples, with comments on the first and last:

> (22) Matt 13:48
> (47) πάλιν ὁμοία ἐστὶν ἡ βασιλεία τῶν οὐρανῶν σαγήνῃ βληθείσῃ εἰς τὴν θάλασσαν καὶ ἐκ παντὸς γένους συναγαγούσῃ· (48) ἣν ὅτε ἐπληρώθη ἀναβιβάσαντες ἐπὶ τὸν αἰγιαλὸν καὶ καθίσαντες συνέλεξαν τὰ καλὰ εἰς ἄγγη, τὰ δὲ σαπρὰ ἔξω ἔβαλον.
> Again the kingdom of heaven is like a net cast into the sea and gathering in some of every kind, which, when it was filled, drawing up onto the shore and sitting they gathered the good ones into containers and threw out the bad ones.

[29] Before the LXX, the total of ἐνεῖδον is 6 (TLG): Th. 1.95.7; 7.36.2, 62.1; S., *Phil.* 854; X., *An.* 7.7.45; [Pl.,] *Ep.* 318d.3. No instances were found by searches in inscriptions (PHI) or papyri (papyri.info).

[30] 4 Kgdms 18:20 (non-Kaige) νῦν οὖν τίνι πεποιθὼς ἠθέτησας ἐν ἐμοί; The others are: 1 Esdras 6:4; 6:10; 4 Macc 11:4; Isa 51:12; 57:11.

[31] Full list of examples: Matt 13:48; Acts 19:25 (Lat.?); 22:5; 27:17; 28:15; Eph 1:13 (2 rel. prnn., 1º Lat.); 2:21; 1 Tim 1:6, 19; 6:10, 21; Heb 11:29; 12:19; 1 Pet 1:8; 2:4 (Lat.); 2 Pet 1:19; 3 John 6 (total 17). See J. A. L. Lee, 'Some Features of the Speech of Jesus in Mark's Gospel', *NovT* 27 (1985), 1–26 at 9, on the literary level of NT books.

Here the participle (ἀναβιβάσαντες) governs the relative (ἥν) but a second participle (καὶ καθίσαντες) has been added, connected to the verb (συνέλεξαν) but not governing the relative.[32] Whether this is clever or inept is hard to decide.

(23) Acts 28:15
κἀκεῖθεν οἱ ἀδελφοὶ ἀκούσαντες τὰ περὶ ἡμῶν ἦλθαν εἰς ἀπάντησιν ἡμῖν ... οὓς ἰδὼν ὁ Παῦλος εὐχαριστήσας τῷ θεῷ ἔλαβε θάρσος.
From there the brethren, having heard about us, came to meet us ... whom seeing Paul giving thanks to God took courage.

(24) 1 Tim 1:19
... ἔχων πίστιν καὶ ἀγαθὴν συνείδησιν, ἥν τινες ἀπωσάμενοι περὶ τὴν πίστιν ἐναυάγησαν.
... holding faith and a good conscience, which some rejecting have been shipwrecked in regard to their faith.

(25) Heb 11:29
πίστει διέβησαν τὴν ἐρυθρὰν θάλασσαν ὡς διὰ ξηρᾶς γῆς, ἧς πεῖραν λαβόντες οἱ Αἰγύπτιοι κατεπόθησαν.
By faith they crossed the Red Sea as on dry land, which attempting the Egyptians were swallowed up.

Grammatically the relative (ἧς) has two possible antecedents (θάλασσαν and γῆς), but neither is the real antecedent, which is the idea of 'crossing' (the Red Sea). To me this one does seem a little clumsy; the other instance in Hebrews is also unusual.[33]

To complete the NT data, let us check on the construction with interrogative (cf. §4.3). It turns out there are just two instances, with identical wording:

(26) Luke 10:25; 18:18
τί ποιήσας ζωὴν αἰώνιον κληρονομήσω;
What doing will I inherit eternal life?

The question is found in two separate accounts of what may or may not be the same event, the questioner being a νομικός in the first, an ἄρχων in the second. The relationship between the accounts is complex, but for

[32] The structure would be improved by deleting καί before καθίσαντες. Some Mss do in fact omit καί: see R. J. Swanson, *New Testament Greek Manuscripts: Variant Readings Arranged in Horizontal Lines against Codex Vaticanus*. 9 vols. (Sheffield: Sheffield Academic Press, 1995–2005), 1:130. The passage occurs in Matt alone, without Synoptic parallel.

[33] Heb 12:19 ἧς οἱ ἀκούσαντες παρῃτήσαντο μὴ προστεθῆναι αὐτοῖς λόγον. None of the commentaries on Hebrews that I have consulted remarks on the construction in either place.

us the point of interest is that the expression is in Luke, and the parallel Marcan account (10:17) shows that Luke's version is a more stylish version of Mark's question, τί ποιήσω ἵνα ζωὴν αἰώνιον κληρονομήσω;[34]

6. Conclusion

The synactical phenomenon in which a relative pronoun is governed by a participle in the relative clause, and a finite verb in the same clause is unattached except through agreement with the participle, had its origin in Classical Greek. It was a stylistic embellishment in the δεινός style, displaying what might be described as 'an artful awkwardness, stylistic bravura, and skirting of incorrectness.' Moreover it is characteristically Greek in the preference for '*hypotaxis* rather than *parataxis* and the use of a participle wherever possible.'[35]

A survey of the evidence down to II AD shows that the construction continued to be used in post-Classical literary Greek authors, appearing also in a documentary text with literary pretensions. My conclusion for the later period is that it was a higher-register feature and a sign of education and competence in writing good-quality Greek.

The construction appears from time to time in literary books of the LXX, and somewhat unexpectedly in the book of Leviticus. In the NT it has a similar distribution, appearing once in the Gospel of Matthew and from time to time in the literary Greek of Acts and some Epistles. The LXX and NT data thus conform to the conclusion of the general survey. The similar construction with an interrogative pronoun governed by a participle shows the same characteristics in the later period. It too occurs in the LXX and NT, where it is even more rare but significantly located. In short, this feature offers a further insight into the complex and variable character of the Greek used by the biblical writers.

JOHN A. L. LEE
5/17–19 Clarke Street,
Bowral, NSW 2576
AUSTRALIA
lee121@bigpond.com

[34] Luke 10:25 || Mark 12:28; Matt. 22:35 (different question). Luke 18:18 || Mark 10:17; Matt. 19:16 τί ἀγαθὸν ποιήσω ἵνα σχῶ ζωὴν αἰώνιον;

[35] I owe these insights to Dr Michael Curran, to whom I am grateful for reading the paper and offering comments. For δεινότης see J. Chr. Th. Ernesti, *Lexicon technologiae graecorum rhetoricae* (Leipzig: C. Fritsch, 1795), 68–70 and (e.g.) G. Kennedy, *The Art of Persuasion in Greece* (Princeton: Princeton University Press, 1963), 281.

𝔓75 and 𝔓4 Reconsidered

PETER R. RODGERS

In recent years the dating of some early Christian papyri has been challenged. Brent Nongbri especially has questioned the value of paleographic dating, noting that several papyri, chiefly 𝔓75, could be placed as confidently in the fourth century as in the second/third. This essay seeks a new criterion for assessing the dates of early Christian manuscripts: *Nomina Sacra*. The abbreviation/suspension of sacred names began with only the four or five, and gradually expanded to include other words treated in this way. Those papyri with fewer *Nomina Sacra* should be dated early, whereas those that include an expanded list should be deemed to be later. The staurogram is also important in this calculation. On this reckoning, 𝔓4 may be placed in the second century, 𝔓75 in the third.

Keywords: Papyri, dating, paleography, Nongbri, *Nomina Sacra, Staurogram.* [1]

One of the most important papyrus discoveries in the twentieth century was 𝔓75, a papyrus containing large portions of Luke and John. 𝔓75 was one of the Bodmer papyri (XIV-XV). It was published in 1961 in a critical edition by Victor Martin and Rodolphe Kasser.[2] The papyrus was assigned a date between 175 and 225 CE. Two studies appeared shortly after this publication which compared the text of 𝔓75 to that of Codex Vaticanus (B). Calvin L. Porter produced a study of the text of 𝔓75 in relation to that of B in John,[3] and Carlo M. Martini presented a study comparing the text of 𝔓75 and B in Luke.[4] Both studies demonstrated a close relationship between 𝔓75 and B. This has led scholars to state that 𝔓75 had been the most important papyrus find in the 20th century.[5] In the early twentieth century scholars had increasingly assumed that the text

[1] I am grateful to Max Botner, Greg Eck, Michael Kares, and Brian Lucas for help with this article. And I am especially grateful to Professor Brent Nongbri for his thorough and thoughtful comments on a draft of this paper, a number of which I have incorporated

[2] Victor Martin and Rodolphe Kasser, *Papyrus Bodmer XIV-XV: Evangiles de Luc et Jean. Evangil de Luc, Chap 3-24,* Cologny-Geneva: Bibliotheca Bodmeriana, 1961.

[3] Calvin L. Porter, "*Papyrus* Bodmer *XV* (𝔓75) *and the text of Codex Vaticanus.*" JBL 81 (1962) 363-76.

[4] Carlo M. Martini, *Il problema della recensionalita del codice B alla luca del papiro Bodmer XIV*, AnBib 26. Rome: Biblical Institute Press. 1966.

[5] Kurt and Barbara Aland, *The Text of the New Testament: An Introduction to the Critical Editions and to the Theory and Practice of Modern Textual Criticism.* Trans. Erroll F. Rhodes, Rev. Ed. Grand Rapids :Eerdmans, 1995, 244. David C. Parker, *An Introduction to the New Testament Manuscripts and their Texts.* Cambridge: Cambridge University Press, 2008, 322.

of Codex Sinaiticus and Codex Vaticanus was not, as Hort and Westcott had argued, a carefully copied text representing very nearly what was the original text, but rather the result of a recension either in the second or the fourth century. With the realization that 𝔓75 was a representative of the B type of text from the second century, the whole picture changed. As Gordon Fee wrote: "The concept of a scholarly recension of the NT text in Alexandria either in the fourth century or the second century, either as a created or a carefully edited text is a myth. The leading MSS of the Egyptian text-type (𝔓75 B) are not themselves recensional - at least not in any meaningful sense of the word."[6] The combination of the early date of 𝔓75 and its textual similarity to the text of B (94 %) has become a trusted north star in the study of the early text of the New Testament. This picture is regularly cited by students of the text of the New Testament.[7]

Recently, however, this secure position has been called into question. In 2016 Brent Nongbri published an article in which he questioned the security of the dating of 𝔓75 in the late second or early third centuries.[8] Nongbri argues that on both paleographic and codicological grounds 𝔓75 might as easily be placed in the fourth century as in the second/third. Indeed, argued Nongbri, 𝔓75 "fits comfortably in a fourth century context, along with the bulk of other Bodmer papyri."[9] Scholars will need to take seriously this challenge to the consensus, and, if Nongbri's arguments are convincing, they will need to call into question whether the 𝔓75 B text represents a textual type or cluster that remained stable and unrevised from the second to the fourth century.[10] A cloud has obscured this north star in NT textual criticism, and new coordinates may need to be found for navigating the earliest history of the text. 𝔓75 may emerge in the end as a second/third century manuscript, but this dating cannot be taken for granted.

In light of these developments, it is worth exploring whether there are other manuscripts among our early papyri that could anchor the 𝔓75 B

[6] Gordon D. Fee "P75, P66, and Origen: The Myth of Early Textual Recension in Alexandria," in Eldon Jay Epp and Gordon D. Fee, *Studies in the Theory and Method of New Testament Textual Criticism:* SD 45, Grand Rapids: Eerdmans, 1993, 247-73, quotation on 272.

[7] See, for example, Juan Hernandez, Jr. "The Early Text of Luke," in *The Early Text of the New Testament,* Edited by Charles E. Hill and Michael J. Kruger, Oxford: Oxford University Press, 2012, 121-38, especially 132.

[8] Brent Nongbri, "Reconsidering the Place of Papyrus Bodmer XIV-XV (𝔓75) in the Textual Criticism of the New Testament. *JBL* 135, no 2, 2016, 405-37.

[9] Nongbri, "Papyrus Bodmer XIV-XV (𝔓75), 405.

[10] See Elijah Hixson, "Dating Myths, Part 1," in Elijah Hixson and Peter J. Gurry, *Myths and Mistakes in New Testament Textual Criticism,* Downers Grove, Ill: InterVarsity Press, 90-109.

text securely in the second century. Among the papyri 𝔓4 stands out as worthy of further study. 𝔓4 is a fragmentary papyrus of several sheets containing the text of portions of Luke 1 – 6. It thus overlaps with 𝔓75 for part of Luke 3-6. The circumstances of its discovery may prove important for our study. The manuscript fragments were found at Coptos in upper Egypt in 1889, concealed in the recess of a wall. The Luke fragments had been re-used to reinforce a book of Philo. It was purchased by the French scholar, Vincent Scheil, who presented the Philo book and Luke fragments to the Bibliotheque National in Paris, where it is numbered MS Suppl. Gr. 1120. Schiel published the Luke fragments in *RB* 1 (1892). They were given a proper critical edition by Jean Merell in 1938.[11]

Fresh attention has been given to 𝔓4 in the last thirty years. The impetus for this has been the proposal that 𝔓4, 𝔓64, and 𝔓67 are all from the same codex.[12] T.C. Skeat subsequently argued that the three fragments were from the earliest example of a four gospel codex, dated to the end of the second century.[13] Skeat's bold proposal has not gone unchallenged. It drew a respectful but thorough critique from Peter M. Head in 2005.[14] Largely on Codicological grounds Head and others challenged the proposal that the three fragments were from the same four gospel codex. My purpose is not to enter into this debate, but to treat 𝔓4 on its own, to compare its text to that of 𝔓75, and to explore the security of its dating in the late second century.[15] Skeat had noted in his 1997 study regarding 𝔓4 that there were "19 agreements (and no disagreements) with 𝔓75, though 9 of these are conjectural."[16] What caught my eye was the claim that there were no disagreements between 𝔓4 and 𝔓75, and this from a seasoned NT textual critic. If true, this observation would be truly remarkable.

A Comparison of 𝔓4 and 𝔓75

Tommy Wasserman conducted a thorough study of 𝔓4 in 2010. His careful textual analysis showed a very close relationship with both 𝔓75

[11] Jean Merell, "Noufragments du papyrus IV " *RB* 47 (1938) 5-22.

[12] Philip W. Comfort, "Exploring the Common Identification of Three New Testament Manuscripts: 𝔓4, 𝔓64 and 𝔓67." *TynBul* 46 1 (1995) 43-54.

[13] T.C. Skeat, "The Oldest Manuscript of the Four Gospels?" *NTS* 43 1 (1997) 1-34.

[14] Peter M. Head, "Is 𝔓4, 𝔓464 and 𝔓67 the Oldest Manuscript of the Four Gospels? A Response to T.C. Skeat. *NTS* 51 3 (2005) 450-57. See also S.D. Charlesworth, "T.C. Skeat, 𝔓64, 𝔓67and 𝔓4 and the Problem of Fiber Orientation in Codicological Reconstruction." *NTS* 53 4 (2007) 582-604.

[15] 𝔓4 and 𝔓75 are both fragmentary. However, there is enough overlap of text that a comparison is warranted. Furthermore, the comparison with B, where there is overlap has proved very useful.

[16] T.C Skeat, "The Oldest Manuscript." *NTS* 43

and B.[17] Wasserman noted a 93% agreement with both P75 and B. He also noted that the same figure for the relationship of P75 to 𝔓4, 93%.[18] The next closest percentage of agreement is with L at 78 %. It is to be noted that these figures are on a par with those presented by Gordon Fee, who found a 94% agreement between 𝔓75 and B.[19]

But how secure is the dating of 𝔓4 to the second century? Indeed, the dating of 𝔓4 has had an interesting career. The first editor, Scheil, dated the manuscript in the sixth century CE.[20] In his 1938 edition Merell re-dated 𝔓4 in the fourth century. Kurt Aland gave it a third century date in 1963.[21] C. H. Roberts further revised the dating in 1979 with a late second century date.[22] These widely differing estimates, largely based on analyses of the handwriting, shows how difficult such a calculation can be. Nongbri's recent work on 𝔓75 confirms this impression, since that manuscript can now be assessed as either a second or a fourth century product. Another criterion must be found, if one is available, for assessing the probable date. Perhaps the circumstances of the discovery of 𝔓4 can help. The study of Philip W. Comfort sought such a criterion.

"We know the terminus date of 𝔓4 because we know about its provenance. It had been used for padding in a codex of Philo's treatises, which was hidden in a house in Coptos to avoid being confiscated during the persecution of A.D. 292 or 303, when Coptos was besieged and sacked by Diocletian. The Philo codex was dated to the third century by both Hunt and Kenyon. The owner of the Philo Codex and the gospel codex was probably a Christian and therefore would have valued the Gospels. He would not have used a newly-copied Gospel for stuffing the padding of Philo's treatises. Rather the Gospel codex must have been well-used and well-worn. In fact, it must have been a discarded copy replaced by another codex. Thus, it is not unlikely that 𝔓4 was made at least as early as hundred years prior to the Philo Codex, if not earlier. As such, we are fairly certain of a second century date."[23]

[17] Tommy Wasserman, "A Comparative Textual Analysis of 𝔓4 and 𝔓64 + 𝔓67. *TC* 15(2010) 1-26. Wasserman built on the earlier work of William F. Warren Jr., 𝔓4 and the 𝔓75 -B Text in Luke'" A paper presented at the Annual Meeting of the Society of Biblical Literature, Orlando, Fl. 22 November 1998.

[18] Wasserman's figures are built on the work of Warren (note 17) and on his own analysis. (pages 6-22).

[19] Gordon D. Fee, "𝔓66, 𝔓75 and Origen," 252.

[20] V. Scheil "Archeologie Varia" *RB* 1, 1892, 113.

[21] K. Aland, *Kurzgefasste Liste Der Griechichen Handschriften Des Neuen Testaments*, Berlin: DeGruyter, 1963, 29.

[22] C. H. Roberts, *Manuscript, Society and Belief in Early Christian Egypt*, London: Oxford University Press, 12-13.

[23] Philip W. Comfort, "Exploring the Common Identification of Three New Testament Manuscripts: 𝔓4, 𝔓64 and 𝔓67," *TynBul*, 46.1, 1995, 52.

The conclusion to which all of this points is that even if 𝔓75 is to be considered a fourth century production, we have in 𝔓4 a solid, if fragmentary, witness to the existence of the 𝔓75 B text in the second century. [24] We are not here dependent on handwriting for the dating, but we can trace the origins of 𝔓4 to the almost certain circumstances of its progress (use, disuse, reuse) in the third century. Once again, the prospect of the text of Codex Vaticanus (i.e. Hort's neutral text) as a fourth or even second century recension might be laid to rest.

Yet again, Nongbri has raised some serious questions regarding 𝔓4. In a chapter of his book *God's Library,* he challenges the story of 𝔓4 being hidden in a wall of a house during the Diocletian persecution.[25] He writes that the town of Coptos recovered after the Diocletian persecution, became a prominent episcopal center in the fourth century, and suffered again in the seventh, ninth and tenth centuries. [26] He does not detail any crisis between the third/fourth and the seventh centuries when the Philo codex and Luke leaves would have been hidden in a wall. The seventh century and beyond would be a long stretch for the codex and leaves to be preserved, even if they are the product of the fourth century. Nongbri also challenges the report that the codex was even found in Coptos. All of this calls into question what seemed a secure dating of the manuscript. Another criterion must be found for anchoring the Luke fragments in the second century. I believe that there is another feature of 𝔓4 that points to an early rather than a later date. This is the *Nomina Sacra.* Scott Charlesworth has suggested the value of *Nomina Sacra* for determining dating. [27] The remainder of this essay will make exploration in this direction.

Nomina Sacra, or the abbreviation of divine names and other important words, is a common feature found in virtually all of the early Christian manuscripts.[28]

[24] The same point has recently been made by Zachary Cole, who notes "a practice of careful copying over time." Chapter 7, "Myths about Copyists," in *Myths and Mistakes in New Testament Textual Criticism,* Edited by Elijah Hixson and Peter J. Gurry, Downers Grove, Ill.:InterVarsity Press, 2019, 132-51, 148.

[25] Brent Nongbri, *God's Library,* New Haven: Yale University Press, 2018, Chapter 7 "Fabricating a Second Century Codex of the Four Gospels." 247-68.

[26] Nongbri, *God's Library*, 262.

[27] Scott Charlesworth, "Consensus Standardization in the Systematic Approach to *Nomina Sacra* in Second- and Third-Century Gospel Manuscripts." *Aegyptus* 86 (2006) 37-68. See 45 note 44. This valuable essay, however, assumes the established dating of early papyri to the second/third centuries, a point the present essay does not assume, but seeks to demonstrate. It is surprising that Larry Hurtado does not mention the *Nomina Sacra* or other early Christian artifacts as potentially useful for dating: see Larry Hurtado, *Texts and Artefacts,* New York: Bloomsbury, 2018, esp. chapter 3, 48-63, where he acknowledges Brent Nongbri's work on the dating of papyri.

[28] The major treatments on the subject are Ludwig Traube, *Nomina Sacra: Versuch einer Gersch*ichte Christlichen Kurnzunh. Munich: Beck, 1907. A.H.R.E Paap, *Nomina*

The following is a list of *Nomina Sacra.* The first four seem to have been regularly contracted from the beginning. The others seem to have been added until the manuscripts of the Byzantine period included fifteen altogether.[29]

God (θεός)
Lord (κύριος)
Jesus (Ἰησοῦς)
Christ (Χριστός)

Son (υἱός)
Spirit (πνεῦμα)
David (Δαυίδ)
Cross (σταυρός)
Mother (μήτηρ)
Father (πατήρ)
Israel (Ἰσραήλ)
Savior (σωτήρ)
Man (ἄνθρωπος)
Jerusalem (Ἰερουσαλήμ)
Heaven (οὐρανός)

A century ago C.H. Turner observed, "The manuscripts which distinguish themselves in respect of limiting the *Nomina Sacra* that are subject to abbreviation represent the earliest types."[30] This seems to be a logical assertion. Of course, there is always the danger of circular reasoning, making a statement about earlier manuscripts containing fewer *Nomina Sacra*, and then finding fewer in the manuscripts we have already considered early. This essay seeks to avoid circularity as much as possible, drawing its deductions from the observable number of *Nomina Sacra* in the various manuscripts. Some surprising results emerge (especially concerning the likely date of 𝔓75). But how do we know that the "original

Sacra in the Greek Papyri of the First Five Centuries A.D.: The Sources and some Deductions. Papyrologia Lugduno-Batava 8, Leiden:Brill, 1959. Jose O'Callaghan, *"Nomina Sacra" in Papyris Graecis Saeculi III Neotestamentariis.* Analecta Biblica 46. Rome: Biblical Institure Press, 1970. Roberts, Colin H. *Manuscript, Society and Belief in Early Christian Egypt.* Schwiech Lectures 1977. London: Oxford University Press for the British Academy, 1979. Larry W. Hurtado, *Earliest Christian Artifacts: Manuscripts and Christian Origins.* Grand Rapids: Eerdmans, 2006, 95-134. Philip Wesley Comfort, *A Commentary on the Manuscripts and Text of the New Testament.* Grand Rapids: Kregel, 2015 31-41. 419-443.

[29] Bruce M. Matzger, *Manuscripts of the Greek Bible: An Introduction to Palaeography.* New York: Oxford University Press, 1981, 36.

[30] C.H.Turner, "A Textual Commentary on Mark 1." *JTS* XXVIII (1927) 145-58, 49.

four" were the earliest? It seems that their almost universal occurrence points in that direction. The discussion of origins of the *Nomina Sacra* may also help.

Larry Hurtado conducted a thorough history of the modern discussion of the background of the *Nomina Sacra.* Of the various different proposals of its origin (Jewish reverence for the divine name, shorthand, readers' aids, early devotion to Jesus -which he goes for) the most plausible seems to be the background in Jewish reverence for the *name.* Our purpose is not to explore the origins of the phenomenon, but to trace the history of its earliest appearance in our New Testament manuscripts, and the development that included other words besides the original four. Nevertheless, a consideration of origins may give clues concerning the development and expansion of the phenomenon. Emanuel Tov has recently traced the procedures for treating the tetragrammaton at Qumran and in the Jewish copies of the scriptures in Greek. He documents the variety of approaches (Paleo-Hebraic script, tetrapuncta, etc).[31] Hurtado re-iterates the observation that the four earliest *Nomina Sacra* were the two key words for God, θεός and κύριος , and the names Christ and Jesus. [32] The Christian practice, which doubtless derived from Jewish procedures, probably began with only one word (κύριος).[33] Gradually other words were added: spirit, son, Jerusalem, David, etc.[34] It is therefore likely, given some variation for local developments, that the manuscripts with the fewer *Nomina Sacra* will be earlier than those with the fuller use of these abbreviations. In 1970 Jose O'Callaghan presented a list of all known *Nomina Sacra* in the larger New Testament papyri of the first three centuries.[35] It is clear from O'Callaghan's list that only a few words are abbreviated in 𝔓4: God, Lord, Jesus, Christ and Spirit. Charlesworth noted that the following words, usually abbreviated in later manuscripts, are written in full in the fragments of 𝔓4 that we possess: son, man, heaven, father and David.[36] On the basis of *Nomina Sacra,* 𝔓4 seems to be more at home in the second century than in the fourth. Skeat observed

[31] Emanuel Tov, "*Divine Names:* Different Approaches and Writing Procedures in the Qumran Scrolls."*Studia Biblica Slovaka, 12/* 2024, 133-158.

[32] Larry W. Hurtado, *The Earliest Christian Artifacts:* 95-134, especially 96-97. To these four Comfort would add πνεῦμα (spirit) *A Commentary,* 427-33.

[33] Scuyler Brown, "Concerning the Origin of the *Nomina Sacra," Studia Papyrologica* 9 (1970), 7-19.

[34] A complete list of *Nomina Sacra* is found in Bruce M. Metzger, *Manuscripts of the Greek Bible: An Introduction to Palaeography.* New York: Oxford University Press, 1981, 14. The fifteen Mertzger lists may not be comprehensive: see P Egerton 2, and the note in Hurtado, *Earliest Christian Artifacs,* 97, which I discuss below. See also 𝔓72.

[35] Jose O'Callaghan, "*Nomina Sacra" in Papyris Graecis Saeculi III Neotestamentariis,* Rome: Biblical Institute Press, 1970.

[36] Charlesworth, "Consensus Standardization," 44.

"the much less developed system of *Nomina Sacra* in 𝔓4." Only God, Jesus, Lord, Christ and Spirit are abbreviated.[37] By way of contrast, a glance at Table 1, at the end of this essay, shows that both Codex Alexandrinus and Codex Ephremi Rescriptus contain 14 of the 15 *Nomina Sacra.* We note here that 𝔓75 has 11, 𝔓66 has 9 of the *Nomina Sacra.* Codex Bezae, produced around the year 400 CE, had a much less developed system of *Nomina Sacra.* David Parker, in his thorough study of Codex Bezae (D) noted the conservatism of this 5th century manuscript, which has added to the original four *Nomina Sacra* three *more:* the words for father, spirit, cross/crucify. The usage also varies among books and copyists in this manuscript.[38]

A perusal of O'Callagan's figure for 𝔓75 is instructive. In addition to the earliest four (or five) terms treated as *Nomina Sacra,* 𝔓75 adds others for a total of 11. This is a more developed system and likely places 𝔓75 in the late third, if not the fourth century. If we consider the use of the first four (or five) as earlier, and the addition of others as of a later date, we may surmise that, other things being equal, 𝔓4 is of a decidedly earlier date than 𝔓75. It is therefore reasonable to consider 𝔓4 to be from the late second century, and 𝔓75 to date from some time in the third or fourth century. [39] In this calculation we need to allow for local differences in the convention, since these papyri may well have come from elsewhere in the empire than from Egypt. But in general, it is safe to conclude that the fewer the *Nomina Sacra* the earlier the date of the manuscript in which they occur. The re-appraisal of dating of early papyri on the basis of *Nomina Sacra* may prove to be an unexpectedly fruitful line of inquiry.[40]

Scribal practice with regard to the *Nomina Sacra* in the early period exhibits two distinct approaches: abbreviation and suspension. So, for example, abbreviation for the name Jesus included the first and last letters of the name (IC); for suspension, the first two or three letters (IH or IHC). Sometimes scribes used both (eg. 𝔓45 Ἰησοῦς) or wrote the name in full and also used *Nomina Sacra* (eg. 𝔓46 for θεός). Variety occurs across

[37] T.C. Skeat, "The Oldest Manuscript..." *NTS* 43 (1997) 6, 31.

[38] D.C. Parker, *Codex Bezae: An early Christian Manuscript and its Text.* Cambridge: Cambridge University Press, 1992, 104. See also Peter E. Lorenz, *A History of Codex Bezae's Text in the Gospel of Mark, Arbeiten zur Neutestamentlichen Textfoschung* band 53. Berlin/Boston: Walter de Gruyter, 2022, 52-58. Lorenz argues for the influence of the old Latin on the Greek column of this earliest New Testament bilingual codex. This may explain the conservatism of D with regard to *Nomina Sacra.* See Traub's table, 188-195.

[39] E.G. Turner, *The Typology of the Early Codex.* Philadelphia: University of Pennsylvania Press, 1977,95.

[40] For another attempt to set manuscript dating on a more scientific footing see "Omnitext." For information see Dr. Pat Sanders at info@omnitext.org. So far this approach has worked for medieval minuscules. But will it be applicable to the early NT papyri?

the early period and is not indicative of an earlier or later date. In fact, it corresponds to the variety of procedures outlined by Tov.

There are also outliers to the general patterns, chiefly P Egerton 2. Dated to the middle or later second century, this non-canonical gospel text offers abbreviations for Moses, Isaiah, and prophet.[41] This text seems to be in this way and others the exception that proves the rule. But perhaps its dating should be re-assessed.

We should also include with the *Nomina Sacra* the curious phenomenon of the Staurogram, the peculiar abbreviation for the word for cross with the combination of the letters tau and rho forming the shape of a crucified figure. (C⳨C)[42] This early Christian symbol/abbreviation is found in 𝔓45, 𝔓66, and 𝔓75. The occurrences of this abbreviated pictogram of the words *cross* and *crucify* are as follows:

𝔓45 (Vienna fragment) Matt 26:2.
𝔓66: John 19:6, 15,16,18,19,25,31.
𝔓75: Luke 9:23,15:27, 24:7.

There is no further occurrence of the staurogram in other early papyri, and it is not used in our mid-fourth century uncial, Codex Vaticanus. Traub lists a few occurrences known to him in 1907: Codex Sinaiticus at Rev. 11:8, P Rainer 8025 at Mark 15:30 and a Coptic manuscript in Paris at Luke 23:26, 24:20.[43] Paap lists several other occurrences, including 0165, P.Vind 29832(a homily of Origen).[44] There are some examples in the Nag Hamadi documents.[45] These occasional occurrences may be indebted to the exemplar they used. Furthermore, it does not appear to have been used in early papyri of the second century. 𝔓46 does not include it. That papyrus manuscript includes an abbreviation of "cross," but not as a Staurogram(ΣΤΡΟΣ). 𝔓90 (P.Oxy 3523) seems to have written out in full the word for "Crucify", such that the line in the verso for John 19:6,

[41] Larry Hurtado, *Earliest Christion Artifacts*, 97.

[42] See Larry Hurtado, *The Earliest Christian Artifactl*, 135-154. Hurtado rightly notes that this is the earliest Christian symbol for the cross, and indeed, probably the earliest Christian symbol. To his credit, Nongbri notes briefly the relevance of the Stourogram to the matter of dating manuscripts, but he does not mention the crucial distinction between the combined tau and rho within the word for cross within manuscripts and the free standing monogram that became popular after the fourth century. B. Nongbri, "The limits of palaeographic dating of literary papyri : some observations on the date and provenance of P. Bodmer II ," Museum Helveticum , 71 (2014), 1-35.

[43] Traub, *Nomina Sacra*, 129.

[44] Paap, *Nomina Sacra*, 98.

[45] Paul Linjamaa, *The Nag Hamadi Codices and their Ancient Readers: Exploring Textual Materialiy and Reading Practice*, Cambridge: Cambridge University Press, 2024, Chapter 6.

which partially includes the word, is too long to have allowed for the stauragram:

ΑΥΤΟΝ ΚΑΙ ΣΤΑΥΡΩΣ**ΑΤΕ ΕΓΩ ΓΑΡ**

Therefore, we may conclude that the staurogram is a third century phenomenon, which only occasionally survived in use into the fourth century and later in our manuscript tradition (except as a free-standing symbol in Christian art)[46] Here is another indication that 𝔓75 may fit more comfortably in the third century than in the fourth(preferably the late third century) Larry Hurtado, writing on his blog in response to Brent Nongbri's attempt to argue for a fourth century date for some early papyri (in this case 𝔓66)[47] notes the following:

By the 4th century, the staurogram had become a free-standing symbol referring to Christ, just as the more well-known Chi-Rho did. But in 𝔓66 and the other papyri dated to the 3rd century, the device is found only as part of abbreviated forms of the Greek words for "cross" and/or "crucify." (C⳨C)[48] This seems to be how the device was first appropriated by Christians (its "pre-Christian" usage was as a symbol for "three" or "thirty" etc.). Then, it seems, after being so used for a while and becoming sufficiently familiar to Christians, it was used as a free-standing "christogram" symbol.[49]

What I am arguing for in this essay is new criteria for assessing the date of early New Testament papyri. I use the plural *criteria*, because I am not arguing for relative dating on the basis of just *Nomina Sacra* or the Staurogram, but the combination of both, taken together.

Because 𝔓4 contains fewer *Nomina Sacra*, it may be dated to the late second(or perhaps, early third) century. Because 𝔓45, 𝔓66 and 𝔓75 use

[46] The occasional instances in manuscripts in the fourth century and later listed by L.Traub, *Nomina Sacra*, 128-30 . The occurrence in Codex Sinaiticus (second hand)may be the result of the scribe following a third century exemplar.

[47] See Brent Nongbri, "The Limits of Paleographic Dating of Literary Papyri: Some Observations on the Date and Provenance of P. Bodmer II (P66)," *Museum Helveticum* 71 (2014): 1-35.

[48] Dieter T.Roth notes the free standing Staurogram in 𝔓80 (a fragment for John 3:34, dated to the third century.) *The Reception of Jesus in the First Three Centuries*. Edited by Chris Keith and others, London: Bloomsbury, T. and T. Clark, 2019. Volume 3, pp.349-58. This scrap is too small to draw any firm conclusions, and the paleographic dating needs to be re-assessed in light of Nongbri's work. See also the free standing staurogram in Codex Sinaiticus at the end of Isaiah (after 66:24)

[49] Larry Hurtado's blog, June 3, 2014. Robin Jensen recognizes that the staurogram in the early papyri is the earliest secure example of the depiction of the cross: Robin M. Jensen, *Understanding Early Christian Art*, Second Editioin, London and New York: Routledge, 2024, 205.

the staurogram *within the words for cross,* the dates for these are best placed some time in the third century, to a time before Christianity became licensed and then official. After that time the staurogram and other christograms were regularly used as free standing symbols.

I conclude by noting that the dating of early Christian papyri will not be determined by paleography (which is too imprecise) and Carbon 14 (which requires the destruction of a portion of the manuscript). A more accurate assessment of the dating of these manuscripts, at least to the century of their production, may be determined by the *Nomina Sacra* and the staurogram. The papyri with fewer *Nomina Sacra* indicate an earlier date than those with an expanded list. The Staurogram within the words for the cross are best seen as a third century phenomenon. So, we may say with some confidence that 𝔓4 may be dated to the second century and 𝔓75 to the (probably late) third century. Codex Vaticanus (B) was produced around the middle of the fourth century. Thus we have in these three documents, 𝔓4, 𝔓75 and B, a witness to a strict and carefully copied text, which scholars usually identify as "Alexandrian," that has been preserved over at least 150 years.

Table 1: *Nomina Sacra* in the larger papyri and the important Uncials till the fifth century. A comprehensive table of *Nomina Sacra* in Greek, Latin, and Coptic manuscripts is beyond the scope of this essay. Traub's list as of 1907, and Paap's 1959 list, are in serious need of a thorough update. The dates given are from NA 28, N = the dates suggested, though not required, by Brent Nongbri. S=Staurogram.

Manuscript	Contents	Date	Nomina Sacra
𝔓4	Luke 1-6	II, N IV	God, Lord, Christ, Jesus, Spirit
𝔓45	EA	III	God, Lord, Christ, Jesus, Spirit, son, father, cross, (S)
𝔓46	P	c.200	God, Lord, Christ, Jesus Spirit, son, cross, (blood), man, Father, savior
𝔓47	R	III	God, Lord, Christ, man, cross, spirit, father
𝔓66	John	c.200, N IV	God, Lord, Jesus, Christ, son, Spirit, father, man, cross, (S)
𝔓72	C	III/IV	God, Lord, Jesus, Christ, Father, Spirit, man, power, Sarah, Abraham, Noah, Michael, Enoch.

𝔓75	Luke/John	175-225/ N IV	God, Lord, Jesus, Christ, spirit, Father, Son, Israel, Jerusalem, Cross, (S) man
𝔓115	R	III/IV	God, Lord, spirit, father, man, heaven, Israel
Codex Sinaiticus (א)	EACPR	IV	God, Lord, Jesus, Christ, spirit, heaven, man, David, Israel, Jerusalem, son, mother, father, cross (S) savior
Codex Vaticanus (B)	EACP	IV	God, Lord, Christ, Jesus, Spirit, heaven, man, David, son, mother
Codex Alexandinus (A)	EACPR	V	God, Lord, Jesus, Christ, Spirit, father, heaven, man, David, Israel, Jerusalem, son, cross, mother
Codex Bezae (D)	EA	V	God, Lord, Jesus, Christ, Father, spirit, cross
Codex Ephraemi Rescriptus (C)	EACPR	V	God, Lord, Jesus, Christ, Spirit, father, heaven, man, David, Israel, Jerusalem, son, savior, mother
LEGEND N=Nongbri. S=Staurogram C⳨C			

Peter R. RODGERS
5810 Cowen PI. NE
Apt 410
Seatle, WA. 98105
USA

Developments in Greek Language Studies: A Review Article

STANLEY E. PORTER

This review article examines three recent volumes that discuss ancient Greek language. Each is a collection of essays, with one concentrating on Greek prepositions, the second focusing on diachronic issues in ancient Greek, and the third offering a tribute to a well-known scholar of classical Greek. Whereas the Greek of the New Testament is only the focus of the first volume, each offers suggestive essays for further Greek study.

Keywords: Postclassical Greek, prepositions, diachrony, synchrony, classical Greek, conceptual metaphor, cognitive linguistics, philology.

Introduction

This review article discusses three relatively recent volumes on ancient Greek that are important in various ways for New Testament Greek studies. These volumes indicate that the field of Greek language studies continues to flourish. Even though not all the work in these volumes addresses the Greek of the New Testament, there is much here to think about regarding how we study the Greek of the New Testament, especially in relation to various approaches to language and linguistics and to how New Testament Greek as representative of Koine Greek fits within the development of the language. In this review, I will treat each volume independently by providing an evaluative overview and then some overall comments on each volume, before concluding with some general statements about the three volumes.

Greek Prepositions

The first volume has the most direct relevance for New Testament Greek studies. Even though it is titled *Postclassical Greek Prepositions and Conceptual Metaphor*,[1] the volume overwhelmingly focuses upon

[1] William A. Ross and Steven E. Runge, eds., *Postclassical Greek Prepositions and Conceptual Metaphor: Cognitive Semantic Analysis and Biblical Interpretation*, Fontes et Subsidia ad Bibliam Pertinentes 12 (Berlin: de Gruyter, 2022). Page numbers for this and the subsequent two volumes reviewed here are given in parentheses within the text.

New Testament Greek (only occasionally citing other examples) by examining prepositions from a cognitive linguistic standpoint (not just in relationship to conceptual metaphor, since various authors also deal with prototypicality and semantic frames, and especially the spatial categories of Trajectory and Landmark, which some will know as figure and ground). I will return to the question of whether the term "postclassical" is a useful one for such Greek studies, although it is highly questionable for this volume.

The book opens with an introduction (1-10) by the editors that notes that this volume is the result of a conference held in 2017 in the UK, although it is noteworthy that two of the major contributors' papers do not appear in the volume (those of Dirk Geeraerts and Anne Thompson). The book shows its colors early when the editors refer to the monographs by Silvia Luraghi and Pietro Bortone on prepositions (and cases)[2] and claim that "there is broad agreement among scholars that Luraghi and Bortone have chosen the ideal theoretical framework for the task of analyzing prepositional semantics, namely Cognitive Linguistics" (2).[3] Only a cognitive linguist probably could or would make such a statement, especially since other linguistic frameworks have addressed prepositions, arguably successfully or at least as successfully as cognitive linguistics. And as becomes clear in this volume, much of cognitive linguistic theory is directly dependent upon, even derived from, traditional locative views of prepositions (as many who have learned Greek know from some of their textbooks, with spatial displays of prepositional meanings).

[2] Silvia Luraghi, *On the Meaning of Prepositions and Cases: The Expression of Semantic Role in Ancient Greek*, Studies in Language Companion Series 67 (Amsterdam: Benjamins, 2003) and Pietro Bortone, *Greek Prepositions from Antiquity to the Present*, Oxford Linguistics (Oxford: Oxford University Press, 2010).

[3] The authors of the introduction make the comment that "Many students and scholars alike tend to work with the languages using basic terminology learned from their teachers (however long ago), a few older introductory texts, and/or what might charitably be called common sense or perhaps instinct" (2). In a footnote, they cite as "popular" sources in this regard James Barr, *The Semantics of Biblical Language* (Oxford: Oxford University Press, 1961); Moisés Silva, *Biblical Words and Their Meaning: An Introduction to Lexical Semantics* (Grand Rapids: Zondervan, 1995); Peter Cotterell and Max Turner, *Linguistics and Biblical Interpretation* (Downers Grove, IL: InterVarsity Press, 1989); and David Alan Black, *Linguistics for Students of New Testament Greek: A Survey of Basic Concepts and Applications*, 2nd ed. (Grand Rapids: Baker, 1995). I cannot imagine that these are the kinds of works that they are thinking of in their previous statement regarding older introductions or commonsense treatments, apart possibly from Black. These remain some of the earliest and still valuable, even if limited, treatments of Greek, even if major advances have since been made. Barr introduced linguistics to biblical studies in a way that made it virtually impossible to ignore (although many did and have tried since). It is true that they are not cognitive linguists, but that is neither here nor there in relation to the previous statement by the authors.

The authors lay out two major commitments of cognitive linguistics, "generalization," by which they mean that "whatever structuring principles hold in one aspect of language hold across all aspects of language," and "cognition," by which they mean that "whatever principles hold in linguistic structures should hold across all aspects of human cognition based on other disciplines," including cognitive studies (3). One should note these explicit commitments, to which I will return below. The authors then identify four implications of the above commitments: (1) "cognition is embodied," (2) "language is not conceptually autonomous," (3) grammar is conceptualization," and (4) "knowledge of language emerges from language use" (4). They then list fourteen "key ideas," which are as much about providing the jargon of cognitive linguistics as they are key ideas, since some are not unique to cognitive linguistics (e.g. construal) and others are simply attempts to provide a shorthand for reference—although some of these involve other jargon that makes some of these key ideas a trip into a rabbit hole rather than an exercise in clarification. One might legitimately wonder whether in fact cognitive linguistics is indeed linguistics, despite passionate claims to be so.

After a summary of the book's contents, there is a list of further reading (with the author Vyvyan Evans's first name misspelled two different ways; typographical errors and inconsistencies are, unfortunately, a regular feature of this book). The authors conclude by saying that, "Although Cognitive Linguistics may be new to most biblical scholars [I doubt it, at least for anyone reading this volume], its application in linguistics proper has more than demonstrated its potential to offer robust explanations to challenging conundrums like the seemingly inexplicable polysemy of Greek prepositions" (9). There is something off-putting about such an unsupported assertion, especially since it is followed by a series of essays offering varied perspectives on Greek prepositions, some more and less informative than others. Others have no doubt believed that they have explicated Greek prepositions, whether they accept polysemy or not (I happen to take a monosemous approach, and have happily defended it).[4] However, the sentence does indicate a primary focus of the book—how to deal with the fact that prepositions appear to have a large number of meanings—although this is not the only focus, since the book also appears to be an apologetic for cognitive linguistics itself, not just a study of prepositions, for which there have been other, previous proposals made.

The bulk of the volume consists of ten chapters, each in some way focused upon Greek prepositions, although not all examples of cognitive

[4] See Stanley E. Porter, "Greek Prepositions in a Systemic Functional Linguistic Framework," *Biblical and Ancient Greek Linguistics* 6 (2017): 17-43; cf. also Porter, *Idioms of the Greek New Testament*, 2nd ed. (Sheffield: Sheffield Academic, 1994), 142-79.

linguistics (an odd feature in a book purporting to present such a position). Some of the essays are relatively introductory and others more advanced in perspective. Most are earnest in their support of cognitive linguistics, although not all. Some are successful, while others are clearly problematic. I can only comment upon a few of these issues.

Richard Rhodes, a retired linguist from thc Univcrsity of California, Berkeley, introduces a cognitive view of prepositions in "Greek Prepositions: A Cognitive Linguistic View" (11-36). The essay problematically begins by citing the diagram of prepositions from the grammar by Dana and Mantey,[5] which Rhodes contrasts with cognitive linguistics in which "meaning arises out of perceptual experience" (12) and such meaning is not objective but constructed. Rhodes appears to be trying too hard, since I doubt that Dana and Mantey thought that their diagram of the relations of the meanings of Greek prepositions was anything other than a construction that arose from their experience of reading Greek texts, especially the New Testament. Rhodes further indicates that he believes that prepositions function similarly in all languages—a claim that will be refuted by essays in this very volume, where contrasts are recognized between English and Greek (see Runge's essay, discussed below). This raises the further question of what "cognitive" means if individuals with the same cognitive apparatus cognitively function differently to the point where an element as basic as a preposition has different construals across languages and even from individual to individual. This chapter is basically an introduction to the notions of Landmark (ground) and Trajector (figure), for which Rhodes provides numerous examples, in which language users impose this structure of Landmark and Trajector "prelinguistically" upon how they perceive the world (35), that is, before thinking about it linguistically (ostensibly to provide an unaffected perception). Rhodes—like the other contributors—provides translations of all examples, but there are many problems with the translations in this essay and in many other essays as well, making one wonder about not just the linguistic argument but the reliability of the perceptions and their construals involved (the heading for figure 2.13 should probably read "radial" rather than "radical," 24).

The next chapter is by Parick James on "The Overlap between ἀπό and ὑπό to Mark Agents: The Trials and Tribulations of a Traditional-

[5] H. E. Dana and Julius R. Mantey, *A Manual Grammar of the Greek New Testament* (New York: Macmillan, 1957 [1927]), 113 (not 1113 as printed). Other readers may be familiar with the similar conception found in Bruce M. Metzger, *Lexical Aids for Students of New Testament Greek*, new ed. (Princeton, NJ: privately published, 1983 [1946]), 80. Cf. also Porter, *Idioms*, 142-79, who uses individual graphic representations of locative meanings.

ist Lexicographic Treatment" (37-65). Despite the author's attempt to argue that he is establishing the problem that the cognitive linguists are attempting to solve regarding prepositions (I thought the introduction made clear that we already knew there was such a problem), this chapter probably does not belong in the volume. Readers may well find many of his observations—some of them diachronic—of some interest but largely irrelevant (did prepositions originally come from content words, and is this pertinent in this discussion?), and some of his claims regarding prepositional usage are at the least questionable. (The publication year for John Lee's book, missing in footnote 16, is 1983).

Rachel Aubrey and Michael Aubrey, in "Spatial Profiling: ἐκ, ἀπό and Their Entailments in Postclassical Greek" (67-83), attempt to explain the differences between the two prepositions. Much of their explanation makes sense, in which the original locative meaning is metaphorically extended—which would appear to explain the apparent polysemous nature of prepositions as not polysemous at all but monosemous. But many scholars probably already knew that, so the question is what cognitive linguistics uniquely provides (apart from use of the language of Landmark and Trajector). Terminology of prototypicality is used, but it is unclear how one arrives at what is prototypical—is it the usual or majority or favorite or writer's or most explanatory use?—and whether such a category is even needed in the discussion.

In chapter 5, Travis Wright explores "The περί Preposition Phrase at the Grammar-Discourse Interface" (86-121), the longest chapter in the book. Despite beginning with the assumption of prepositional polysemy, Wright ends up showing how a basic locative sense provides the basis for a variety of metaphorical extensions based on function, which one might well argue is not polysemy at all but monosemy. However, Wright's larger interest is how the preposition περί functions in discourse, especially in relation to topic. He claims that linguists have found that topic identification varies across languages, which I believe poses a problem for cognitive linguistics, especially if cognition implies a similar cognitive apparatus. Nevertheless, he attempts to show how περί functions in such environments. Whether he is correct in putting so much weight on a single preposition is certainly debatable.

William Ross then writes on "Construals of Faith in ἐν and ἐκ Prepositional Constructions" (123-52). By this he does actually mean "faith," as this is a chapter that has biblical interpretive goals, in fact, probably theological goals, as its primary aim. Ross approaches the question of prepositions from a different angle than most of the essays (at least previously in the book) and takes examples of two prepositions that are used with πίστις (note probable confusion of word and concept, a Barrian fallacy). He then works with a similar framework of locative meaning being metaphorically extended (most of the conclusions are predictable), with the result being polysemous meaning (which is not necessarily an entailment of such a theory). Ross also invokes prototype theory (without defining it or making clear how one is meant to arrive at a prototype), family resemblance (from Ludwig Wittgenstein, but that notion has fallen on hard times, since resemblances do not necessarily mean relations only points of posited similarity), and of course Trajector and Landmark. Ross's theological orientation is made clear when he expresses surprise at arriving at an understanding of "πίστις as a cause of justification" (143). He inevitably refers to the πίστις Χριστοῦ debate especially regarding the use of prepositions in such phrases but fails to cite the work by Porter and Pitts that has already discussed this issue at some length (although not from a cognitive perspective).[6] There are also a few problems with some of the translations and some misunderstanding regarding verbal aspect (144). Ross closes by invoking the phrase "choice implies meaning" (149), which I believe is a misconstrual, and probably a misunderstanding, of the longstanding linguistic notion of meaning implying choice, found in other and earlier linguistic theories, in which meaning is realized in language, rather than the other way around.[7]

In chapter 7, Bonnie Howe presents "'Why Do You Eat and Drink with Tax Collectors and Sinners?': How Prepositions Shape Social Space and Norms in Luke" (153-78). Howe emphasizes application of cognitive linguistic views of prepositions to the New Testament. She makes clear at the outset, however, that she will utilize a variety of cognitive linguistic theories, not just the more limited Trajector and Landmark concepts of others, by invoking mental spaces, conceptual networks, conceptual blending, semantic frames, and of course prototypicality, among others. Her goal is to provide insights into social spaces in Luke's Gospel (Luke 5:29-32; 7:36-49; 15:1-2; 19:4-6, although some of the headings seem out of sync). The result is, unfortunately, what appears to be much overread-

[6] Stanley E. Porter and Andrew W. Pitts, "Πίστις with a Preposition and Genitive Modifier: Lexical, Semantic, and Syntactic Consideration in the Πίστις Χριστοῦ Discussion," in *The Faith of Jesus Christ: Exegetical, Biblical, and Theological Studies*, ed. Michael F. Bird and Preston M. Sprinkle (Peabody, MA: Hendrickson, 2009), 33-53. The work is listed in the bibliography but not discussed in the main text, where it is pertinent.

[7] Is this phrase from Stephen H. Levinsohn, *Discourse Features of New Testament Greek: A Coursebook on the Information Structure of New Testament Greek*, 2nd ed. (Dallas: SIL International, 2000), viii, as cited by Runge on p. 182 in the reviewed volume? Ross does not say. The notion of meaning implying choice was apparently first formulated by Charles Bazell, *Linguistic Form* (Istanbul: Istanbul Press, 1953), 81, with many linguists since using similar language, including M. A. K. Halliday, "Meaning as Choice," in *Systemic Functional Linguistics: Exploring Choice*, ed. Lise Fontaine, Tom Bartlett, and Gerard O'Grady (Cambridge: Cambridge University Press, 2013), 15-36.

ing of several passages based upon attempting to say more than should or can legitimately be said about a given use of a preposition (such as ἐν, διὰ τί, μετά, εἰς), to the point that she might appear to be creating a word-theology. This is extended beyond prepositions, such as her use of metonymy. In light of this, I found it odd that she then calls for a very restrained view of interpreting compound verbs (although there has been much more written on this topic than she cites).[8] She also makes appeal to what she calls "the bare prototypical meaning" of the use of ἐπί in Luke 19:4 (174), which seems incongruous with her overall treatment of prepositions and implies something unusual about prototypes. (There seem to be more typographical problems in this chapter than in many of the others.)

Steven Runge's chapter, "Land Forms, Weapons, and Body Parts: How Mismatches in Preferred Construals Have Shaped Our Understanding of Greek Prepositions" (179-207), addresses supposed mismatches between Greek prepositions and English understandings and translations. After (again) reviewing the presuppositions of cognitive linguistics (a feature of too many of the essays in this volume), as well as invoking "choice implies meaning" (attributed this time to Levinsohn) and reviewing ways to understand the varied semantics associated with Trajectors and Landmarks (container, path, etc.), Runge turns to two groups of nouns, those with restricted spatial profiles (mountains, bodies of water, and military forces) and those with few restrictions on spatial profiles (hands, fire, and weapons), and how these have been understood in English translations. One would expect there to be differences among languages, at least I would. However, some of the explanations of the Greek meanings seem to push a bit hard, such as the use of ἐν with words for fire indicating that ancient Greeks viewed fire as a container (199). Runge concludes from his examination that "Such prelinguistic preferences about how to profile spatial relationships vary between languages and dialects" (205). Besides "prelinguistic" being a buzzword for some in this book (meaning before linguistic reflection upon such usage), the conclusion appears at odds with the idea that humans, as humans, process language similarly. This seems like a conclusion based upon social rather than cognitive findings. Social factors no doubt play a role in language use and even construction, but what that relationship is remains unclear in this volume but also in cognitive linguistics as a whole. The invocation of prototype theory, and, with it, family resemblance, does nothing to mute the fact that the

[8] For example, see Stanley E. Porter, *Verbal Aspect in the Greek of the New Testament, with Reference to Tense and Mood*, Studies in Biblical Greek 1 (New York: Peter Lang, 1989), 66-70, for discussion of one issue regarding compound verbs. There are other discussions.

idea of meanings having metaphorical extensions is not unique to cognitive linguistics. There are also numerous problems with the translations provided in this chapter, including issues regarding how to render or understand compound verbs, repeated prepositions, and even simple phrasing or individual words (e.g. Josh 10:28 in Greek seems to be translated according to the Hebrew text rendered by the NRSV). (Runge also uses several times the annoying phrase "the bare dative," which sounds more like a contemporary musical band than a useful grammatical category; cf. "bare prototypical meaning" above.)

Michael Aubrey and Rachel Aubrey (the same two authors as above, but in reverse order) also contribute "Construing Agency and Cause in Passive Constructions" (209-40). This chapter appears to be an example of over-reading literalistic locative understandings to establish metaphorical meanings, such as being under (ὑπό), a spatial position, indicating power and control (and hence agency). They deal with several other prepositions in this regard (ἐκ, ἀπό, and διά). They sometimes create unnecessary problems, such as how they handle passives of intransitive verbs, because they apparently follow the active/passive transformation criterion. This article discusses δικαιόω and passivization, where ὑπό is not used for agency, except in one instance in their corpus from Shepherd of Hermas (which unfortunately the authors identify as a classical text, rather than probably second-century Christian text that it is, 225). I am not sure that their treatment of δικαιόω benefits in any significant way from cognitive linguistics, despite their appeal to semantic frames as a way of raising questions regarding whether the background of the term is Jewish or Hellenistic—itself probably a false dichotomy and problematic in dealing with the Greek language. (The article also has some questionable and problematic translations, as well as a problem with accent on πνεῦμα.)

Erin Heim's chapter, "The 'Ins' and 'Outs' of Matthew 15:1–20: Insights on Prepositions from Prototype Theory and Metaphor Theory" (241-58), takes far too long to introduce the topic of cognitive linguistics and especially of metaphor in a book that focuses upon these. To her credit, Heim does attempt to differentiate cognitive linguistics, prototype theory, and conceptual metaphor, without necessarily defining them all sufficiently but instead arguing that they can work together to enhance biblical exegesis. However, I am not sure that she is fully on topic all the time in her discussion. For example, she includes Gregory Fewster's work on creation language in Romans as an example of studies that make use of metaphor theory and cognitive linguistics (241 note 1).[9] Fewster indeed mentions

[9] Gregory P. Fewster, *Creation Language in Romans 8: A Study in Monosemy*, Linguistic Biblical Studies 8 (Leiden: Brill, 2013).

cognitive linguistics but only to treat it in relationship to monosemy. His emphasis is upon grammatical metaphor within Systemic Functional Linguistics. Heim also seems to rely a lot upon Janet Martin Soskice, even though her view of metaphor is traditional and rooted in classical thought.[10] Heim also makes the claim that some conceptual metaphors that she is discussing are not linguistic, which raises further questions about what cognitive linguistics is. Her example of Matt 15:1–20 raises the question regarding what cognitive linguistics adds that we don't already know or can surmise about this passage. (She oddly refers twice to a clause as a "phrase" and, unfortunately, sometimes puts the Greek wording in quotation marks.)

The final chapter, by Jonathan Pennington on "Cognitive Linguistics and Greek Prepositions: A New Testament Perspective" (259-67), appears to be designed to bring the volume to a close from the standpoint of an avowedly exegetically and translationally oriented scholar who is not a committed cognitivist. Pennington approaches his task through Umberto Eco's *Experiences in Translation*,[11] in which the question of linguistic determinism is raised because of the difficulty if not impossibility of translation without recognizing that language affects how we perceive and reflect reality (260). So far, most cognitive linguists would probably agree with this. The problem, however, is that such a viewpoint is based more on language as a communal or cultural property and not on the cognitive capacity of the individual. What is the relationship between the two? Would one expect such differences in language if all humans share the same cognitive apparatus? How do we know? Shouldn't we know if we are going to make statements about each? Pennington, like several others, cannot resist the opportunity to introduce theological discussion, in his case the uses of the prepositions ἐν and ἐκ in 1 John, where he identifies origin language. One of the conclusions that Pennington arrives at is that, "Using Cognitive Linguistics categories, the prototypical idea of ἐν appears to be locative"—no surprise there!, but he is not done—"though there are certainly many other uses including temporal, instrumental, and respect, even if one understands these as derivative from the locative" (264). Did we need cognitive linguistics to tell us this, or does it tell us this any better, or is it simply using (or is it?) some cognitive linguistic categories or language?

[10] Janet Martin Soskice, *Metaphor and Religious Language* (Oxford: Clarendon, 1985). Soskice defines metaphor as "that figure of speech whereby we speak about one thing in terms which are seen to be suggestive of another" (15, italics in original), in other words a substitutionary view of metaphor, arguably quite different from that of cognitive linguistics.

[11] Umberto Eco, *Experiences in Translation*, trans. Alastair McEwen (Toronto: University of Toronto Press, 2001).

The volume concludes with a bibliography that appears to be redundant, since each chapter has its own bibliography. One or the other would be sufficient. There is also a list of contributors, an ancient sources index, and a topic index. The topic index includes both topics and people (a modern author index would have been better to include separately).

After reading this volume, I was perplexed and even frustrated at having spent so much time for so little return. I wondered whether the problem was with me or with cognitive linguistics (I know how some will answer this). In 2016, Ewa Dabrowska, herself a cognitive linguist, published an article in the journal *Cognitive Linguistics* (incidentally, also published by de Gruyter and a journal she formerly edited) entitled "Cognitive Linguistics' Seven Deadly Sins."[12] She first outlines three major premises of cognitive linguistics: language is meant to convey meaning (a premise that many other linguists would also affirm), linguistic description reflects human psychological reality (a distinctive of cognitive linguistics, even if it does not hold to Chomsky's "language organ"), and grammar reflects usage (another premise that many linguists would adhere to). However, Dabrowska also lists seven major problems in cognitive linguistics (using her headings): (1) "excessive reliance on introspection," where she cites the work of especially early cognitive linguists, such as Gilles Fauconnier, George Lakoff, Mark Johnson (and their joint work on metaphor), Ronald Langacker, and Leonard Talmy;[13] (2) "not treating the cognitive commitment seriously," that is, not referring to the latest research in neuroscience and cognitive processing and related areas; (3) "not enough serious hypothesis testing," especially in terms of alternative hypotheses; (4) "ignoring individual differences" in an attempt to formulate generalizations without understanding the importance of differences (such as how individuals can communicate if they perceive the world differently); (5) "neglecting the social aspects of language," even though cognitive linguistics claims to be attentive to cultural and social factors, to the point of it needing to become (according to Dabrowska) a "social Cognitive Linguistics" (486); (6) "assuming that we can deduce mental representations

[12] Ewa Dabrowska, "Cognitive Linguistics' Seven Deadly Sins," *Cognitive Linguistics* 27.4 (2016): 479-91. Her article, as one might expect, caused a reaction. For one response, see Lin Gan, "Is Cognitive Linguistics Deadly Sinful? On the Pros and Cons of Cognitive Linguistics and Its Development," *Forum for Linguistic Studies* 3.1 (2021): 52-66.

[13] Representative works are Gilles Fauconnier, *Mental Spaces: Aspects of Meaning Construction in Natural Language* (Cambridge, MA: MIT Press, 1985); George Lakoff, *Women, Fire and Dangerous Things: What Categories Reveal about the Mind* (Chicago: University of Chicago Press, 1987); Lakoff and Mark Johnson, *Metaphors We Live by* (Chicago: University of Chicago Press, 1980); Ronald Langacker, *Foundations of Cognitive Grammar*, 2 vols. (Stanford, CA: Stanford University Press, 1987-1991); and Leonard Talmy, *Toward a Cognitive Semantics* (Cambridge, MA: MIT Press, 2000).

from patterns of use" drawing upon corpus linguistics, when explanation is required; and (7) "assuming that distribution equals meaning," when there may be other valid explanations not associated with distribution.

I won't attempt to evaluate each article according to the seven criteria. I simply note that the volume relies heavily upon the highly introspective theories of especially Lakoff and Johnson (after Luraghi, the two most frequently cited authors, but all the above are cited numerous times each), as well as relying upon the introspective theories of the individual authors as they hypothesize about the development of the semantic origins, characteristics, and metaphorical extensions of various prepositions. Some of the hypotheses are interesting and some may be accurate, but too many of them remind me of folk etymologies. There is very, very little reference by any of the authors to research in cognitive science, with only the occasional reference here and there (Rhodes includes references to four or five sources, most by one author). There does not appear to be any significant first-hand knowledge of neuroscience by the authors and little indication of a desire to know more. As for hypothesis testing, especially in terms of alternative hypotheses, this is clearly a shortcoming of the volume. From the outset, the widespread and working assumption is that cognitive linguistics provides the answer to whatever question is being posed, and then an explanation is offered. The only evidence resembling a test is the citation of another passage that purportedly confirms the hypothesis (often by means of translation). One of the surprising results of this volume is that it has a high degree of uniformity throughout, with most authors singing very tight harmonies from the same songbook. There are a couple of exceptions, such as James and Heim, but their alternatives are not necessarily in support of cognitive linguistics. The importance of the social aspects of language is one that is admittedly in tension with the cognitive assumption that language reflects psychological reality. This volume does not attempt to resolve that tension. This volume recognizes cultural difference—hence efforts in some essays to explain prepositions that may be translated in ways that do or do not fit their Greek usage—but never comes to terms with the relationship of cognitive function to communal, and differing communal, language use. This remains a major issue for cognitive linguists. On the one hand, if the cognitive apparatus is the same for each human (barring disability) why is there so much linguistic diversity? On the other hand, if cognition is individual, then how are humans able to communicate at all? The social and cultural factors seem to be overwhelmingly important, to the point that one may not even need to appeal to cognition in the formulation of an answer. Several of the essays use corpus-linguistic like features as a means of speculation regarding mental representation. Many of the conclusions are similar, although that is not a guarantee that they are correct. There may be other, better explanations, but they are rarely explored here. However, since so many of the conclusions seem to reflect past knowledge regarding prepositions—such as their locative origins and meaning, polysemy, metaphorical or other types of extensions—one wonders how much cognitive linguistics has contributed to the discussion, apart from introducing "new" language for categorization (Trajector and Landmark). Several of the chapters also rely upon distribution as explanation, even to the point of formulating theological conclusions. For all the reasons above, one must be careful with such conclusions.

A Historical Study of Ancient Greek

The second reviewed volume is likewise styled as a treatment of issues in postclassical Greek: *Postclassical Greek: Contemporary Approaches to Philology and Linguistics*.[14] This volume is perhaps more appropriately called postclassical in orientation than the first, since it covers a much wider range and period of authors than the previous volume, although calling it linguistic is more problematic. Most of the studies—though not all—are historical and philological, with abundant references to secondary literature that can only be characterized as prelinguistic (here used as a term to describe their development before modern linguistics).

The first essay, by the editors, is on "Postclassical Greek: An Overview" (1-15). I will spend some time on this essay as it provides an accurate introduction to the volume. From the outset, the authors reveal that they themselves, and presumably other contributors and readers, are not certain what the term "postclassical" refers to. They would be correct. The primary distinction they make is between classical and postclassical Greek. But this won't do. The authors admit also to archaic and classical periods in Greek, so what has happened to archaic in their bifurcation? The term classical is itself problematic. Here it usually seems to indicate Attic (or Attic-Ionic) Greek, but that was only one of the dialects of the dialect period. The editors also include all Greek from 323 BC (Alexander) to AD 1453 (fall of Byzantium) within postclassical Greek, but they should, to be fair, also include Greek up to the present as it too is postclassical. In any case, this period is too long and contains too much to provide a useful term (as recognized by Chiara Gianollo, 41 note 1). Further, calling the period postclassical privileges classical Greek (or in

[14] Dariya Rafiyenko and Ilja A. Seržant, eds., *Postclassical Greek: Contemporary Approaches to Philology and Linguistics*, Trends in Linguistics Studies and Monographs 335 (Berlin: de Gruyter Mouton, 2020).

this case Attic Greek) in an unlinguistic way. Just because one city or region over a short few centuries happened to develop as it did so as to host some of the arguably most important Greek authors (others, and I would be one, would argue that there are examples of later Greek that are just as important literarily and even linguistically) does not linguistically privilege them or their variety of Greek. To the contrary, one might well argue that Hellenistic/Roman period Greek, what is often called Koine Greek—when Greek became a world language whose influence extended far beyond Greece—should be the reference point for any discussion of the history of Greek, with preceding and following Greek compared to it (so far as it can be characterized as a lingua franca or even standard language). In other words, reference to postclassical Greek as it is used in this volume is a bit like referring to contemporary English as post-Renaissance or post-Shakespearean English. The term recognizes an important literary period in English, but it is linguistically inappropriate. This volume, however, does make reference to a broader expanse of texts that extend over a longer period than the previous volume—focused predominantly on the New Testament (the only two authors in the first volume who seem to use more appropriate terminology are the second article by the Aubreys, somewhat, and the article by Heim)—which makes the use of the term postclassical even more inappropriate.

Since the major set of texts often examined by those writing on "postclassical" Greek are biblical (New Testament and Septuagint), it is surprising, especially in this second volume, how relatively little appears to be known by the various authors of scholarship by linguistically-informed biblical Greek scholars (although some of the older comparative works, such as Blass and Debrunner, are still often cited). For example, in the introduction the authors speak about the "chronological periodization" (1) of Greek, recognizing that Koine Greek was the lingua franca of the Hellenistic/Roman period and providing a tabular formulation of various proposals regarding the periodization of Greek—but without reference to any New Testament (or Septuagint) Greek scholars, even though they have written extensively on this topic.[15] Similarly, the authors refer to

[15] As examples that I am immediately aware of, see Bruce M. Metzger, "The Language of the New Testament," in *The Interpreter's Bible*, ed. George Arthur Buttrick, 12 vols. (Nashville: Abingdon, 1951-1957), 7:43-59, esp. 44-45; E. C. Colwell, "The Greek Language," in *The Interpreter's Dictionary of the Bible*, ed. George Arthur Buttrick, 4 vols. (Nashville: Abingdon, 1962), 2:479-87, esp. 479-82; Chrys C. Caragounis, *The Development of Greek and the New Testament: Morphology, Syntax, Phonology, and Textual Transmission*, WUNT 17 (Tübingen: Mohr Siebeck, 2004), 21-60, esp. 22; and Stanley E. Porter, "Greek Language," in *The New Interpreter's Dictionary of the Bible*, ed. Katharine Doob Sakenfeld, 5 vols. (Nashville: Abingdon, 2006-2009), 2:673-81, esp. 674. I apologize at the outset for referring to my own published works as much as I do in this review, but I am most aware

registers of Greek. They make the strange comment that "This new common language, the Koiné, started developing different registers" (2), as if registers had not existed before. The authors appear to be confused over the difference between register and dialect, since they then go on to talk about Atticism, but they also talk about higher and lower forms. Again, what is missing in this discussion is citation of New Testament Greek scholars, even though register has been a topic within New Testament Greek studies since at least the late 1980s.[16] The authors even refer to the Greek of the New Testament as representing "an excellent example of contemporary Koiné" (3), yet again without citation of any New Testament Greek scholars on this issue.[17] They also speak of language contact, especially "Greek-Coptic language contact" being "the best attested instance of language contact in antiquity" (3), but without reference to any biblical scholars who have addressed this or the related issue of Semitisms, especially in the Septuagint but also in the Greek New Testament.[18] The authors oddly claim that "The language of the Septuagint closely matches the Hebrew Bible" (4), a view that is at the least highly controversial and arguably disputed by many Septuagint scholars.[19]

The authors of the introduction also offer a brief conspectus of the grammar of what they call postclassical Greek. In their discussion, their neat bifurcation between classical and postclassical Greek encounters further problems when they make their own distinctions between various dialects, such as Attic and Ionic. They also make the unsupported

of these essays and their availability. Other New Testament Greek scholars could be cited as well, as evidenced in this note.

[16] In particular, see Porter, *Verbal Aspect*, 153, who may have been the first to introduce the concept of register to New Testament Greek studies, referred to by several scholars in subsequent research. See also Porter, "Greek Language," 675-76.

[17] As an example known to me, see Stanley E. Porter, "New Testament," in *Encyclopedia of Ancient Greek Language and Linguistics*, ed. Georgios K. Giannakis, 3 vols. (Leiden: Brill, 2014), 2:497-500; cf. Porter, "Septuagint," in *Encyclopedia of Ancient Greek*, 3:287-90.

[18] For a history of discussion to the point of writing, see Porter, *Verbal Aspect*, 111-56. The discussion of Semitic influence on the Greek of the New Testament goes back to at least the seventeenth century but has been brought up to date in recent discussion in terms of language contact, multilingualism, and diglossia. For a recent treatment, see Sung Min Park, *The Prestige Language of Christianity in the Book of Acts: Historical Sociolinguistic Approaches to Multilingualism*, Linguistic Biblical Studies 29 (Leiden: Brill, 2025).

[19] See Stanley E. Porter, "History of Scholarship on the Language of the Septuagint," in *Die Sprache der Septuaginta/The Language of the Septuagint*, ed. Eberhard Bons and Jan Joosten, LXX.H 3 (Gütersloh: Gütersloher Verlagshaus, 2016), 15-38, esp. 32-36, where I cite recent advocates of the Koine Greek hypothesis of the Septuagint (opposed to the view expressed above), including such scholars as Moisés Silva (biblical scholar), John A. L. Lee (classicist), Greg Horsley (classicist), Trevor Evans (classicist), and Geoffrey Horrocks (classicist), the last well-known and often cited in the review volume, and most recently Takamitsu Muraoka, the author of the first complete Greek grammar of the Septuagint.

claim that "the aorist and perfect—originally distinct tense-aspect categories [a point with which I strongly agree]—came increasingly to be used interchangeably" during the classical period and in Koine Greek (what happened to the postclassical period?), to the point of there being "one perfective past category with largely stylistically conditioned allomorphy" (5). Such a theory has been disputed, by both New Testament and classical Greek scholars.[20] I also think that their too facile dismissal of a distinction between middle and passive voices calls for further reexamination (see also below).[21]

A category widely invoked in this volume is grammaticalization, although it is more invoked than readily defined. Many of the examples the authors offer must be questioned. For example, they utilize what I consider a much too broad category of periphrasis that encompasses use of not just structures with εἰμί but those with ἔχω and, for the possible "future tense" (a category debatable in itself), periphrases with ὀφείλω and μέλλω. The authors confuse periphrasis—which I narrowly equate with constructions with the aspectually vague verb εἰμί—with various other collocations (or colligations), including catenative verbal constructions.[22] As for "future" forms, there is first of all the question of whether Greek even has a future-referring form (I do not believe that it does) and whether the proposed alternative constructions are syntactical or semantic substitutes (I do not believe that they are, but that they are more likely catenative constructions or similar, in which the verbal aspect of the finite and non-finite

[20] The most notable of the classical Greek scholars to argue for the semantics of the perfect tense-form, perhaps, are J. P. Louw, "Die Semantiese Waarde von die Perfektum in Hellenistiese Grieks," *Acta Classica* 10 (1967): 23-32; and K. L. McKay, "The Use of the Ancient Greek Perfect down to the End of the Second Century A.D.," *Bulletin of the Institute of Classical Studies* 12 (1965): 1-21; McKay, "On the Perfect and Other Aspects in the Greek Non-Literary Papyri," *Bulletin of the Institute of Classical Studies* 27 (1980): 23-49; and McKay, "On the Perfect and Other Aspects in New Testament Greek," *Novum Testamentum* 23 (1981): 289-329.

[21] See Stanley E. Porter and Matthew Brook O'Donnell, "The Greek Verbal Network Viewed from a Probabilistic Standpoint: An Exercise in Hallidayan Linguistics," *Filología Neotestamentaria* 14 (2001): 3-41, where ergativity is introduced along with transitivity into the Greek voice (causality) system; Porter, *The Pastoral Epistles: A Commentary on the Greek Text* (Grand Rapids: Baker, 2023), 11-12; and especially David L. Mathewson, *Voice and Mood: A Linguistic Approach*, Essentials of Biblical Greek Grammar (Grand Rapids: Baker, 2021), esp. 7-73.

[22] This reviewed volume does not refer to aspectually vague verbs or catenative constructions, so far as I can see. They are discussed in Porter, *Verbal Aspect*, 442-47, 487-92. On periphrasis itself, see Porter, *Verbal Aspect*, 441-78. My proposals have been responded to by Klaas Bentein, *Verbal Periphrasis in Ancient Greek: Have- and Be- Constructions* (Oxford: Oxford University Press, 2016), esp. 67-68, although I believe that his objections to my view are not compelling. Regardless, his definition of periphrasis remains too expansive and seems to be based upon conceptual equation rather than syntactical configurations.

verbs are maintained, unlike in a periphrasis).[23] The authors, returning to the perfect tense-form (see comments above), also claim that the perfect "no longer attested its original 'perfect' functions" (7)—whatever these are they do not say—but have become a "past tense" (7). They call this an "aspectual change" (7). This is not an aspectual change but a temporal change, at the least a debatable issue within Greek linguistics. There appears to be confusion over the notions of tense and aspect and how they apply to the semantics of the perfect tense-form (which is arguably not temporal at all, until much later in the development of Greek than the Hellenistic and Roman periods).[24] In all this discussion, there is no reference to any New Testament (or Septuagint) Greek scholars, pro or con, so far as I can see—and they have productively written on all these topics.

The authors of the introduction seem to accept a valency approach (argument structure) to their discussion of cases and prepositions. There is no obvious recognition that other approaches have been used to study Hellenistic and Roman period Greek.[25] Even though many of the observations here are correct (such as so-called prepositional cases [prepositional phrases] becoming more frequent than non-prepositional cases [an odd way of formulating it, but better than "bare dative"]), the authors in referring to essays within the volume show that there is a tendency to invoke distributional arguments and to infer semantics from these. They set the barrier for distributional differentiation at 60% (10), whereas some linguists might argue for a greater differentiation (as in Halliday's probabilistic grammar). Some typical and perhaps unhelpful statements include reference to possible Semitic influence on prepositions. (I am unaware of the category of "inessive" cited on 9.)

The authors conclude with a section on other phenomena treated within the volume, noted individually below but still meriting comment here. One issue is negation, where the authors claim that "Negative

[23] On the meaning of the future form as neither a tense nor a mood, but as an aspectually vague indicator of expectation, see Porter, *Verbal Aspect*, 403-39.

[24] For a recent discussion of some of these issues, including the meaning of the perfect tense-form in New Testament Greek, see Constantine R. Campbell, Buist M. Fanning, and Stanley E. Porter, *The Perfect Storm: Critical Discussion of the Semantics of the Greek Perfect Tense Under Aspect Theory*, ed. D. A. Carson, Studies in Biblical Greek 21 (New York: Peter Lang, 2021); cf. also Robert Crellin, "The Semantics of the Perfect in the Greek of the New Testament," in *The Greek Verb Revisited: A Fresh Approach for Biblical Exegesis*, ed. Steven E. Runge and Christopher J. Fresch (Bellingham, WA: Lexham, 2016), 430-57 (a volume with some other essays that might be pertinent to some of the issues raised in this review). I argue for Greek being a tenseless language, including in the indicative, a view first argued in Porter, *Verbal Aspect*, but in many works since. This perspective has been widely debated.

[25] For example, see the first reviewed volume above. See also the early work by J. P. Louw, "Linguistic Theory and the Greek Case System," *Acta Classica* 9 (1966): 73-88.

concord gives rise in Koiné Greek to double negation" (10), citing the example of Mark 16:8. There are, indeed, instances of double negation in Koine Greek, but negation is far more complex, including in Koine Greek, than the authors state. The authors would have benefited from an article that appeared just before their volume, in which both paradigmatic and syntagmatic axes of the Greek language are considered.[26] The rank scale in relation to types of negation results in syntactical descriptions that realize both negative constituents but also negative scope (resulting in negative spread) across units. As a result, determining negation in Greek is more difficult than simply counting negatives, but involves considering the types and functions of negation within each clause and its components. Another comment concerns auxiliary verbs where other categories, such as catenative constructions, could have proved enlightening. A further consideration is information structure and its relationship to word order (a slight misnomer, since we are speaking of clausal constituent order, not simply verb, etc.), where it is questionable whether there has been a clear OV to VO shift (I hesitate to use these indicators, but they are the terms used).[27] The situation is far more complex. The authors unfortunately refer to the "definite article" (11), which ancient Greek does not have—article yes, definite article no.

The authors conclude their introduction with a strange juxtaposition between what they call "'pure' linguistics" and "variational factors," by which they seem to be contrasting theoretical or formalist linguistics with sociolinguistics (12). They are indeed right that such variationist and other sociolinguistic factors not only should but must be considered. However, I am not sure how this relates to their advocacy of rephilologizing historical linguistics, when less philologizing and more use of functional linguistic models might be more productive. The essay closes with a bibliography that has several errors, including listing Blass and Debrunner's grammar as 1898, when it was first published in 1896 (in either case, it is unclear why this work continues to be so widely used), and not listing Eideneier 1999.[28]

[26] Stanley E. Porter and Christopher D. Land, "Modeling Negation in Ancient Greek," *Filología Neotestamentaria* 32 (2019): 3-20.

[27] For a recent discussion of some of the issues concerning so-called word order, see Stanley E. Porter and Matthew Brook O'Donnell, *Discourse Analysis and the Greek New Testament: Text-Generating Resources*, Library of New Testament Greek 2 (London: T&T Clark, 2024), 184-88.

[28] Friedrich Blass, *Grammatik des Neutestamentlichen Griechisch* (Göttingen: Vandenhoeck und Ruprecht, 1896), mostly used in the form of Friedrich Blass and Albert Debrunner, *A Greek Grammar of the New Testament and Other Early Christian Literature*, trans. Robert W. Funk (Chicago: University of Chicago Press, 1961). Presumably Hans Eideneier, *Von Rhapsodie zu Rap: Aspekte der griechischen Sprachgeschichte von Homer bis heute* (Tübingen: Narr, 1999).

Section one of two concerns grammatical categories. The first essay, by Giuseppina di Bartolo, "Purpose and Result Clauses: ἵνα-hína and ὥστε-hōste in the Greek Documentary Papyri of the Roman Period" (19-38), appears to argue for what is probably already widely accepted (extended to other conjunctions and their constructions), although the author is often insistent in her observations. These commonplaces include the fact that the Egyptian papyri have some phonological differences or differences from classical Greek and that the Greek language has developed (reference to the "bare indicative" is unnecessary). There are, however, some problems, such as the author's reliance upon Edwin Mayser, Blass and Debrunner, and A. N. Jannaris as three of her four primary repositories of information (all are dated prelinguistic works);[29] her lack of describing the modal system as a system, but instead treating the moods in isolation; the assumption that purpose and result can so easily be distinguished in earlier Greek; the ability to make differentiations between purpose and result primarily on the basis of translation; and some confusion over whether she is defining the meaning of conjunctions or clauses (or moods). I am not convinced that the use of ἵνα with the indicative is simply a matter of phonology and morphology (29) and suspect that the distinction between ὥστε and the indicative or infinitive was never as strong as some may think. (Di Bartolo repeatedly refers to Palme 1980, when she means [L. R.] Palmer 1980; Jannaris 1968: 417, not 416, refers to the New Testament data; there are many other typographical errors.)

Chiara Gianollo writes on "Syntactic Factors in the Greek Genitive-Dative Syncretism: The Contribution of New Testament Greek" (39-70). This is one of the most interesting articles in the collection. Gianollo begins with some questionable assumptions regarding the limitations of so-called postclassical Greek—limited availability of non-literary language (what of the documentary papyri?), literary conservativeness (the Greek New Testament?), and lack of clear language contact data (Palestine? Egypt?). Nevertheless, she argues that the major increase in adnominal genitives in the Greek New Testament (a factor already long recognized by research in New Testament Greek)[30] restricts other kinds

[29] Edwin Mayser, *Grammatik der Griechischen Papyri aus der Ptolemäerzeit*, vol. 2 in 3 parts (Berlin: de Gruyter, 1926-1934); Blass and Debrunner, *Greek Grammar*; and A. N. Jannaris, *An Historical Greek Grammar Chiefly of the Attic Dialect* (London: Macmillan, 1897).

[30] Whether these studies would have been informative or not, see Stanley E. Porter, "The Adjectival Attributive Genitive in the New Testament: A Grammatical Study," *Trinity Journal* NS 4 (1983): 3-17; and Ghassan Elia Khalaf, *The Adnominal Genitive in the Pauline Corpus*, ed. J. William Johnston, Studies in Biblical Greek 19 (New York: Peter Lang, 2022), based on a dissertation from 2001.

of genitive, with prenominal genitives (as evidenced in pronouns) taking the previous role of datives as non-core arguments of verbs and hence leading to restriction and eventual disappearance of the dative case. This theory is supported by Wackernagel's law regarding clitics (54, although his work is not specifically cited).[31] Gianollo attributes this transformation—which she admits is presaged in earlier Greek—to a progressiveness in New Testament Greek. I am not sure she has considered all the pertinent evidence regarding the forms of genitive attribution in the Greek found in the New Testament, but her argument is provocative and interesting. (Notes 10 and 11 should either be combined or reconfigured; the final verb in the gloss of example 17 is 2sg.)

In "Future Periphrases in John Malalas" (71-96), Daniel Kölligan treats synthetic and other future forms for the analytic future, especially in this early Byzantine writer. The assumption is that there is such a thing as an analytic future (tense) in Greek and what it means. Köllingan discusses the present used for the future and a variety of so-called periphrases that are, to my mind, highly questionable and perhaps better explained otherwise.

Joanne Stolk, in "Combining Linguistics, Paleography and Papyrology: The Use of the Prepositions *eis*, *prós* and *epí* in Greek Papyri" (97-109), discusses these prepositions in relation to use of the dative case in the documentary papyri and uses her findings to influence how to decipher the papyri.

Liana Tronci returns to future forms in "Future Forms in Postclassical Greek: Some Remarks on the Septuagint and the New Testament" (111-43). Tronci attempts to address some of the major issues regarding the future form, including voice—a much bigger topic than one single chapter can handle. The chapter seems to me limited in many of its perspectives and so does not satisfactorily resolve the issues. Some of the problems include the fact that Tronci never asks the fundamental question of what is the future form, that is, what are its semantics and functions? Her history of discussion does not address those who take the future form as not being a tense-form.[32] Further, Tronci takes a very heavily lexical-additive view of morphology (this is seen in her interlinear glosses that follow her morphological analysis) and so limits voice choices primarily to two (active-middle), with the passive a restricted form based on the theta in

[31] See N. E. Collinge, *The Laws of Indo-European* (Amsterdam: Benjamins, 1985), 217-19, citing the original source: Jacob Wackernagel, "Über ein Gesetz der indo-germanischen Wortstellung," *Indogermanische Forschungen* 1 (1892): 333-436.

[32] She gives one confusing citation of Porter, *Verbal Aspect* (137), but does not respond to his and similar arguments regarding the non-aspectual and non-temporal semantic features of the future form. See Porter, *Verbal Aspect*, 403-39.

some contexts, clearly not aware of recent debate about this topic in other arenas (Thucydides 3.40 not being an exception).[33] She also pursues the notion of deponency (here unnecessarily called *media tantum* futures), again an area where recent investigation has called the category itself into question—although even the New Testament Greek grammarian A. T. Robertson did so a century ago.[34] As mentioned above, I also question whether some of the syntactic constructions posited as periphrases (such as with μέλλω and θέλω) should actually be called periphrases or other types of constructions such as catenatives (with periphrasis restricted to the auxiliary εἰμί), although Tronci rightly questions their function. Very few of the larger issues involved are discussed in this chapter, although her conclusion that challenges the widespread use of periphrasis is probably sound. However, I question her sociolinguistic analysis that opts for a so-called "hieratic register" (138-39), which sounds much too much like a form of Jewish Greek,[35] and her conclusion that Septuagint Greek is "an artificial language" (139). (Tronci refers to Blass and Debrunner 1898, when it is 1896; Emmanuel, Tov; and several times to the "definite article," which Greek does not have.)

In "Greek Infinitive-Retreat versus Grammaticalization: An Assessment" (145-62), Brian Joseph examines the example of infinitive clauses being replaced by *na*-clauses as an example not of grammaticalization but of degrammaticalization. Based upon Martin Haspelmath's definition of grammaticalization—with such a definition being rarely found in these volumes—Joseph points out that this development does not result in "stronger internal dependencies" (142) according to Haspelmath's

[33] See Porter and O'Donnell, "Greek Verbal Network"; and Mathewson, *Voice and Mood*, cited above. Tronci also does not discuss Rachel Aubrey, "Motivated Categories, Middle Voice, and Passive Morphology," in *Greek Verb Revisited*, 563-625.

[34] See esp. Jonathan Pennington, "Deponency in Koiné Greek: The Grammatical Question and the Lexicographical Dilemma," *Trinity Journal* NS 24 (2003): 55-76; Pennington, "Setting Aside 'Deponency' and Rediscovering the Middle Voice for New Testament Studies," in *The Linguist as Pedagogue: Trends in the Teaching and Linguistic Analysis of the Greek New Testament*, ed. Stanley E. Porter and Matthew Brook O'Donnell, New Testament Monographs 11 (Sheffield: Sheffield Phoenix, 2009), 183-205; and Pennington, "The Greek Middle Voice: An Important Rediscovery and Implications for Teaching and Exegesis," in *Linguistics and New Testament Greek: Key Issues in the Current Debate*, ed. David Alan Black and Benjamin L. Merkle (Gand Rapids: Baker, 2020), 83-102, with a history of discussion. See A. T. Robertson, *A Grammar of the Greek New Testament in the Light of Historical Research*, 4th ed. (Nashville: Broadman, 1934), 332, who says the term deponency "should not be used at all." Others even earlier had raised questions. See now also Mathewson, *Voice and Mood*, 70-71.

[35] The notion of Jewish Greek has been widely discussed and usually dismissed. For a summary of opinions and representative essays on forms of Semitic Greek, see Stanley E. Porter, ed., *The Language of the New Testament: Classic Essays*, Journal for the Study of the New Testament Supplement Series 60 (Sheffield: Sheffield Academic, 1991).

definition, but a looser one found in a dependent clause.[36] Joseph thereby disputes the unidirectionality of grammaticalization.

Nikolaos Lavidas and Dag Haug explore backward control in "Post-classical Greek and Treebanks for a Diachronic Analysis" (163-202). This is a difficultly organized article, but the part I am concerned with is the Greek of the New Testament. The authors contend that there is an increase in continuous constructions from Herodotus to the Greek of the New Testament but also an increase over the same span in discontinuous constructions with the subject of the participle being placed within the participle clause. Their definition of backward control includes a lower-level element controlling a higher-level element (170) and only the subject in Greek being interposed in the participle clause (172). The first seems to depend on transformational generative grammatical theory, while the second seems to me to require more proof. The problem for New Testament Greek seems to be that the subject in Greek is not a lower-level element, as it is in the main or matrix clause (e.g. Mark 2:5; 172). I also don't understand their analysis of Matt 1:24 (173), where their translation, "When Joseph woke up from sleep, he did [...]," seems to argue against their claim that the participle structure is not discontinuous (the Greek text they print does not include the article with Joseph, ὁ Ἰωσήφ).

The second section of the volume concerns sociolinguistic aspects and variation. In the first chapter, "The Perfect Paradigm in Theodosius' Κανόνες: Diathetically Indifferent and Diathetically Non-Indifferent Forms" (205-20), Marina Benedetti examines Theodosius's canons on inflection of nouns and verbs. She concentrates on voice or diathesis, where she notes that Theodosius argues for three voices, active, middle, and passive, against contemporary views that at least morphologically the perfect only has active and non-active (middle–passive) forms (what the author equates with *-a* and *-mai* endings). Theodosius also has a different understanding of the middle voice, although subject-affectedness, which Benedetti begrudgingly accepts, certainly calls for and has elicited further discussion, especially recently in terms of ergativity (mentioned above). She concludes that Theodosius evidences a more theoretical than philological approach to Greek, although it comes at the expense of chronological and variational factors.

Carla Bruno, in "Forms of the Directive Speech Act: Evidence from Early Ptolemaic Papyri" (221-44), examines various directive speech acts beyond use of the imperative in the papyri. In particular, she addresses

[36] Joseph cites Martin Haspelmath, "Directionality in Language Change, with Special Reference to Unidirectionality in Grammaticalizatioan," in *Up and Down the Cline*, ed. Olga Fischer et al. (Amsterdam: Benjamins, 2004), 17-44.

such utterances as performatives with δέομαι and ἀξιόω, καλῶς ποιέω, and χάρις-constructions. She also examines the relative relationships of the participants involved in the various constructions. Bruno does not address the question of semantic/pragmatic mismatch, where a theory of grammatical interpersonal metaphor might have been useful. In many ways, this is an extension of the work of Porter and O'Donnell in their examination of various linguistic features of a selected corpus of papyri.[37]

In the next chapter, Robert Crellin's "What's in a (Personal) Name? Morphology and Identity in Jewish Greek Literature in the Hellenistic and Roman Periods" (245-82), the author surveys a variety of Jewish Greek authors to describe how they adapt Jewish names to Greek literature. Rather than following literary levels, the adaptation of names seems, according to Crellin, to reflect whether the author writes from (or wishes to be seen writing from) a Greco-Roman or Jewish context and by doing this helps to create Jewish identity. Perhaps this works for Josephus and his wanting to be fully integrated within his Greco-Roman context (he is the most thorough adapter), but does this explain the Pentateuch where the names are not adapted, in light of traditions surrounding the origins of the Septuagint?

Sonja Dahlgren and Martti Leiwo, in "Confusion of Mood or Phoneme? The Impact of L1 Phonology on Verb Semantics" (283-301), argue against the usual view that the vowel interchange of the documentary papyri demonstrates poor command of Greek. They cite similar vowel confusion in indigenous Egyptian texts of the time. They therefore conclude that rather than inferior knowledge of Greek, there was a lack of differentiation and even relative significance of vowels in the Egyptian that led to nonstandard usage in Greek. This is an interesting proposal regarding language contact in Egypt that also has strong implications for how various phonetic spellings are viewed in Koine Greek.

In the final chapter, García Ramón José Luis writes on "Change in Grammatical and Lexical Structures in Postclassical Greek: Local Dialects and Supradialectal Tendencies" (303-36), a fitting chapter in the section on sociolinguistics and variation. Luis shows the relevance of written evidence for there being various regional dialects and "supradialectal languages" (304), which include various forms of Koine Greek (including that based on Attic-Ionic) in the third to first centuries BC. The patterns vary according to region, but many of them reflect the supradialectal structures and create hyperdialectal forms (333).

Since each chapter ends with its own bibliography, there is no conclud-

[37] Stanley E. Porter and Matthew Brook O'Donnell, "Building and Examining Linguistic Phenomena in a Corpus of Representative Papyri," in *The Language of the Papyri*, ed. T. V. Evans and D. D. Obbink (Oxford: Oxford University Press, 2010), 287-310.

ing bibliography. The volume concludes with a single topical index that includes no references to ancient sources or modern authors, a serious shortcoming in a book full of references to primary and secondary literature.

As in any collection of individual contributions, some are stronger than others. I note that many of the authors, despite whatever they may claim about postclassical Greek, tend to use the Greek New Testament as a primary corpus for study of Greek of this period. However, despite some instances throughout, many of the essays would benefit from knowledge of and reference to studies done by New Testament Greek scholars who have already touched upon many of the topics discussed in this volume. I am not sure why these studies have not been used, since at least some of the authors are aware of at least a few biblical scholars who have written on matters of Greek language and linguistics. This volume is also diachronic in orientation. Besides the fact that some of the essays are poorly organized, the argument often loses sight of bigger and, arguably, more important synchronic questions regarding language. This collection also limits the linguistic models that are used mostly to historical linguistics, with some traces of some other frameworks. Some of the most interesting current research in New Testament Greek studies is being done in functional linguistics, an area that is not well-represented in this volume.

A Major Festschrift

The third and final volume reviewed here is on *Synchrony and Diachrony of Ancient Greek.*[38] This Festschrift published in honor of Emilio Crespo, one of the leading Spanish classical scholars over the last nearly fifty years, opens with a recounting by the lead editor, Georgios Giannakis, of Crespo's career and contributions to Greek studies. These include the areas of Homer and epic poetry, syntax, sociolinguistics and language policies, Greek dialectology, the *Encyclopedia of Ancient Greek Language and Linguistics*, as well as his other scholarly activities, followed by a list of his publications, beginning in 1977 to 2019. This volume is a fitting tribute to one who has done so much for Greek language studies.

The volume is divided into five parts: epigraphy and dialectology; lexicon, onomastics, morphology, and morphophonology; syntax and clause structure; pragmatics and discourse; and the linguistics and philology interstices. I will only deal with a small number of the 36 chapters that

[38] Georgios K. Giannakis, Luz Conti, Jesús de la Villa, and Raquel Fornieles, eds., *Synchrony and Diachrony of Ancient Greek: Language, Linguistics and Philology. Essays in Honor of Emilio Crespo*, Trends in Classics—Supplementary Volumes 112 (Berlin: de Gruyter, 2021).

have some direct or mostly indirect relevance for New Testament Greek studies.

Panagiotis Filos writes on "Reflexes of Koineization in Ancient Epirote Feminine Names" (11-31). This chapter is not directly concerned with the New Testament, but with the koineization process in one admittedly distant region of ancient Greece. The significance is seeing how, at least in this region, a supra-dialectal variety of Koine emerged from the convergence of local and other dialects (e.g. Attic-Ionic Koine), in particular personal names. This may well offer insights for those curious about the origins of the Greek of the New Testament.

In a single-page contribution, Michael Meier-Brügger writes on "Μνημονεύω" (183). This was no doubt written more as a tribute than as a substantive contribution. Nevertheless, Meier-Brügger does raise the interesting question of how memory—as indicated by the meaning of this lexeme—functioned in an oral culture that relied upon those with good memories, with the implication that this verb may not have been understood as we might tend to think.

In "Main Phonetic Changes in Ancient Greek Obscuring the PIE Ablaut" (193-211), Georgios Papanastassiou traces the development of ablaut and inflection in PIE until ablaut is functionally eliminated. Since phonetic changes are still evident in New Testament Greek, this chapter provides a helpful overview of them for those wishing to know more.

Vit Bubenik treats absolute constructions in "Reconstructing (Late) Proto-Indo-European Syntax: Absolute Constructions" (215-26). He provides a useful explanation of the origin of absolute constructions in Greek. However, his definition of absolute constructions is stricter than that used by many, since he does not include coreferentiality within the matrix clause of an element of the possible absolute construction. This definition, if used, would have interpretive implications for the Greek of the New Testament, where some research has doubted the absoluteness of absolute constructions.[39]

In "Γίγνομαι as the Lexical Passive of the Support Verb ποιέω in Ancient Greek" (227-40), María Dolores Jiménez López examines examples of event nouns with supporting verbs that she analyzes as a single verbal unit. Based on the lack of clear evidence of ποιέω in the passive in such constructions, the author posits γίγνομαι as the lexical passive. She cites two possible examples in the New Testament (Acts 20:3 and Matt 24:20)

[39] See Lois K. Fuller Dow, "The 'Genitive Absolute' in New Testament/Hellenistic Greek: A Proposal for Clearer Understanding," *Journal of Greco-Roman Christianity and Judaism* 3 (2006): 142-67.

based upon the translation in the Vulgate. Jiménez López attempts to show how use of γίγνομαι has passive syntactical consequences, but then one must wonder whether this is a lexical passive. The question for the New Testament examples is whether this is a lexical passive or simply a matter of translation.

Nikos Liosis, in "On Negation, Jespersen's Cycle, and Negative Concord in Post-Classical Greek" (253-64), takes a syntactical view of negation at the clause level. The article first tests and affirms in modified form Otto Jespersen's negation cycle, but nowhere actually cites Jespersen.[40] Liosis then examines two competing tendencies in Greek: negative concord shifts from non-strict negative concord (negative words only post the negator itself) to strict negative concord (negative words either before or after). Liosis claims that this takes place in the second century AD, based in part upon a citation from the Septuagint, Hos 2:12 (261). Since Hosea was probably translated in the first or second centuries BC, one must wonder how this would shift Liosis's perspective. Liosis also does not consider paradigmatic negation features, such that negation of the word or group is different than of the clause, so that negated groups within the clause do not negate the clause.[41]

In "A Construction Grammar Approach to Ancient Greek Argument Structure Constructions" (265-77), Silvia Luraghi examines the second arguments of two-place verbs and argues that the use of accusative, dative, and genitive structures is the result of "constructional polysemy" with some influence of "constructional homonymy" (265) based upon syncretism of the earlier eight-case system and various homonymous constructions realized by the same forms.

Jesús de la Villa, in "Relative Time and Narrative in Herodotus and Thucydides" (291-305), discusses how narratives temporally order events. The ordering elements noted include: adverbs/adverbial phrases, prepositional phrases, and temporal subordinate clauses (although he does not give examples of the last to clarify what he means). De la Villa also mentions "aspectual themes" (292) and their role in such temporal reconstruction, although he is unclear what is meant by "aspectual themes" (apparently tense-forms) and how they function. In a footnote, the author mentions that the "relationship between verb tenses and narrative structure has also been studied" (292 note 2) by some listed authors, but he does not say what the outcome of this study has indicated. Nevertheless, de la Villa

[40] See Otto Jespersen, "Negation in English and Other Languages" (1917), repr. in *Selected Writings of Otto Jespersen* (London: Routledge, 2010), 3-151. This work on negation first appeared as a separate book.

[41] See Porter and Land, "Modeling Negation in Ancient Greek."

is concerned with something else, what he calls “the iconic presentation of events” (292), in other words the presentation of events as they occur, contending that such has never been systematically studied before. Based on samples from Herodotus (6.87-103) and Thucydides (6.42-53), he concludes that linear order is maintained in 88.4% and 94.3% respectively. He notes that when subordinate clauses refer to previous action they tend to be placed before the main clause and subsequent action after (simultaneous events may be either). The few exceptions in main clauses are accounted for by means of explanatory clausal conjunction (e.g. γάρ), with subordinate clauses based upon what the author refers to as “aspectual values” (300) (the aorist is used of “concluded” events related out of order, 300). De la Villa is not clear on his understanding of tense and aspect.[42] The attempt to link participle clauses to tense-forms is less successful. The example in Thucydides 6.50 with an aorist participle clause following the main verb arguably indicates concurrent or possibly logically subsequent rather than preceding action as de la Villa claims (“immediately, having filled sixty ships from the whole and having taken daily provisions, the generals set sail toward Naxos, leaving behind the other troops in Rhegium,” my translation, rather than de la Villa’s). The infinitive functions as an extension of its modal-like main verb (probably not based upon the tense-form as de la Villa seems to say). De la Villa seems to have confused aspect and tense in his analysis, thus problematizing his findings (after all, his analysis is roughly 90%, not 100%, and admittedly subject to further analysis). It is unclear how de la Villa’s proposal would work in expository rather than narrative texts. More likely is that participle clauses are a way of organizing material by placement in relation to the main (matrix) verb, not based upon tense-form, even if there are some general patterns.[43]

In the only essay exclusively focused upon the New Testament, Rafael Martínez writes on “Discourse Markers, Interpretation, and Translation in the *Lord’s Prayer*” (357-66). He identifies the wording ὡς καί in the third and fifth petitions of the prayer as having been largely misunderstood. In the third petition, Martinez does not take the phrase as

[42] There are a range of views on tense and aspect in Greek, including New Testament Greek, where New Testament scholars have made a major contribution. Some of the most important works are Porter, *Verbal Aspect*, esp. 75-109; Buist Fanning, *Verbal Aspect in New Testament Greek*, Oxford Theological Monographs (Oxford: Clarendon, 1990); and Constantine R. Campbell, *Verbal Aspect, the Indicative Mood, and Narrative: Soundings in the Greek of the New Testament*, Studies in Biblical Greek 13 (New York: Peter Lang, 2007). A comparison of these authors is found in Douglas S. Huffman, *Verbal Aspect Theory and the Prohibitions in the Greek New Testament*, Studies in Biblical Greek 16 (New York: Peter Lang, 2014), 511-15.

[43] See Porter, *Verbal Aspect*, 377-88.

indicating equal status on earth and heaven, but as additive with the presupposition (God's will in heaven) and the added focus (God's will on earth). In the fifth petition, where the two words appear together, he sees the relationship as, somewhat like γάρ in Luke 11:4, one of justification, that is, with the presupposition connected to the assertion by ὡς. This construction can take a variety of forms in the New Testament (e.g. Matt 5:48; John 13:34; Luke 11:1; and Matt 18:33). In that sense, the use of καί is arguably redundant, at least in translation, since it has a discourse rather than an equative or additive function.

In the final essay I will discuss, Georgios Giannakis treats "The Concept of 'Emphasis' in Ancient Greek and Indo-European" (413-37). Giannakis's discussion of emphasis as part of information structure begins not with the Prague School of linguistics (even though later he uses the term foreground), as one might expect, but with a footnoteless quotation from Harm Pinkster and two English dictionary definitions. No doubt defining emphasis is problematic, as is the varied terminology, but I think we can do better than this. Giannakis then offers a compendium of means of emphasis in ancient Greek, including lexical (emphatic words, triads, totality, scalarity, particles, deictics), morphological (augmentation, diminutives, suffixes, intensives, plurality), phonetic (repetition, alliteration, etc.), and syntax/stylistic features (deviation from normal word order, figures of speech, repetition, elatives, anacolutha, ellipsis). This is an attempt at a reasonably comprehensive list within a short space, but it lacks several very important elements, such as emphatic values of verbal aspect, modality, and causality, among several others. More problematic, however, is the failure to offer a definition that provides for assessment and evaluation of emphasis and its relative contextual values. For example, does phonetic emphasis function to the same degree and in the same way as morphological or syntactic? Most works in ancient Greek will contain a variety of these identified emphatic features. How do we assess which ones are important and in which ways in which contexts? Some scale of emphasis is needed, along with an indication of the scope of the emphasis. For example, does a given emphatic element only emphasize its local construction or does it have larger clausal or discourse implications? What are these implications, other than simply drawing attention to themselves? There is much more to be done on such issues.[44]

This third volume concludes with a list of contributors and a single general index that includes neither ancient sources nor modern authors.

[44] See, for example, Porter and O'Donnell, *Discourse Analysis*, esp. 128-89, for a treatment of what Giannakis would call "emphasis," labeled as linguistic highlighting (and separate from information structure, 96-127). This chapter on linguistic highlighting attempts to provide guidelines for determining and evaluating what Giannakis calls emphasis.

My comments on this volume need not add much to what I have said above. Most of the essays are not directly addressed to the Greek of the New Testament, but several of them have implications for how New Testament Greek might be studied. However, I also note that there are some places where greater knowledge of recent developments in New Testament Greek study might have enhanced the contributions of individual essays.

Conclusion

In light of the review of these three volumes, I conclude with several overall comments. I first offer two positive comments before offering some final evaluations. The first positive comment is that there is a lot of excellent work represented in these volumes. That is not to be denied. There is much to be learned from each of them. It is rewarding to see the results of continued study of the Greek language. I am very thankful for the opportunity to have worked through these varied chapters, even if I approach Greek differently and have some serious questions about some of the findings. I still learned much. The second positive comment is that I am thankful that there are still publishers—and in this case de Gruyter in particular—interested in producing good books that contribute to serious scholarship, especially such collections of essays that are now often shunned by other publishers. All three volumes are well-produced as physical books and a pleasure to hold and read.

I have offered points of criticism about the individual essays and volumes above, so I need not reproduce these here. I do wish, however, to make some closing statements. The first is that there needs to be greater editorial control exercised over the production of such volumes. Several of the volumes, the first two in particular from what I noticed, had a larger number of typographical errors and other stylistic inconsistencies than I would have expected in such volumes. There were an especially large number of errors in bibliographical information. I also notice that indexes are a disappearing entity, at least in such volumes. Only one of the volumes (on prepositions) has an ancient source index, when the primary purpose of each volume is to discuss ancient sources! I found that frustrating and altogether unhelpful. None of the volumes has a dedicated modern authors index either (one volume, the one on prepositions, includeds modern authors in the topic index). In collections of essays, such as these, access not just to ancient source references but to the authors who talk about them is, to my mind, essential. Each of the essays had a topical index, which is helpful, to be sure, but probably the least valuable in a series of individual essays that are clearly marked for their content.

A second criticism is that many of the essays seem to have been written in isolation or without regard to their audience or possible audiences. This is not as true of the first volume, which is dedicated to cognitive linguistics and the New Testament, although even so not everyone seems to have had a similar understanding of cognitive linguistics or their task in relationship to it. Regarding the other two volumes, I believe that it is incumbent upon authors to make clear what linguistic approach they are using, especially in a diverse collection of essays. Even the second volume, which was diachronically oriented, evidenced a variety of linguistic methods within it that could have used elaboration. One cannot assume that such a linguistic approach is self-evident, and one certainly cannot assume that others will necessarily agree with or even understand such a linguistic approach (especially for non-linguistically oriented readers who might be interested more in matters of Greek language than in linguistics). I think that many of the essays would have been better served by making clear at the outset their linguistic orientation, perhaps with some words of helpful clarification to ensure that readers have as much access to the essay as possible. This can only help the essay to have greater impact.

A third criticism is that I found it unfortunate that, apart from a select few historical or well-known recent works, New Testament Greek linguistic scholarship was often overlooked in the second and third volumes, even though essays within them, especially the second volume, often discussed the Greek New Testament. In fact, in that volume, the Greek of the New Testament as a representative Koine corpus was selected to best exemplify the Greek of the time. New Testament Greek linguistic study has been a highly productive area of research over the last thirty to forty years, and many of the studies, especially in the second and third volumes, could have benefited at least from knowledge of this work, even if they disagree with it.

Finally, considering the comments above, I hope that we can perhaps get a reprieve from the term "postclassical Greek," especially when something far more specific is often meant by the term than is at first indicated. For most of the essays that use the term, such as in the first volume, postclassical essentially means the Greek of the New Testament; for the second volume, it sometimes includes the New Testament, but rarely goes much further than the early medieval or Byzantine period; and even for the third volume, it only occasionally means modern Greek (although excluded from the definition in the second volume introduction). If these three volumes teach us anything, it is that Greek from all periods and places, including that of the few centuries on either side of the turn of the millennia, and especially so-called Koine Greek, offers plenty of excellent linguistic data for discussion, and to prejudice or even disparage it by referring to it as "postclassical" does it an injustice. Based upon the diachronic trajectories recounted and the many synchronic discussions contained within these volumes, privileging one regional dialect of Greek (classical) as the primary point of comparison, especially considering the Greek language's later history as a world language, does a disservice to the study of ancient Greek in all its varieties and registers.

STANLEY E. PORTER
McMaster Divinity College
1280 Main St. W.
Hamilton, ON L8S 4K1
CANADA
porters@mcmaster.ca

History of the Text and Johannine Exegesis: Jn 13.14 as Test Case

DAVID PASTORELLI

The idea of a single-form text is misleading. For this reason, we advocate a decompartmentalisation of low and high criticism. The aim of this paper is to provide some elements for reflection based on an example from the account of the washing of the feet: Jn 13.14 is treated as a test case. Our thesis is that these elements have an impact on exegesis and that the commentator benefits from paying attention to them. It requires bringing together three fields of research: textual criticism with its methodology; exegesis; and the history of reception.

The 'Western' variants deserve attention from the point of view of the history of the text, because they are repeatedly the oldest and the most widespread. Here the history of reception requires giving due consideration to versions and patristic quotations, particularly in the Syriac and Latin traditions, and the testimony of the *Diatessaron* (c. 170) in favour of the 'Western' text is decisive. This is why the exegete should be encouraged to comment not only on the Alexandrian text, followed by the current editions, but also to take into account this other form of the text. Here, there are two possibilities. If the 'Western' reading is considered secondary, because it appears very early in the second century, the exegete gains by taking it into account with regard to the history of the reception of the text. If the 'Western' reading is considered original with regard to the establishment of the text, the exegete must comment on it.

Keywords: Jn 13.14, Footwashing, History of the Text, Johannine Exegesis, Textual Criticism, History of Reception, 'Western' Text, Alexandrian Text, Old Latin and Old Syriac Versions, Tatian's *Diatessaron.*

In the eighteenth century, low criticism and high criticism were carried out by the same scholars. It was not until the twentieth century that the two types of analysis were definitively separated, both chronologically and quantitatively. Chronologically, because the textual critic is expected to first establish and edit the text that the exegete will then adopt for his or her interpretation, after checking the critical apparatus. Quantitatively, because the textual critic must take into account a wide range of sources: Greek manuscripts (papyri, uncials, minuscules, lectionaries), early versions (Latin, Syriac, Coptic, Armenian, Georgian, Ethiopian, etc.) and patristic quotations. The exegete, for their part, is confronted with multiple, complementary or competing interpretative approaches, and consequently needs a single Greek text for their analyses.

With the advent of printing, textual criticism sought first of all to fix and edit the New Testament text once and for all. However, the idea of a single-form text is misleading. Once the errors of copying and spontaneous corrections have been eliminated, a significant number of variants remain, forming part of the history of the text. A single text-form was not imposed in Antiquity, the Middle Ages or the Renaissance. For this reason, we advocate a decompartmentalisation of low and high criticism, and reconstructing the history of the text should, in our view, be the primary task of New Testament textual criticism rather than reconstructing even an 'initial' text. The aim of this paper is to provide some elements for reflection based on an example from the Johannine farewell discourses (John 13–17). Our thesis is that these elements have an impact on exegesis and that the commentator benefits from paying attention to them. It requires bringing together three fields of research: textual criticism with its methodology; exegesis; and the history of reception. We will proceed in three stages.

(1) Textual criticism of the New Testament would be much simpler if the 'Western' text, represented above all by Codex Bezae (D.05), did not exist. This is why consensus is so rare. It is therefore necessary to give a brief history of the 'Western' text, which has been considered corrupt since Westcott and Hort (§1.1); Westcott's about-turn, about which very little is known in research (§1.2); and the criterion of geographical diffusion behind this about-turn (§1.3).

(2) How is the history of the Johannine text to be written? To provide a framework for such a history, we summarise the conclusions of our research on the classification of the main Greek manuscripts of five chapters, John 13–17 (§2.1). We then present our own method of treating a variation-unit (§2.2). It should be said at the outset that, far from seeking to innovate, we are using the methodological criteria of classical philology, developed and tested since the eighteenth century.

(3) Finally, an example is taken from the account of the washing of the feet: Jn 13.14 is treated in detail as a test case (§3–4) and the exegetical implications are outlined in a conclusion (§5).

The history of reception is a guiding principle of this article. Indeed, we pay particular attention to versions and patristic quotations, because there we gather the most reliable historical clues for locating a variant in time and space. Insofar as we are concentrating on the 'Western' or Syro-Latin readings, readers will not be surprised by the importance given to the Old Latin and Old Syriac versions, as well as to Latin authors (Ambrose and Augustine, for example) and Syriac authors (Aphrahat, *Liber Graduum*, Ps-Ephrem). Moreover, because of its antiquity (around 170), Tatian's *Diatessaron* occupies a significant place in the discussion.

The history of the text thus invites the exegete to comment not only on the Alexandrian text, as adopted by the current editions, but also to take account of another state of the text, that read in Christian communities in the first half of the second century.

1. The 'Western' text in the textual criticism of the New Testament

1.1. The 'Western' text since B.F. Westcott and F.J.A. Hort: a 'corrupt' text

Because the readings of Codex Bezae are early and widespread, they are at the origin of the hypothesis of a free text in the second century. Where does this theory come from?[1] Brooke F. Westcott and Fenton J.A. Hort were the first to link the age and diffusion of the 'Western' readings with their corruption[2]. They describe them as including paraphrase, the addition of traditions or apocryphal sources and above all, harmonisations[3]; in short, they characterise the text as one that is certainly early and widespread, but strongly corrupted and unscrupulous with regard to the apostolic writings:

> In surveying a long succession of Western readings by the side of others, we seem to be in the presence of a vigorous and popular ecclesiastical life, little scrupulous as to the letter of venerated writings [...] During that part of the Ante-Nicene period of which we have any direct knowledge 'Western' texts were at least dominant in most churches of both East and West, and [...] whatever may be the merits of individual Western readings, the Western texts generally are due to a corruption of the apostolic texts[4].

This textual corruption would not have affected the text preserved in Alexandria, the 'neutral' text as Westcott and Hort then called it. Consequently, their edition of the Greek text of the New Testament follows codex Vaticanus (B.03), as do the successive editions of Nestle-Aland and the *Editio critica maior*.

Westcott and Hort's assessment of the 'Western' text had a profound influence on twentieth-century textual critics. An example is Ernest C.

[1] L.D. Bell, *The Early Textual Transmission of John. Stability and Fluidity in Its Second and Third Century Greek Manuscripts* (NTTSD 54; Leiden/Boston: Brill, 2018) 8–12, provides a history of the textual instability thesis.

[2] B.F. Westcott and F.J.A. Hort, *The New Testament in the Original Greek. Introduction. Appendix* (Cambridge/London: Macmillan, 1896²) 148–9. 'On all accounts the Western text claims our attention first. The earliest readings which can be fixed chronologically belong to it. As far as we can judge from extant evidence, it was the most widely spread text of Ante-Nicene times' (120).

[3] Westcott and Hort, *New Testament*, 122–4.

[4] Westcott and Hort, *New Testament*, 126–7.

Colwell, for whom 'the general nature of the text in the earliest period (to A.D. 300) has long been recognized as "wild," "uncontrolled," "unedited"'[5]. Bart D. Ehrman takes textual fluidity for granted: 'The fluidity of the textual tradition in the early period of transmission [...] has long been recognized within the field'[6]. He adds: 'It should be emphasized, however, that the instability of the text in the early centuries is equaled by the instability of the scribes'[7]. Similarly, George D. Kilpatrick argues that the period of textual fluidity predates 200: 'Most deliberate changes, if not all, were made by A.D. 200'[8]. Furthermore, David C. Parker considers the 'Western' text to be a free text existing before 150. Among the extant witnesses, the first known attempt at a controlled text is the Alexandrian text of papyrus P^{75} in the last decade of the second century. Before that, Parker believes that the text was free. The best witness to this free text is Codex Bezae, which contains on each page singular readings, numerous harmonisations and rewritings of the text in a informal style. Parker thus places the 'Western' text at the centre of the discussion about the earliest form of the NT. Addition to Codex Bezae, the 'Western' text includes the old Syriac and Latin versions; it emerges in the course of the second century, at a time when the Alexandrian and Byzantine types are not attested. Parker concludes:

> Although it has sometimes been claimed that the free-text form of Codex Bezae is of a late date – the work of the manuscript's scribe, or of "an outstanding early theologian of the third/fourth century" – there is substantial evidence that it is as old as the second century. The evidence most perplexing to those who believe that the Alexandrian text is the best, and to those who continue to favour the Byzantine form, is that the second-century materials available to us show no knowledge of either. It is with such texts as Codex Bezae, the Old Syriac and some Old Latin witnesses – all those considered most aberrant by later standards – that second-century witnesses concur most regularly. The reconstruction which emerges from current study is that the text represented by Codex Bezae was formed in Rome in about the middle of the second century[9].

[5] E.C. Colwell, 'Hort Redivivus: A Plea and a Program', *Studies in Methodology in Textual Criticism of the New Testament* (NTTS 9; Leiden: Brill, 1969) 166 n. 3.

[6] B.D. Ehrman, *The Orthodox Corruption of Scripture. The Effect of Early Christological Controversees on the Text of the New Testament* (Oxford/New York: Oxford University Press, 1993) 42 n. 92.

[7] Ehrman, *Orthodox Corruption*, 277.

[8] G.D. Kilpatrick, 'Atticism and the Text of the Greek New Testament', *The Principles and Practice of New Testament Textual Criticism. Collected Essays of G.D. Kilpatrick* (ed. J.K. Elliott; BETL 96; Louvain: Presses Universitaires de Louvain, 1990) 19.

[9] D.C. Parker, *The Living Text of the Gospels* (Cambridge: Cambridge University Press, 1997) 202.

For their part, Kurt and Barbara Aland defend the thesis of a 'free' text in the second century, while asserting the parallel presence of a 'normal' text, which deviates from its model only occasionally, and above all that of a 'strict' text, like that of P[75]. They are simply repeating the thesis of Westcott and Hort: the existence of a pure text, the Alexandrian type, not contaminated by the 'Western' text which, in constrast, is corrupted and 'free'[10]. Papyri witnesses occupy a privileged position in the Aland's historical reconstruction. The age of the manuscripts takes primacy over the age of the text. On the other hand, the Alands reject the existence of text-types in the second/third centuries on the basis of a historical argument that is surprising, to say the least. They postulate a correlation between the production of a text-type and the need for institutional organisation. According to them, this kind of ecclesial organisation did not exist before the fourth century, and neither did the text-types: 'The text of the early period prior to the third/fourth century was, then, in effect, a text not yet channeled into types, because until the beginning of the fourth century the churches still lacked the institutional organization required to produce one'[11]. The Alands' rejection of any text-type before the fourth century allows them to avoid any discussion of an Alexandrian recension at the end of the second century. For them, the 'strict' text goes back to the 'original' text and cannot be the result of a recension. Their main argument lies in the discovery in 1961 of papyrus P[75], copied around 200 AD and whose text is very close to Codex Vaticanus (B.03). The hypothesis of an Alexandrian recension in the fourth century is no longer valid. But the continuity between the Alexandrian text of the late second century (P[75]) and that of the fourth century (B.03) does not resolve the question of a recension. It merely shifts the question one hundred and fifty years earlier. As far as the 'emergence' of the presumed Alexandrian recension is concerned, Jean Duplacy refuses to trace it back to the 'original' text: 'From the point of view of the history of the text, there is currently no valid reason to situate this "emergence" with certainty very early in the second century and, from this point of view, the "Western text" retains the advantage over "P[75]–B"'[12].

[10] K. Aland and B. Aland, *The Text of the New Testament. An Introduction to the Critical Editions and to the Theory and Practice of Modern Textual Criticism* (Grand Rapids: W.B. Eerdmans, 1989[2]) 59.

[11] Aland & Aland, *Text*, 64.

[12] J. Duplacy, 'P[75] (*Pap. Bodmer XIV–XV*) et les formes les plus anciennes du texte de *Luc*', *Études de critique textuelle du Nouveau Testament* (BETL 78; Leuven: Leuven University Press, 1987 (1973)) 168: 'Du point de vue de l'histoire du texte, il n'y a actuellement aucune raison valable de situer avec assurance cette "apparition" très haut dans le IIe siècle et, de ce point de vue, le "texte occidental" garde l'avantage sur "P[75] – B"'.

1.2. Westcott's about-face

William L. Petersen takes a critical view of the Alexandrian text-type. Contrary to the majority opinion, he does not identify it with the 'original text', but with the recension known in Egypt around 180. What is his position on the other most debated text-type, the 'Western' text? In 2012, Jan Krans and Joseph Verheyden brought together thirty-two major studies by Petersen, who died prematurely in 2006 at the age of 56. The answer can be found in the last study, which is unpublished and is based on a paper given at the *Annual Meeting of the Society of Biblical Literature* in San Francisco in November 1992: 'The Syro-Latin Text of the Gospels, or How the "Western Text" Became a Phantom'[13].

The study begins with the observation that the two main handbooks of textual criticism of the New Testament, those of Bruce M. Metzger and of Kurt and Barbara Aland, accord little importance to the 'Western' text. Petersen regrets that the term 'Western' has not been replaced by 'Syro-Latin'. He then points out – and this is the core of his study – that these handbooks have overlooked the high esteem in which the 'Western' text was previously held, including in the eyes of Westcott:

> In view of the inadequacy of Semler's (and later, Griesbach's) designation, it is odd that the term "Syro-Latin" has not been adopted. Even more puzzling, however, is the failure of the handbooks to disclose the high opinion distinguished textual critics – *including Sr. Westcott himself* – had of the Western Text[14].

Petersen then expresses his admiration for Frederic Henry Chase's *The Syro-Latin Text of the Gospels*, which he considered to be 'one of the most important works in the history of New Testament textual criticism'[15]. Chase labels the text-type 'Syro-Latin' and shows that many of its readings are found not only in Codex Bezae (D.05) and in the Old Latin and Old Syriac, but also in Irenaeus, Marcion and Justin. He therefore concludes that the 'Western' text is very old, dating from the first half of the second century:

> The Syro-Latin text was no doubt a gradual growth. The tendencies of which it is the result were active in the first half of the second century. Syro-Latin readings, which occur in Codex Bezae, are found, as has just been

[13] W.L. Petersen, 'The Syro-Latin Text of the Gospels, or How the "Western Text" Became a Phantom', *Patristic and Text-Critical Studies. The Collected Essays of William L. Petersen* (ed. J. Krans and J. Verheyden; NTTSD 40; Leiden/Boston: Brill, 2012) 581–9.

[14] Petersen, 'Syro-Latin Text', 584.

[15] Petersen, 'Syro-Latin Text'.

> noticed, in Irenaeus, Marcion, and Justin [...] The coincidences between the Bezan text and the Diatessaron forbid our assigning the former to an earlier date than 170 A.D.[16]

Petersen observes that Chase's dating is interesting because it makes the Syro-Latin text the oldest form of text that can be reconstructed. But current handbooks do not mention Chase and few textualists today know his name, as Petersen humorously points out[17]. Ignorance of his work might explain why the 'Western' text has always been held in such low esteem, but Petersen's investigation demonstrates otherwise. In the second edition of the second volume of *The New Testament in the Original Greek* (1896), Westcott added six pages of additional notes, even though Hort had died in the meantime. We can read:

> The Essays of Dr Chase on *The Syriac Element in Codex Bezæ*, Cambridge, 1893, and *The Syro-Latin Text of the Gospels*, Cambridge, 1895, are a most important contribution to the solution of a fundamental problem in the history of the text of the New Testament. The discovery of the Sinaitic MS of the Old Syriac raises the question whether the combination of the oldest types of the Syriac and Latin texts can outweigh the combination of the primary Greek texts. A careful examination of the passages in which syr.*sin* and *k* are arrayed against ℵB would point to the conclusion[18].

Petersen notes that the concession made by Westcott is astonishing, since it is his publication cited here that defends the idea, accepted and applied by the main current editions, that B.03 contains the primitive form of the text[19]. Yet in 1896, Westcott himself came out in favour of the Old Syriac-Old Latin agreements, in preference to the ℵ.01-B.03 agreements. Let us add to the data collected by Petersen that the discovery of Old Sinaitic Syriac (sy^{s}) was the main reason for the second edition and for Westcott's change of position. The 1896 preface is explicit in this respect:

> The present volume is a reprint of the first Edition (1881), with the correction of a few errata and the addition of some supplementary Notes

[16] F.H. Chase, *The Syro-Latin Text of the Gospels* (London: Macmillan, 1895) 132.

[17] Petersen, 'Syro-Latin Text', 585: 'When I cited his work in the text critical seminar of the SNTS at its Milan meeting in 1990, one of the editors of the UBS edition was not familiar with his work: What had he written? What was that name again?'

[18] Westcott and Hort, *New Testament*, 328.

[19] Westcott and Hort, *New Testament*, 205–51: 'It will be evident from the foregoing pages that B must be regarded as having preserved not only a very ancient text, but a very pure line of very ancient text, and that with comparatively small depravation either by scattered ancient corruptions otherwise attested or by individualisms of the scribe himself'.

> required by the discovery of fresh documents. Of these documents the most important is the Sinaitic palimpsest of the Old Syriac Version of the Gospels (Syr.*sin*); and I desire to offer my hearty thanks to Mr F. C. Burkitt, M.A., of Trinity College, Cambridge, for inserting the evidence of this MS in the "Notes on Select Readings," and for contributing other independent notes of considerable interest which deal mainly with questions suggested by Syriac authorities[20].

In other words, the additional notes and the preface to the second edition are by the hand of Westcott and not Burkitt. Burkitt is only responsible for adding the new data in the appendix at the end of the volume, which contains notes on a selection of variants.

Petersen's conclusion on the 'Western' text is unequivocal:

> The Syro-Latin text of the New Testament not only "deserves a hearing," but some (not all) of its readings deserve to be taken as – and I quote Alexander Souter – "the correct text." Or, as Burkitt put it in 1899: "the question at issue is what right we have to reject the oldest Syriac and the oldest Latin reading when they agree" [...] The question – the most burning question in New Testament textual Criticism – was posed a century ago. We know the consequences of answering it. And because we don't really *want* to recover the earliest form of the text, we not only refuse to answer it, we do even worse: we have refused to even record asking of the question in our histories of the discipline[21].

1.3. The criterion of geographical diffusion

Westcott's change of position in favour of the Syro-Latin agreements stems from a fundamental criterion in biblical and classical philology: the criterion of geographical diffusion. In view of the methodological importance of this criterion for New Testament textual criticism, a few historical milestones for its development are useful. The criterion first appeared in 1713 with Richard Bentley (1662–1742). He drew attention to the value of readings attested independently by manuscripts from Egypt, Asia and the Western churches. He deserves to be quoted:

> 'Tis a good providence and a great blessing, that so many manuscripts of the New Testament are still amongst us; some procured from Egypt, others from Asia, others found in the Western churches. For the very distances of places as well as numbers of the books demonstrate, that there could be no

[20] Westcott and Hort, *New Testament*, V.

[21] Petersen, 'Syro-Latin Text', 588–9.

> collusion, no altering nor interpolating one copy by another, nor all by any of them[22].

The essence of the criterion's underlying principle is expressed by Bentley's statement: the distance between geographical areas is a guarantee against contamination and the number of manuscripts is a guarantee against accidental agreement. For his part, Johann Albrecht Bengel (1687–1752) developed the theory of the principle. He was the first to recognise several textual groups in the manuscript tradition: the 'Asiatic' family (Constantinople), which includes the largest number of witnesses, and the 'African' family, which is subdivided into the 'Alexandrian tribe' and the 'Latin tribe', with a smaller number of witnesses and an older text[23]. Bengel discerned in this classification a reliable criterion for choosing variants, thereby abandoning 'the old and deceitful criterion of the majority of manuscripts', as Sebastiano Timpanaro pointed out:

> The important thing is not that a reading be attested by the majority of the manuscripts but by the majority of the families; only within each family does the majority of the manuscripts have a value for reconstructing its ancestor's reading [...] Further on Bengel repeats even more explicitly that it is the consensus of manuscripts *belonging to different families* that guarantees the antiquity of a reading[24].

Johann Salomo Semler (1725–91) adopted Bengel's groups, but with a new terminology: the Alexandrian recension, the Western recension and the Eastern recension (1764). Johann Jacob Griesbach (1745–1812) took up this model in his second edition of the Greek text (1796–1806), with the Alexandrian, Western and Constantinopolitan groups. In short, in less than a century the foundations of the main text-types we know today ('Western', Alexandrian, Byzantine) were laid. It was with the New Testament that textual criticism made its greatest advances in the eighteenth century and the criterion of geographical diffusion was thus linked to text-types from the outset.

Timpanaro gives a masterly summary of the scope of this criterion:

> What is involved is an elementary calculation of probability: if two witnesses at a great distance from one another agree with one another with

[22] Quoted and translated in S. Timpanaro, *The Genesis of Lachmann's Method* (Chicago/London: The University of Chicago Press, 2005) 86.

[23] J.K. Elliott, 'Histoire du texte grec imprimé', *Manuel de critique textuelle du Nouveau Testament*. Vol. 1: *Introduction générale* (ed. C.-B. Amphoux; Langues et cultures anciennes 22; Bruxelles: Safran, 2014) 330.

[24] Timpanaro, *Genesis*, 66.

> little or no possibility of communication, and if the agreement is such that it can hardly be attributed to chance (that is, to polygenesis of innovations), then it must be concluded that they preserve a genuine tradition. This is how Lachmann (and already Bentley and Bengel, as we have seen) understood the geographical criterion[25].

Timpanaro also lists the two cases that invalidate the criterion: contamination (or dependence) and accidental agreement. Once these two possibilities have been ruled out, the criterion is extraordinarily effective, which explains Westcott's about-face. The agreements between two distant and independent geographical areas – Syriac-speaking Syria and the Latin West – cannot be explained by contamination, and they are too frequent to be accidental. They clearly point to an early stage – the earliest that can be reached – in the transmission of the Gospel text. The concession made by Westcott is astonishing because, we recall, it is precisely his publication that defends the idea, accepted and applied by the main current editions, that B.03 contains the primitive form of the text. The concession has been ignored by New Testament philology for over a century.

2. How to write the history of the Johannine text?

2.1. The classification of manuscripts

The starting point of our research is a classification of the main Greek manuscripts on the basis of the variation-units of John 13–17. Thanks to Reuben J. Swanson's edition of the Gospel of John, in which the manuscripts are read continuously and synoptically, we have listed all the variation-units of John 13–17 involving the following 43 witnesses[26]:

- 2 papyri: P^{66} P^{75} (often lacunose);
- 24 majuscules: ℵ.01 A.02 B.03 C.04 D.05 E.07 F.09 G.012 H.013 K.017 L.019 M.021 N.022 S.028 U.030 W.032 Y.034 Γ.036 Δ.037 Θ.038 Λ.039 Π.041 Ψ.044 Ω.045;
- 17 minuscules: 1 2 13 28 33 69 118 124 157 565 579 700 788 1071 1346 1424 1582.

There is a total of 506 variation-units, distributed as follows:

[25] Timpanaro, *Genesis*, 81–2.

[26] R.J. Swanson, *New Testament Greek Manuscripts. Variant Readings Arranged in Horizontal Lines against Codex Vaticanus. John* (Sheffield: Sheffield Academic Press, 1995) 185-237.

	John 13	John 14	John 15	John 16	John 17	**Total**
Number of variation-units	128	100	74	113	91	**506**

The following 10 Old Latin witnesses and the Vulgate have been added to the list of Greek manuscripts[27]:

VL2(*e*) VL3(*a*) VL4(*b*) VL5(*d*) VL6(*c*) VL8(*ff*^{2}) VL10(*f*) VL11(*l*) VL13(*q*) VL14(*r*^{1}) vg

together with the Syriac versions: the Sinaitic (sy^{s} – the Curetonian is deficient), the Peshitta (sy^{p}) and the Harklean (sy^{h}) [28].

To classify the 43 Greek manuscripts, statistical methods from the hard sciences are used. As early as 1975, Jean Duplacy explained and successfully applied the statistical methods of Data Analysis to the textual criticism of the New Testament[29]. A summary of the method is presented here, the results obtained with regard to John 13–17 being a priority[30]. The first step is to calculate the distances between the readings, and then between the witnesses. This involves quantitatively characterising the relative weight of a variant. Unlike the binary counting of agreements (1 or 0), the distance between readings shows that not all variations are equivalent. According to the type of variation and the length of the variation-unit, the distance between two readings varies between 0 and 12. Furthermore, we can see that if a manuscript A is the closest to a manuscript B, the latter is not necessarily the closest to A. This observation helps us to understand that a percentage of agreements between two manuscripts only makes sense within the set of all witnesses (in this case 43). It is only within this network of interrelations (43 x 42 / 2 = 903) that a comparison is possible. The 'classification' method ('Hierarchical

[27] The text of the Old Latin witnesses is available at www.iohannes.com, as part of the *Vetus Latina* edition of the Gospel of John.

[28] We have used the edition by G.A. Kiraz, *Comparative Edition of the Syriac Gospels Aligning the Sinaiticus, Curetonianus, Peshîtta and Harklean Versions*. Vol. 4: *John* (Piscataway: Gorgias Press, 2004).

[29] J. Duplacy, 'Classification des états d'un texte, mathématiques et informatique: repères historiques et recherches méthodologiques', *Études* (1975) 193–257.

[30] For details of statistical procedures, see D. Pastorelli, 'The *Chester Beatty* I Papyrus (P[45]) and the Main Greek Manuscripts of Mark 6 and 9: A Classification Based on a New Quantitative Method', *Reading New Testament Papyri in Context. Lire les papyrus du Nouveau Testament dans leur contexte* (ed. C. Clivaz and J. Zumstein; BETL, 242; Leuven/Paris/Walpole: Peeters, 2011) 281–305; Id., 'A Classification of Manuscripts Based on A New Quantitative Method. The Old Latin Witnesses of John's Gospel as Text Case', *Journal on Data Mining and Digital Humanities* (Episciences.org, 2017) 1–48, *Special Issue on Computer-Aided Processing of Intertextuality in Ancient Languages* <halshs-01557447>).

Ascendant Clustering'), which analyses hundreds of distances, fulfils this objective. It makes it possible to form homogeneous groups or clusters to which the philologist then assigns a meaning. These methods, which are similar to stemmatology, bring out clusters that the interpreter immediately identifies with text-types known elsewhere.

The groups obtained at the end of the quantitative analysis of John 13–17 are:

Group 1: A.02 E.07 F.09 G.012 H.013 K.017 M.021 N.022 S.028 U.030 Y.034 Γ.036 Δ.037 Θ.038 Λ.039 Π.041 Ω.045 2 28 157 565 700 1424
Group 2: P[66] P[75] ℵ.01 B.03 C.04 L.019 W.032 Ψ.044 33 579 1071
Group 3: D.05
f[1]: 1 118 1582 and *f*[13]: 13 69 124 788 1346

The textual critic has no difficulty in recognising the Byzantine (group 1) and Alexandrian (group 2) text-types, as well as the 'Western' text represented by D.05 (group 3).

2.2. Method for treating a variation-unit

The method we use to treat a variation-unit is based on three stages: (1) verbal criticism, (2) external criticism and (3) internal criticism[31].

(1) *Verbal criticism.* The aim of verbal criticism is to eliminate copying errors, which are generally involuntary and result from textual transmission, as well as intentional variants such as spelling, grammatical or harmonising corrections, conflated readings or explanatory glosses.

(2) *External criticism.* External criticism takes into account all available witnesses, i.e. Greek manuscripts, ancient versions and patristic quotations. The textual critic seeks to establish a chronology or dating of the different text forms for a given variation-unit. This anchoring in time is inseparable from a geography of witnesses. Jean Duplacy sums up the fundamental criterion of this investigation as follows: 'From the point of view of the history of the text, the variant that is most likely to correspond to the original text is the one whose attestations are the oldest and the most geographically widespread (with no close dependency)'[32].

[31] For a presentation of the method used in New Testament textual criticism, see D. Pastorelli, 'Le traitement des variantes', *Manuel de critique textuelle du Nouveau Testament.* Vol. 1: *Introduction générale* (ed. C.-B. Amphoux; Langues et cultures anciennes 22; Bruxelles: Safran, 2014) 213–47.

[32] J. Duplacy, 'À propos d'un lieu variant de 1 Co 11, 24: Voici mon corps (-, rompu, donné, etc.) pour vous', *Études*, 343: 'Du point de vue de l'histoire du texte, la variante qui a le plus de chances de correspondre au texte original est celle dont les attestations sont les plus anciennes et les plus dispersées géographiquement (sans dépendance proche)'.

(3) *Internal criticism.* Unlike external criticism, internal criticism takes into account the content of the readings. It uses two complementary but distinct approaches. The first looks for the best source-variant, i.e. the variant that best explains the origin of the others without itself being explained by the other readings. For a sound method, each variant must be considered as a potential source-variant in order to highlight the decisive arguments for or against its elimination. The second approach takes into account the context in looking for the original reading. 'The critic must select the variant which best fits with the general tendencies of the author'[33], i.e. his language, vocabulary, style, ideas, way of composing, etc. The variant that best conforms to the context, both in form and content, has the best chance of being original. This principle is based on the following presupposition: the text produced by an author at a given moment in history shows a homogeneity in both form and content that is undermined by variants from different backgrounds and eras.

(4) *Conclusion.* At the end of the analysis, the philologist is led to bring together the results produced by the external and internal criteria in what is known as the 'eclectic method'[34]. It seeks to strike a balance between external and internal criticism. Nevertheless, philologists are ultimately led to favour one or the other, especially when the results do not coincide on the reading to be adopted. It is regrettable that many textual critics favour external criteria, and Jean Duplacy's warning is still valid today: 'A critical choice should never, except in the absence of any other argument, be based on the "value" of a manuscript or a text-type, as is still too often done'[35].

3. External criticism of Jn 13.14

After the washing of their feet, Jesus commands his disciples to wash one another's feet. A variation-unit is located precisely at this point: 'If I, then, the Lord and the Teacher, have washed your feet, *you too* (var. 1) *how much more you too* (var. 2) ought to wash one another's feet' (Jn 13.14: εἰ οὖν ἐγὼ ἔνιψα ὑμῶν τοὺς πόδας ὁ κύριος καὶ ὁ διδάσκαλος, *καὶ ὑμεῖς* (var. 1) *πόσῳ μᾶλλον καὶ ὑμεῖς* (var. 2) ὀφείλετε ἀλλήλων νίπτειν τοὺς πόδας). Our treatment of this variation-unit will follow the

[33] L. Vaganay and C.-B. Amphoux, *An Introduction to New Testament Textual Criticism* (Cambridge: Cambridge University Press, 1991) 83.

[34] See D. Pastorelli, 'Traitement des variantes', 239–41.

[35] J. Duplacy, 'Histoire des manuscrits et histoire du texte du N.T. Quelques réflexions méthodologiques', *Études* (1965–1966) 54 n. 1: 'Jamais, sauf à défaut de tout autre argument, un choix critique ne devrait être fondé sur la "valeur" d'un manuscrit ou d'un type de texte, comme on le fait encore trop souvent'.

above method in detail. These variants are intentional and cannot be subjected to verbal criticism. They must first be analysed using external criticism, based on the following inventory:

Variant 1: και υμεις
P[66] א.01 A.02 B.03 C.04 L.019 W.032 Ψ.044 33 579 1071 Byz rell
Origen Basil of Caesarea Cyril of Alexandria John Chrysostom

Variant 2: ποσω μαλλον και υμεις
D.05 Θ.038
a d ff^2 *l r*^{1} VL24 VL29 sy^{s,p} NF Syr. 39
Ambrose of Milan Pseudo-Augustine
Aphrahat *Liber Graduum* Ps-Ephrem Diat^{ar} Diat^{p} Diat^{l}

3.1. Variant 1

Variant 1 is attested by all the Alexandrian witnesses of the Gospel of John (P[66] א.01 B.03 C.04 L.019 W.032 Ψ.044 33 579 1071 sa bo). Quotations from Origen[36] and Cyril of Alexandria[37] confirm this. With the evidence of the Papyrus Bodmer II (P[66]), we can conclude that variant 1 existed in Egypt from the end of the second century.

Moreover, it is read by a large number of Byzantine witnesses. John Chrysostom attests to it around 391 at Antioch in his *In Joannem homilia* LX.6[38]. In Asia Minor, Basil of Caesarea (c. 330–379) attests to it four times in his *Regulae Morales*[39].

Variant 1 is attested by the Vulgate and dominates the medieval Latin world. In North Africa, it was read by Cyprian of Carthage (early 3rd century–258)[40], and also Augustine of Hippo (354–430)[41].

In short, this variant is attested from the end of the second century and is widely spread in the West and North Africa, Egypt, Greek-speaking Syria and Asia Minor.

[36] B.D. Ehrman, G.D. Fee and M.W. Holmes, *The Text of the Fourth Gospel in the Writings of Origen* (SBL. The New Testament in the Greek Fathers 3; Atlanta: Scholars Press, 1986) 277, note no less than five quotations from Origen.

[37] P.E. Pusey, *Sancti Patris nostri Cyrilli Archiepiscopi Alexandrini in D. Joannis Evangelium accedunt fragmenta varia necnon tractatus ad Tiberium Diaconum duo*, vol. 2 (Oxford: Clarendon, 1872) 352 (lemma and commentary).

[38] *PG* 59 (1862) 335.

[39] *PG* 31 (1857) 825 (LXX.10), 837 (LXX.24), 856 (LXXV.2), 860 (LXXX.1).

[40] *Testimonia ad Quirinum* III.39; *Epistula* XIV.2.3.

[41] *Speculum* XXVIII.

3.2. Variant 2

Variant 2 is attested by Codex Bezae (D.05), a Greek witness to the 'Western' text, as well as by the Codex Koridethi (Θ.038), generally classified as a witness to the 'Caesarean' text-type.

No fewer than seven Old Latin witnesses attest to the 'Western' reading (*quanto magis*): *Vercellensis* (*a*, VL3), *Bezae* (*d*, VL5), *Corbeiensis* (*ff*², VL8), *Brixianus* (*f*, VL10), *Usserianus primus* (*r*¹, VL14), *Fragmentum Milanense* (VL24), *Sangermanensis secundus* (*g*², VL29). When quoting Jn 13.14, Ambrose of Milan (333/4–397) reads this variant[42]. It should be remembered that Ambrose used Greek manuscripts and that his New Testament text is related to the European text-type according to Bonifatius Fischer. Ps-Augustine should also be noted[43]. The 'Western' reading continued to be attested in the medieval West, notably with Heiric of Auxerre (841–c. 876)[44], Peter Damian (c. 1007–1072)[45], Rupert of Deutz (c. 1070–1129)[46], Bernard of Clairvaux (1090–1153)[47], Frowin of Engelberg (–1178)[48].

The 'Western' reading (var. 2) is also attested by the Old Sinaitic Syriac version (sy^{s}), by the New Finds manuscripts Syr. 39 (folio 4)[49], and by the Peshitta (sy^{p}). It is firmly rooted in the Syriac tradition, with several patristic quotations. The first author to be mentioned is Aphrahat (c. 270–after 345). In his *Twenty-Three Expositions*, written between 337 and 345 in the Persian Empire, he quotes at length from the account of the washing of the feet (Jn 13.6–7a, 11b–15), which rules out any quotation from memory:

> Our Saviour took water and poured [it] into a footbath, took a cloth, secured his waistband, and began to wash the feet of his disciples. When he came to Simon Peter, he said to him, "*You, my Lord, are washing my feet for me? You will never wash my feet for me!*" Jesus said to him, "*If I do not wash for you, you will have no reward with me!*" Simon said to him, "*Then, my Lord, do not wash only my feet for me, but also my hands and my head!*" Jesus said to him, "*Whoever has bathed needs only his feet to be washed.*" When he had

[42] *De mysteriis* VI.33; *De uirginitate* X.57.

[43] *Liber de diuinis scripturis siue Speculum* 141.

[44] *Homiliae per circulum anni pars hiemalis* 64.

[45] *Epistulae* 110.

[46] *Liber de diuinis officiis* V.

[47] *Liber de gradibus humilitatis et superbiae* 20 (1127).

[48] *Tractatus de ueritate* 494.

[49] S.P. Brock, 'Two Hitherto Unattested Passages of the Old Syriac Gospels in Palimpsests from St Catherine's Monastery, Sinai', *Δελτίο Βιβλικῶν Μελετῶν* 31A (2016) 7–18, identified a third Old Syriac version, based on multi-spectral images produced by the Sinai Palimpsests Project, not yet edited but available online (see www.sinaipalimpsests.org).

> washed the feet of his disciples, he took up his garments, reclined, and said to them, "*You call me 'Rabbi' and 'Lord', and I am. But if I, your Rabbi and your Lord, wash your feet for you,* **how much more** [*kmā'*] *ought you to wash each other's feet? I have shown you this example so that you will do as I have done.*" (*Demonstrations* XII.10)[50].

The *Liber Graduum* (circa 400), an anonymous collection of ascetic treatises, contains three quotations constructed around 13.14:

Liber Graduum II.8:

> Likewise, our Lord said: If I then, your Lord and teacher, who have not sinned or erred, have lowered myself so much, **how much more** [*kmā' yatir*] ought not you, who are servants and sinners, to lower yourselves. For since I have lowered myself before evildoers, **how much more** [*kmā'*] ought not you to lower yourselves before evil people![51]

Liber Graduum XVI.5:

> 'For if I, who am your Lord and your Teacher' have made myself Sin through my lowliness, **how much more** [*ḥad kmā' yatir*] still must you lower yourself?[52]

Liber Graduum XXII.13:

> If I, who am without law, am your Lord and Master, have humbled myself in this way, **how much more** [*kmā'*] ought you who are beneath God to bring yourselves to be humbled **more than me** [*yatir meny*], the Lord and Master.[53]

These three passages unquestionably refer to Jn 13.14: they have in common the double title 'your Lord and Master' and the paralleling of the disciples ('you') with the notion of humbling oneself, which refers to the washing of the feet. In addition to Aphrahat, the *Liber Graduum* adopts the expanded formula *kmā' yatir*, which is a copy of the Greek πόσῳ μᾶλλον. Similarly, Ps-Ephrem, *Sermones in Hebdomadam Sanctam* IV.3, quotes v. 14 with the full formula *ḥad kmā'... yatir*[54].

[50] Syriac text in J. Parisot, *Patrologia Syriaca* I.1 (1894) 532, and translation by A. Lehto, *The Demonstrations of Aphrahat, the Persian Sage* (Gorgias Eastern Christian Studies 27; Piscataway: Gorgias Press, 2010) 287.

[51] Syriac text in M. Kmosko, *Patrologia Syriaca* I.3 (1926) 44, and translation by R.A. Kitchen and M.F.G. Parmentier, *The Book of Steps. The Syriac* Liber Graduum (Cistercian Studies Series 196; Kalamazoo: Cistercian Publications, 2004) 21.

[52] Syriac text in Kmosko, *Patrologia Syriaca*, 397, and translation by Kitchen and Parmentier, *Book of Steps*, 163.

[53] Syriac text in Kmosko, *Patrologia Syriaca*, 664, and translation by Kitchen and Parmentier, *Book of Steps*, 262.

[54] Syriac text in T.J. Lamy, *Sancti Ephraem Syri Hymni et Sermones*, vol. I (Mechelen: H. Dessain, 1882) 413.

Was this reading present in Tatian's *Diatessaron*? The Arabic[55] and Persian[56] harmonies, the two main Eastern witnesses, attest to it. On the Western side, the Liège harmony is a witness in its favour[57]: '"Met rechte" is probably the rendering of *quanto magis* (*et uos debetis alter alterius lauare pedes*)'[58]. On the basis of the criterion of geographical diffusion, several authors answer affirmatively: variant 2 is diatessaronic. Thus Frederic Henry Chase: 'In the Bezan text then we have here an Old Syriac and Tatianic reading'[59]. Similarly, in their reconstruction of the text of the *Diatessaron*, Theodor Zahn (1881) recognised the reading attested by Aphrahat[60] and Ignatius Ortiz de Urbina (1967), that of Ps-Ephrem (*ḥad kmā'... yatir*)[61]. Tjitze Baarda also admits variant 2 as diatessaronic, but he hesitates between the two Syriac forms: 'My impression is that the conjecture of Zahn is preferable to that of the last editor of the Diatessaron, but nothing can be proved here'[62].

The history of the text in the Syriac tradition can be summarised as follows. The Syriac *Diatessaron* was composed by Tatian around 170 and was adopted by the Syriac-speaking churches until at least the fifth century. This is the text quoted by Aphrahat and commented on by Ephrem in the fourth century, and it influenced the Old Syriac versions. Variant 2 meets all these criteria. It is also attested by the Peshitta. 'This continuity

[55] A.-S. Marmardji, *Diatessaron de Tatien. Texte arabe établi, traduit en français, collationné avec les anciennes versions syriaques, suivi d'un évangéliaire diatessarique syriaque et accompagné de quatre planches hors texte* (Beyrouth: Imprimerie Catholique, 1935) 423: 'Si donc moi, qui suis votre Seigneur et votre Grand, je vous ai lavé les pieds, combien il est nécessaire que les uns d'entre vous lavent les pieds aux autres?'.

[56] G. Messina, *Diatessaron Persiano. I. Introduzione. II. Testo e traduzione* (Biblica et Orientalia 14; Rome: Pontificio Istituto Biblico, 1951) 315: 'Quando io, che sono vostro signore e grande (= maestro), lavai i vostri piedi, quanto più è conveniente a voi che laviate i piedi gli uni degli altri'.

[57] D. Plooij, C.A. Phillips, A.H.A. Bakker and A.J. Barnouw, *The Liège Diatessaron.* Parts I–VIII, (Verhandelingen der koninklijke Akademie van Wetenschappen te Amsterdam. Afdeeling Letterkunde, Nieuwe Reeks, Deel XXXI.1–8; Amsterdam: Uitgave der koninklijke Akademie van Wetenschappen te Amsterdam, 1929–70) 639: 'En ochic dan hebbe vwe voete geduegen die here ben en meester • So motti dan deen den andren sine voete met rechte dua en'.

[58] D. Plooij, *A Further Study of the Liège Diatessaron* (Leiden: Brill, 1925) 36.

[59] Chase, *Syro-Latin Text*, 26.

[60] T. Zahn, *Tatian's Diatessaron* (Forschungen zur Geschichte des neutestamentlichen Kanons und der altkirchlichen Literatur 1; Erlangen: Andreas Deichert, 1881) 203: 'Wenn also ich, euer Meister und euer Herr, eure Füsse euch gewaschen habe, wie müsst dann ihr Einer des Anderen Füsse waschen?'

[61] I. Ortiz de Urbina, *Vetus Evangelium Syrorium et exinde excerptum Diatessaron Tatiani* (Biblia Polyglotta Matritensia 6; Madrid: Consejo superior de investigaciones científicas, 1967) 280: 'Si, pues, yo vuestro maestro y vuestro señor he lavado vuestro pies, cuánto más os es más justo que os lavéis uno a otro'.

[62] T. Baarda, *The Gospel Quotations of Aphrahat The Persian Sage. I. Aphrahat's Text of the Fourth Gospel* (Vrije Universiteit Amsterdam; Amsterdam: B.V. Meppel, 1975) 195.

between the Old Syriac and the Peshitta indicates that the diatessaronic inheritance lasted for a long time and only gradually disappeared'[63]. The Greek text attested by the Peshitta is mixed with 'Western' and above all Byzantine readings, whereas the literal Harklean version is based on a Byzantine Greek text[64].

3.3. Conclusion on external criticism

Variant 1 (Alexandrian and Byzantine) is ancient (Papyrus Bodmer II), dating from the end of the second century. It is also widespread (Egypt, Greek-speaking Syria, Asia Minor, the West, North Africa).

Variant 2 ('Western') meets the criterion of geographical diffusion: it is firmly attested in two distant and independent geographical areas, Syriac-speaking Syria and the Latin West. Moreover, the *Diatessaron's* testimony in its favour confirms its existence at an early stage in the transmission of the Gospel text, probably the first half of the second century or at least the middle of the second century.

For these reasons, from the point of view of antiquity, the 'Western' variant has more in its favour.

4. Internal criticism of John 13.14

4.1. The search for the best source-variant

Let's examine the content of the two variants in order to determine which variant best explains the genesis of the other. We shall analyse the arguments in favour of one and the other.

4.1.1. Hypothesis 1: Variant 1 is original

We assume that variant 1 is original. How then can we explain the emergence of variant 2 with the addition of πόσῳ μᾶλλον?

Most commentators ignore this variation-unit and read only the Alexandrian variant. Those who mention the existence of the 'Western' reading immediately reject it as a deviance of the 'Western' text. Thus Rudolf Schnackenburg: 'The expression occurs only once in John and

[63] J. Joosten, 'Le *Diatessaron* syriaque', *Le Nouveau Testament en syriaque* (ed. J.-C. Haelewyck; Études syriaques 14; Paris: Paul Geuthner, 2017) 61: 'Cette continuité entre la Vieille syriaque et la Peshitta indique que l'héritage diatessaronique perdure longtemps et ne disparaît que graduellement'.

[64] For an overview of the Syriac versions, see J.-C. Haelewyck, 'Les versions anciennes', *Manuel de critique textuelle du Nouveau Testament*. Vol. 1: *Introduction générale* (ed. C.-B. Amphoux; Langues et cultures anciennes 22; Bruxelles: Safran, 2014) 100–111.

probably indicates the tendency of the 'Western' text to expand'[65]. The question then is how to explain the shift from variant 1 to variant 2. Why does the 'Western' text add πόσῳ μᾶλλον? Is it an interpolation? – An explanatory gloss aims to improve understanding of a difficult text; yet v. 14 presents no textual difficulty here. A harmonising correction? – No parallel passage can be cited. A grammatical or stylistic correction? – The phrase πόσῳ μᾶλλον frequently appears in the apodosis of a conditional sentence (Matt 7.11; 10.25; Luke 11.13; 12.28; Rom 11.12, 24; Heb 9.14)[66]. Could this stereotypical construction be applied to variant 1 to develop or improve it? The syntactic argument alone is not decisive. In the end, none of these avenues provides a convincing answer.

The final possibility is the observation of parallelism between v. 14a (ἐγώ / ἔνιψα / ὑμῶν τοὺς πόδας) and 14b (ὑμεῖς / νίπτειν / ἀλλήλων... τοὺς πόδας): the syntactic construction would prompt the 'Western' text to strengthen the feature. The strengthening with πόσῳ μᾶλλον would be paraphrasing. However, nothing could be less certain. In fact, two patristic authors, witnesses to variant 1, indulge in such a paraphrase. Having just quoted the Alexandrian reading, Cyril of Alexandria comments on v. 14 with the following paraphrase: ὥσπερ ἐγὼ ἔνιψα ὑμῶν τοὺς πόδας, οὕτω καὶ ὑμεῖς ὀφείλετε ποιεῖν[67]. Similarly, John Chrysostom: Εἰ οὖν ἐγὼ ὁ Κύριος καὶ ὁ διδάσκαλος ἔνιψα ὑμῶν τοὺς πόδας, οὕτω καὶ ὑμεῖς ὀφείλετε ἀλλήλοις ποιεῖν[68]. In both cases, the paraphrase uses a comparison of equality, not superiority: 'since I, the Lord and Master, have washed your feet, in the same way (οὕτω) you must also wash one another's feet'. Both the Alexandrian and Antiochian patristic traditions, when they develop the text, move towards a comparison of equality between Jesus and the disciples, and not towards a comparison of superiority ('how much more'). Another disturbing fact is that, as far as we know, there is no example of a similar paraphrase in the Greek manuscript tradition. In other words, when they read the Alexandrian reading, the copyists did not spontaneously or in isolation give way to paraphrasing. Variant 1 does not allow for this. In the end, the value judgement of the

[65] R. Schnackenburg, *The Gospel According to St. John*, vol. 3 (New York: Crossroad, 1990) 402 n. 65. Likewise B. Mathew, *The Johannine Footwashing as the Sign of Perfect Love. An Exegetical Study of John 13:1–20* (WUNT 2. Reihe 464; Tübingen: Mohr Siebeck, 2018) 403 n. 251: 'See the variations D Θ VL[pt] sy in other manuscripts. These could be attributed to the tendency of Western text to expand'.

[66] W. Bauer, F.W. Danker, W.F. Arndt and F.W. Gingrich, *A Greek-English Lexicon of the New Testament and Other Early Christian Literature* (Chicago: The University of Chicago Press, 2021) 544: 'Very oft. a conditional clause (εἰ) precedes it [...] εἰ... πόσῳ μ. *if ... how much more surely*'.

[67] Pusey, *Cyrilli*, 352.

[68] *De Christi precibus, Contra Anomoeos, homilia* 10 (*PG* 48 (1862) 786).

'Western' text on its tendency to develop is not sufficient in this case to explain how variant 2 would arise from variant 1.

4.1.2. Hypothesis 2: variant 2 is original

Let us now test the hypothesis that variant 2 is original. How can we explain the emergence of variant 1 with the omission of πόσῳ μᾶλλον?

The syntactic formulation εἰ... πόσῳ μᾶλλον... is a classic turn of phrase in Greek rhetoric. It is an argument *a maiore ad minus* or argument *a fortiori*, which corresponds to the adage 'who can do more can do less'. This argument is based on logic and involves reasoning built on a graduated scale. The gradation scale associates facts in the same category within a hierarchy agreed by the speakers. The gradation may go from the general to the particular, from the largest to the smallest, from the whole to the part, from the strongest to the weakest, and so on. These are all logical relationships that structure the hierarchy in this way.

The argument *a maiore ad minus* is also firmly rooted in ancient Judaism. 'There is evidence that this procedure was developed on the Jewish side in pre-Christian times, and it is listed as one of the seven exegetical rules promoted by Hillel'[69]. Several commentators link the 'Western' reading to the rabbinic exegetical rule *qal wâḥômer*, i.e. the fact of concluding from minor to major, from light to heavy ('all the more reason')[70]. Let us quote Rudolf Schnackenburg again: 'The version + πόσῳ μᾶλλον before καὶ ὑμεῖς (D Θ VL[pt] sy) makes the final rabbinical procedure *a minori ad maius*'[71]. The Jewish roots of the 'Western' text, which can be seen particularly in the Acts of the Apostles, and the antiquity of variant 2 go together with this background.

In these circumstances, how can we explain the omission of πόσῳ μᾶλλον? In v. 13a the disciples acknowledge Jesus (ὑμεῖς φωνεῖτέ με) as Master and Lord, as the one with authority over them, and this is confirmed by Jesus in v. 13b (καὶ καλῶς λέγετε). Jesus' eminent position constitutes the mainspring of the argument *a maiore ad minus*. Indeed, the logical link rests above all on the difference in status of the subjects, ἐγώ in v. 14a, ὑμεῖς in v. 14b: 'If he who is endowed with the highest authority exercises it by washing the disciples' feet, how much more must

[69] R. Jewett, *Romans. A Commentary* (Hermeneia; Minneapolis: Fortress Press, 2007) 362. J. Bonsirven, *Exégèse rabbinique et exégèse paulinienne* (Bibliothèque de Théologie historique; Paris: Beauchesne, 1939) 81.

[70] For a detailed account with references, consult H.L. Strack and P. Billerbeck, *Kommentar zum Neuen Testament aus Talmud und Midrasch*, vol. 3 (Munich: Beck, 1926) 223–6.

[71] Schnackenburg, *John*, 402 n. 65.

those who claim to be under him submit to this practice'[72]. The gradation thus relates more to the subjects than to the action itself. The premise contained in the protasis ('Jesus, the Lord and Master, washed the feet of his disciples') is a fact regarded as true and irrefutable by the speakers. In fact, εἰ followed by the aorist indicative ἔνιψα (v. 14a) here characterises an action carried out in view of the disciples[73]. This protasis may even have the meaning of a causal relation[74]. In any case, if the first proposition is accepted as true, the second is not yet admittted[75]. For the latter to be accepted as true, the argument *a maiore ad minus* must require it by means of the gradation scale. In the present case, the scale has an absolute degree that cannot be exceeded: Jesus, who occupies the highest position, is going to perform an action usually carried out by a slave, by someone in the most humble social position. The scale of gradation is pushed to its paroxysm. And if that was not already enough, the wording of v. 14b adds an obligation: it doesn't simply say 'how much more you also wash one another's feet', but 'how much more you also *must* (ὀφείλετε) wash one another's feet'. This reinforces the obligatory nature of the footwashing[76]. The risk incurred by variant 2 is to divert the attention from Jesus, a model for the disciples (as v. 15 immediately goes on to say), towards the washing of the feet itself. In other words the omission of πόσῳ μᾶλλον has the effect of curbing a literalism where the logical argument *a maiore ad minus* would leave room for ecclesial controversies or an over-emphasis on footwashing in churches that practice it. Variant 1, with its comparison of equality between Jesus and the disciples, avoids any drift towards a comparison of superiority in the action of washing feet.

The history of reception provides clues to the risk raised by variant 2. Ambrose of Milan, who reads variant 2, echoes such controversies.

[72] J. Zumstein, *L'Évangile selon saint Jean (13–21)* (Commentaire du Nouveau Testament 4b; Genève: Labor et Fides, 2007) 29: 'Si celui qui est nanti de la plus haute autorité l'exerce en lavant les pieds des disciples, à combien plus forte raison, ceux qui se réclament de lui doivent-ils se soumettre à cette pratique'.

[73] H. von Siebenthal, *Ancient Greek Grammar for the Study of the New Testament* (Oxford: Peter Lang, 2019) 529, comments on John 13.14 as follows: 'The condition is fulfilled: it refers to something that has just been put into action (by the speaker)'.

[74] BDF § 372 (1). In the same way E.A. Abbott, *Johannine Grammar* (London: A. & C. Black, 1906) § 1931 (39): '"If I (emph.), then, have washed your feet – *the lord and the teacher...*" (perhaps generally interpreted as meaning "*though* I am the lord and the teacher, " but possibly meaning "*because* I am the lord and the teacher, " if Christ assumed that it was the attribute of the lord to serve)'.

[75] Jewett, *Romans*, 362: 'It is a form of enthymeme in which the premise is provided in what has already been accepted as true and the inference is drawn to what has not yet been accepted as true'.

[76] Mathew, *Footwashing*, 403–6.

He describes the rites of initiation in Milan, on the eve of Easter, in two of his works, *De sacramentis* and *De mysteriis*. Immediately after baptism and anointing, John 13 was read (*Sacr.* III.4; *Myst.* VI.31) and the feet of the newly baptised were washed by the bishop and priests (*Sacr.* III.4). At the core of his commentary on John 13, Ambrose mentions the divergence with the Church of Rome, which did not practise footwashing:

> We are not unaware of the fact that the Church in Rome does not have this custom, whose character and form we follow in all things. Yet it does not have the custom of washing the feet. So note: perhaps on account of the multitude this practice declined. Yet there are some who say and try to allege in excuse that this is not to be done in the mystery, nor in baptism, nor in regeneration, but the feet are to be washed as for a guest. But one belongs to humility, the other to sanctification. Finally, be aware that the mystery is also sanctification: "If I wash not thy feet, thou shalt have no part with me. " So I say this, not that I may rebuke others, but that I may commend my own ceremonies. In all things I desire to follow the Church in Rome, yet we, too, have human feeling; what is preserved more rightly elsewhere we, too, preserve more rightly (*De sacramentis* III.5)[77].

In this way, Ambrose gives a literal reading of v. 14 and relies on the 'Western' reading and on its argument *a maiore ad minus* in order to justify his practice against that of Rome:

> At the same time note that the mystery itself consists in the ministry of humility. For He says: "If I have washed your feet, I the Lord and Master, " *how much more* [*quanto magis*] "ought you also to wash one another's feet." For since the very Author of salvation has redeemed us through obedience, *how much more* [*quanto magis*] ought we, His servants, to offer the service of humility and obedience (*De mysteriis* VI.33)[78].

V. 14 is central to Ambrose's literal interpretation, which extends the argument *a fortiori* from humility (the meaning of footwashing) to obedience (the actual practice of footwashing). In his *Letter to Janvier, Epistle* LV.33, Augustine also echoes the quarrels raised by the footwashing. These were of two kinds: on the one hand, the refusal to practise it, and on the other, the date to be used in the Easter liturgy to distinguish it from baptism:

[77] Translation by R.J. Deferrari, *Saint Ambrose. Theological and dogmatic works* (The Fathers of the Church. A New Translation 44; Washington D.C.: The Catholic University of America Press, 1963) 291–2.

[78] Translation by Deferrari, *Ambrose*, 17.

> As to the feet-washing, since the Lord recommended this because of its being an example of that humility which He came to teach, as He Himself afterwards explained, the question has arisen at what time it is best, by literal performance of this work, to give public instruction in the important duty which it illustrates, and this time [of Lent] was suggested in order that the lesson taught by it might make a deeper and more serious impression. Many, however, have not accepted this as a custom, lest it should be thought to belong to the ordinance of baptism; and some have not hesitated to deny it any place among our ceremonies. Some, however, in order to connect its observance with the more sacred associations of this solemn season, and at the same time to prevent its being confounded with baptism in any way, have selected for this ceremony either the eighth day itself, or that on which the third eighth day occurs, because of the great significance of the number three in many holy mysteries[79].

These liturgical quarrels are still perceptible in Aphrahat. At the end of the quotation of the Johannine narrative with the 'Western' reading, reported above, he immediately adds the following comment: 'After he had washed their feet and reclined, he gave them his body and his blood. [They] were not like the Israelites, who were baptized into the cloud and into the sea after eating the Passover sacrifice' (*Demonstrations* XII.10)[80]. Aphrahat, for his part, would have been in favour of footwashing before baptism, not afterwards. In short, the omission of πόσῳ μᾶλλον attempts to counter a literalism that fuels ecclesial controversies over footwashing.

4.2. The context

The context carefully elaborates the scale of gradation on which the *a fortiori* argument in v. 14 is based. The difference in status between Jesus and the disciples runs through verses 13–17: Jesus is Master and Lord (13, 14); as Jesus did to them, so the disciples must do (15); the servant is not greater than his master (16). The context argues in favour of variant 2.

[79] Translation in P. Schaff, *The Confessions and Letters of St. Augustin, with a Sketch of his Life and Work* (NPNF, 1.01; New York: Christian Literature Publishing, 1886) 446.

[80] Syriac text in Parisot, *Patrologia Syriaca*, 532, and translation by Lehto, *Demonstrations*, 287. M.-J. Pierre, *Aphraate le Sage Persan. Les Exposés.* Tome II. *Exposés XI-XXIII* (Sources Chrétiennes 359; Paris: Cerf, 1989) 584, comments: 'Faut-il le faire avant ou après le baptême, qui a lieu lors de la veillée pascale? Si c'était le cas, Aphraate trancherait en faveur de la première solution' (note 11).

5. Conclusion: exegetical implications

The mainspring of the second interpretation of the footwashing (13.12–17) lies in the *a fortiori* argument of v. 14 and the scale of gradation taken to its climax. However, v. 15 transforms the footwashing into a community principle: 'For I have given you an example, that you also should do as I have done to you.' The example of love accomplished by Jesus becomes a general norm for the disciples. Indeed, the verb ποιέω is recurrent in this passage (vv. 12, 15, 15, 17): it is a matter of doing that goes beyond the footwashing alone (νίπτω) and excludes any controversial literalism.

Contemporary exegesis, however, reveals a paradox in the interpretation of v. 14. On the one hand, variant 1 is adopted as original, with little discussion about the 'Western' variant, which is considered secondary from the outset. On the other hand, the latter is tacitly accepted in the commentaries when the argument *a maiore ad minus* is highlighted. For example, Jean Zumstein's interpretation, quoted in 4.1.2. above, uses the formula 'how much more' ('à combien plus forte raison'), corresponding to πόσῳ μᾶλλον. Likewise George R. Beasley-Murray: 'If he whom they acknowledge as "Teacher" and "Master" (revered terms) stooped to perform a slave's task for them, how much more readily should the disciples do the like for each other!'[81] Or Johannes Beutler: 'If the one whom the disciples rightly call "Lord" and "Master" washes their feet, how much more must they be ready to wash one another's feet'[82]. In the end, although it is not adopted in the current editions, the 'Western' reading is in fact favoured by commentators.

Our conclusion is not that the 'Western' variants are always original, but that they deserve attention from the point of view of the history of the text. The standard criteria of textual criticism indicate that these readings are repeatedly the oldest and the most widespread. Here the history of reception is of the utmost importance: it requires giving due consideration to versions and patristic quotations, particularly in the Syriac and Latin traditions. The testimony of the *Diatessaron* (c. 170) in favour of the 'Western' text is decisive. Another testimony from the second century could be cited[83]: that of Heracleon, a Valentinian who wrote a commentary on John's Gospel around 160, probably in Rome.

[81] G.R. Beasley-Murray, *John* (Word Biblical Commentary 36; Waco: Word Books, 1987) 235–6.

[82] J. Beutler, *A Commentary on the Gospel of John* (Grand Rapids: W.B. Eerdmans, 2017) 355.

[83] See D. Pastorelli, 'Liberté de l'Évangile et lecteur averti. Réflexions à partir de Jean 4,17', *Études Théologiques et Religieuses* 95 (2020) 491–3.

Bart Ehrman classifies Heracleon's text in relation to known text-types and concludes that his basic text is 'Western' (D.05, א.01).[84] It is not unlikely, moreover, that Valentinus, Heracleon's teacher and who taught in Rome in the 140s, used the 'Western' text, as did Justin, Tatian's teacher. In sum, the 'Western' text of John's Gospel was read in the first half of the second century.

This is why the exegete should be encouraged to comment not only on the Alexandrian text, followed by the current editions, but also to take into account this other form of the text. Here, there are two possibilities. If the 'Western' reading is considered secondary, because it appears very early in the second century, the exegete gains by taking it into account with regard to the history of the reception of the text. If the 'Western' reading is considered original with regard to the establishment of the text, the exegete must comment on it. In either case, the commentator's quest for meaning leads them to be open to other possible meanings than the usual reading of the edited text.

David PASTORELLI
63 chemin de l'Onde
84140 Montfavet (Avignon)
FRANCE
dpastorelli@yahoo.fr

[84] B.D. Ehrman, 'Heracleon and the "Western" Textual Tradition', *NTS* 40 (1994) 178.

Lexicography of Ἐνίστημι and the Eschatology of 1 Corinthians 7.25-26 and 2 Thessalonians 2.1-2

SIMON GATHERCOLE

This article analyses the meaning of the perfect tense of the Greek verb ἐνίστημι. This verb is controversial because of its usage by Paul and its relevance to early Christian eschatology.

The first debated use comes in 1 Cor. 7.26, which has been interpreted as referring either to a *present* crisis or to an *impending* crisis, depending on the meaning of the perfect participle of ἐνίστημι. The second comes in 2 Thess. 2.2, according to which the Thessalonians are anxious that the day of the Lord either *is here* or *is imminent*, depending on the meaning of the perfect indicative of ἐνίστημι.

This article aims to demonstrate beyond reasonable doubt that, where the perfect of ἐνίστημι has temporal connotations, it has a present not a future sense. A comprehensive analysis of the usage of the perfect of ἐνίστημι in the LXX, NT, the Apostolic Fathers, Philo, Josephus and Jewish Documentary Papyri provides no examples of the perfect of ἐνίστημι with a sense "be imminent" / "be impending". This is followed by a critical evaluation of various Greek lexica from the fifteenth century to the present. Evaluation of the parallels adduced over the centuries for the "impending" sense of the perfect of ἐνίστημι are shown to be inaccurate.

All the linguistic evidence points to a consistent sense of the perfect of ἐνίστημι as meaning "be present" / "be here". There is also a legal usage of the perfect of ἐνίστημι, but the formula refers to cases "in process" rather than "pending".

Keywords: ἐνίστημι, perfect, 1 Cor. 7.26, 2 Thess. 2.2, imminent, impending, crisis, eschatology.

Introduction

There has been long-standing disagreement over the meaning of the perfect of ἐνίστημι. This might seem like an obscure technicality, but that meaning is central to two important eschatological passages in the New Testament:

> "Now concerning virgins, I have no commandment from the Lord, but I give my opinion as one who by the Lord's mercy is faithful. Therefore I consider this to be good διὰ τὴν ἐνεστῶσαν ἀνάγκην: it is good that a person remain as he is." (1 Cor. 7.25-26)

> "Concerning the coming of our Lord Jesus Christ and our being gathered to him, we ask you, brothers and sisters, not to become quickly unsettled or alarmed by the opinion allegedly from us – whether by a spirit or word of mouth or by letter – ὡς ὅτι ἐνέστηκεν ἡ ἡμέρα τοῦ κυρίου." (2 Thess. 2.1-2)

In the former, the question is of whether it is the imminence of the parousia which has implications for Paul's view of marriage; in the latter, at issue is what the eschatological problem was in the letter. The central linguistic question is: does the perfect of ἐνίστημι have a present sense, or can it have either a present or an imminently future sense? This scholarly uncertainty has led to the divergent translations of these two passages. In the case of 1 Corinthians 7, does Paul take the view that it is good to remain as one is "in view of the *impending* crisis" (NRSV), or "because of the *present* crisis" (NIV)? In the case of 2 Thessalonians 2, is the misconception in Thessalonica that the day of the Lord "is at hand" (KJV) or that it "has come" (ESV)? Similarly, scholars can be found on both sides, but they tend to cite only a few parallels, especially those elsewhere in the New Testament.[1]

The aim of this present article is to bring clarity to this question by a fairly broad treatment of parallel instances of the perfect of ἐνίστημι. The aim is to demonstrate beyond reasonable doubt that, where the perfect of ἐνίστημι has temporal connotations,[2] it has a present not a future sense.[3] The treatment below covers most of the corpora usually taken into account in establishing the meanings of New Testament terms (LXX, Apostolic Fathers, Philo, Josephus, Jewish documents); in these it seeks to be exhaustive. Classical and Hellenistic authors are also taken into account, as are papyri and epigraphic evidence, but in these cases a comprehensive analysis is not feasible and so the focus in the discussion of these corpora will be on those instances which have been alleged (by commentators or lexica) to give evidence for a future sense. Despite the lack of complete coverage, however, well over a hundred passages are considered.[4] At the end we will draw conclusions about these two passages cited above.

[1] See the discussion of New Testament scholars in sections 3 and 4 of this article.

[2] The aspect of ἐνίστημι in the perfect will be considered later.

[3] As can be seen from a glance at a lexicon, the perfect of ἐνίστημι can obviously have other senses as well.

[4] NT: 7x (6x perf.); LXX: 13x (7x perf.); Apostolic Fathers 6x (5x perf.); Philo 28x (11x perf.); Josephus 58x (24x perf.); other Jewish texts 31x (30x in perf.): total 143x (83x perf.). Additionally, 41 passages are discussed in §2.

1. Ἐνίστημι in Contemporaneous Jewish and Christian Literature

1.1. The Perfect of Ἐνίστημι Elsewhere in the New Testament

Paul's usage elsewhere is unambiguous, as is that of the wider New Testament (ἐνίστημι 7x in NT; perf. 6x). In the perfect tense, the participle of ἐνίστημι is used substantivally to refer to "the present" or "what is present". For Paul, "neither things present nor things future" (οὔτε ἐνεστῶτα οὔτε μέλλοντα) can separate us from the love of God (Rom. 8.38). Paul uses the same pairing in a list in 1 Cor. 3.22: "whether Paul or Apollos or Cephas, whether the world or life or death, *whether things present or things future*" (εἴτε ἐνεστῶτα εἴτε μέλλοντα). In these cases ἐνεστῶτα is contrasted with μέλλοντα, and therefore emphatically present. The participle can also be used adjectivally, to refer to "the present evil age" (τοῦ αἰῶνος τοῦ ἐνεστῶτος, Gal. 1.4), or "the present time" (τὸν καιρὸν τὸν ἐνεστηκότα, Heb. 9.9).

Only two of the seven NT uses of ἐνίστημι are not perfect participles: one is 2 Thess. 2.2 (in the perfect indicative); the other is a future indicative, which unsurprisingly does refer to future time: "there will be terrible times" (ἐνστήσονται καιροὶ χαλεποί, 2 Tim. 3.1). This last instance is the only case where the verb is not used to describe a present reality. The terrible times coming are future, however, because the verb ἐνστήσονται is in the future tense; this is not therefore evidence that ἐνίστημι in 2 Tim. 3.1 means "*be imminent*", as some dictionaries propose: the point is not that, in last days, the terrible times will be imminent.[5] Leaving 1 Cor. 7.26 and 2 Thess. 2.2 for the moment, the consistent usage elsewhere in the New Testament of the perfect of ἐνίστημι is therefore to refer to a present reality.

1.2. Ἐνίστημι in the Septuagint

The body of evidence is only slightly expanded in the Septuagint (ἐνίστημι 13x; perf. x7). The evidence for ἐνίστημι here is notable because

[5] *Contra* George Pasor, *Lexicon Graeco-Latinum in Novum Domini Nostri Jesu Christi Testamentum* (London: Edward Griffin, 1650), 372; Samuel Thomas Bloomfield, *A Greek and English Lexicon to the New Testament* (London: Longman, 1840), 127; Edward Robinson, *A Greek and English Lexicon of the New Testament* (New York: Harper & Brothers, 1855), 254: "to be at hand, to impend, 2 Thess. 2, 2. 2 Tim. 3, 1"; Samuel Christoph Schirlitz, rev. by Theodor Eger, *Griechisch-deutsches Wörterbuch zum neuen Testamente* (Giessen: Roth, [5]1893), 143: "dabeistellen, dann bevorstehen, in Kürze da sein, 1 Cor. 7, 26; 2 Thess. 2, 2; 2 Tim. 3, 1"; Adalbert Schulte, *Griechisch-Deutsches Wörterbuch zum Neuen Testamente* (Limburg: Steffen, 1918), 160: "bevorstehen 2 Th 2, 2; 2 Ti 3, 1; 1 Ko 7, 26"; also F. Wilbur Gingrich, rev. Frederick Danker, *Shorter Lexicon of the Greek New Testament* (Chicago: University of Chicago Press, [2]1983), 66, additionally commenting that the present sense is possible.

all the instances are unparalleled in the canonical Hebrew text; therefore most if not all are composed rather than translated Greek. The first is the Greek expansion of 1 Kgs 12.24, and the rest of the cases are from non-canonical Greek compositions. There is again a great consistency in the sense of the verb, according to the tense in which it appears.

1 Kgs 12.24 LXX. This is the only LXX case in the present tense. Here we find a standard usage of ἐνίστημι, referring to when a period of time "begins": Rehoboam mustered his army "at the beginning of the year" (ἐνισταμένου τοῦ ἐνιαυτοῦ). As we will see, this is a standard way to refer to a season beginning.[6] It is not clear to me how Fitzmyer can cite this verse as an example of ἐνίστημι meaning "to be threatening, being imminent".[7]

1 Esdr. 5.46 and 4 Macc. 2.8. The same meaning appears in some of the cases in the aorist, e.g. "when the seventh month *began*" (ἐνστάντος δὲ τοῦ ἑβδόμου μηνός, 1 Esdras) or "when the seventh year *began*" (τῶν ἑβδομάδων ἐνστασῶν, 4 Maccabees).

In the other aorist cases, similar to those meaning "begin" are other instances where the best single glosses are perhaps "arrive", "take place", or "happen".

2 Macc. 4.43. "Charges were brought against Menelaus about these incidents (περὶ δὲ τούτων ἐνέστη κρίσις πρὸς τὸν Μενέλαον)." Here ἐνέστη κρίσις (with the aorist) means "an accusation *was lodged*", or "charges were brought".[8] There is no sense here that the charges are merely pending.[9] We have just seen the terrible actions of Menelaus (4.23-42); there is then the report that a charge was brought (4.43: ἐνέστη κρίσις); then the case is made (4.44: δικαιολογίαν ἐποιήσαντο); only by bribery does Menelaus avoid his sentence (4.45-47).

[6] See e.g. Philo below, where the present participle of ἐνίστημι is used to refer to times or seasons *beginning* (*Leg.* 1.6; *Mos.* 1.115; *Spec.* 1.183; 2.210, 220). Cf. also Theophrastus, *Hist. Plant.* 9.8.2 (4th-3rd cent. BCE): τοῦ ἐνιστάμενου θέρους ("with the beginning of summer"). This probably also underlies the sense of πόλεμος + ἐνίστημι referring to the outbreak of war. See fn. 11 below.

[7] Joseph A. Fitzmyer, *First Corinthians: A New Translation with Introduction and Commentary* (Anchor; New Haven: Yale University Press, 2008), 315. Similarly Bruce W. Longenecker & Timothy A. Brookins, *1 Corinthians 1-9: A Handbook on the Greek Text* (Waco: Baylor University Press, 2016), 179: "ἐνεστῶσαν as 'imminent'; as in 1 Macc 12:44; LXX 1 Kgs 12:24."

[8] For the latter, see Daniel R. Schwartz, *2 Maccabees* (CEJL; Berlin: De Gruyter, 2008), 210.

[9] *Contra* Karl Gottlieb Bretschneider, *Lexicon Manuale Graeco-Latinum in Libros Novi Testamenti* (Leipzig: Barth, [3]1840), 142: "insto, quasi in conspectu iam sto vel versor, i.e. proxime insto, immineo, 2 Thess. 2, 2. 2 Tim. 3, 1. 1 Macc 12, 44. 2 Macc. 4, 43. 12, 3. Ioseph. ant. 4, 8, 12"; Bloomfield, *A Greek and English Lexicon*, 127; Robinson, *A Greek and English Lexicon*, 254.

1 Macc. 8.24. Conzelmann cites this passage as an instance of the meaning “to be immediately impending”.[10] The passage is a copy of a letter written by the Romans to the Jews cementing an alliance:

> “May all go well for the Romans and for the nation of the Jews by land and sea forever, and may sword and enemy be far from them. *But if war does come first to Rome* (ἐὰν δὲ ἐνστῇ πόλεμος Ῥώμῃ προτέρᾳ) or to any of their allies in their whole empire, then the nation of the Jews shall act as their allies wholeheartedly, as the occasion demands.” (1 Macc. 8.23-25)

The scholarly confusion, according to which the verb is thought to imply imminence, has perhaps arisen here because the decree is contemplating a possible scenario in the future. But it would clearly be irresponsible to translate ἐὰν δὲ ἐνστῇ πόλεμος Ῥώμῃ προτέρᾳ as “If war is immediately impending against Rome first...”. In fact, πόλεμος + ἐνίστημι is a standard way of referring to the outbreak of war.[11] This is in line with the sense of “begin” above. Here the form of the verb is also aorist.

3 Macc. 3.24. This passage is a source of similar confusion (*pace* Conzelmann), in the course of Ptolemy Philopator’s decree to arrest the Jews:

> “Therefore, fully convinced by these indications that they are ill-disposed toward us in every way, we have taken precautions so that, *if a sudden disturbance later breaks out against us* (αἰφνιδίου μετέπειτα ταραχῆς ἐνστάσης ἡμῖν), we shall not have these impious people behind our backs as traitors and barbarous enemies.”

The point here in this genitive absolute clause is that the Egyptians are taking care in case, “a tumult having happened to us hereafter”, the Jews turn out to be enemies. Again, the meaning is hardly “a tumult immediately impending against us hereafter”. As in the previous example, the decree is envisaging a hypothetical scenario in the future. The

[10] Hans Conzelmann, *1 Corinthians: A Commentary on the First Epistle to the Corinthians* (Hermeneia; Philadelphia: Fortress Press, 1975), 132 n. 14.

[11] See James Diggle, ed. *The Cambridge Greek Lexicon* (Cambridge: Cambridge University Press, 2021), s.v. ἐνίσταμαι: “2 (of a war) break out”. Note e.g. Isocrates (5th/4th cent.), *Or.* 5.2; Demosthenes, *Cor.* (*Or.* 18) 89 and 139; Aeschines 2.58; Philo, *Legat.* 30: διὰ τοὺς ἐνισταμένους πολέμους (“on account of the wars which break out”); *Virt.* 47 : ἐνστάντος πολέμου ῥᾳδίως τῶν ἐχθρῶν περικρατήσεις (“if war breaks out, you will easily overcome your enemies”). Instances in the perf. often refer to a war having broken out, therefore underway: see *IG* II^2 1299.57; *IScM* III 7.11-12; *ILindos* II 2 xxxvii.98-99; *ICrete* III iii 3,A.74-76; *IG* XIV 1297.33-34. For the transitive usage, see Franz Passow, *Handwörterbuch der griechischen Sprache*, vol. 1 (Leipzig: Vogel, ^{3}1828), 516: ἐνίστημι + πόλεμον means “einen Krieg beginnen”.

prospective sense of the future is communicated by the adverb μετέπειτα, not by the semantics of the verb which is in the aorist.

When we consider ἐνίστημι in the perfect tense, it invariably means "to be present":

Esth. 3.13: To the existing text "on the fourteenth day of the twelfth month", the translator adds the gloss "of the present year" (τοῦ ἐνεστῶτος ἔτους).

1 Esdr. 9.6: The assembled Judahites and Benjaminites are shivering "because of the bad weather at the time" (διὰ τὸν ἐνεστῶτα χειμῶνα).

1 Macc. 12.44: Trypho objects to Jonathan that the people have laboured so hard "even though we are not at war", or literally, "even though *a war is not present to us*" (πολέμου μὴ ἐνεστηκότος ἡμῖν). There is no sense of the verb meaning "to be immediately impending" here.[12]

2 Macc. 3.17: Terror and trembling make known to the onlookers "the pain present in the heart" (τὸ κατὰ καρδίαν ἐνεστὸς ἄλγος) of the high priest.

2 Macc. 6.9: A decree that some Greek cities should compel the Jews to participate in the sacrifices to Dionysus and change their laws made "the present misery" (τὴν ἐνεστῶσαν ταλαιπωρίαν) of the Jews plain to see. The author illustrates this misery: two women, arrested for circumcising their chilldren, were hurled off the city wall, and others who had secretly observed the sabbath were burned alive.

2 Macc. 12.3: The people of Joppa tricked the Jews, acting in pretence "*as if there were no ill-will at all present towards them*" (ὡς μηδεμιᾶς ἐνεστώσης πρὸς αὐτοὺς δυσμενείας).[13]

3 Macc. 1.16: The priests prays that God will help them "*in the present circumstances*" (τοῖς ἐνεστῶσιν), namely Philopator's decision to enter the temple and thereby desecrate it.

It is striking that all the LXX instances in the perfect tense are participles (like the case in 1 Cor. 7.26). There is, as in the various New Testament cases, a remarkable consistency in meaning. Hence there is an important interim conclusion to be drawn here. As in the New Testament, there is not a single instance of the meaning "to be impending" or "to be imminent". Using the perfect participle of ἐνίστημι is again a conventional way of talking about the present. Contra Bauer's claim that the imminent sense is supported by "LXX", the major Septuagint Lexica confirm the present sense.[14]

[12] *Contra* Bretschneider, *Lexicon Manuale Graeco-Latinum*, 142; Conzelmann, *1 Corinthians*, 132 n. 14; Fitzmyer, *First Corinthians*, 315; Longenecker/Brookins, *1 Corinthians 1-9*, 179.

[13] *Contra* Bretschneider, *Lexicon Manuale Graeco-Latinum*, 142.

[14] Clearly, T. Muraoka, *A Greek-English Lexicon of the Septuagint* (Leuven: Peeters,

1.3. The Apostolic Fathers

The cases of ἐνίστημι from the artificial corpus of the Apostolic Fathers are quite straightforward (ἐνίστημι 6x; perf. 5x). Four of the six contrast present time with the past and/or the future. The prophets tell us of "what is past, what is present, and the first-fruits of what is to come" (τὰ παρεληλυθότα καὶ τὰ ἐνεστῶτα καὶ τῶν μελλόντων ... ἀπαρχάς) in *Barn.* 1.7. In *Barn.* 4.1, the author contrasts the present and future age with different language (τοῦ νῦν καιροῦ / τὸν μέλλοντα), but at the same time urges his readers to "investigate closely the present circumstances" (περὶ τῶν ἐνεστώτων ἐπιπολὺ ἐραυνῶντας); they should recognise the signs in the present that the end is near. Shortly thereafter, in *Barn.* 5.3, God has similarly revealed "what is past... and about the present ... and for what is future" (καὶ τὰ παρεληλυθότα ... καὶ ἐν τοῖς ἐνεστῶσιν ... καὶ εἰς τὰ μέλλοντα). Then the author of the epistle talks of the difficulty of writing to his audience "about the present or the future" (περὶ τῶν ἐνεστώτων ἢ μελλόντων) (*Barn.* 17.2). Despite the claims of some editions of Bauer's Lexicon,[15] the reference here in *Barn.* 17.2 seems clearly to the present, not least because of the previous usages in chapters 1, 4 and 5; other similar passages juxtapose present and future in the same way.[16] Ignatius offers the Ephesians (*Eph.* 11.1) only two choices: "Let us either fear the wrath to come, or love the grace which is present" (ἢ γὰρ τὴν μέλλουσαν ὀργὴν φοβηθῶμεν ἢ τὴν ἐνεστῶσαν χάριν ἀγαπήσωμεν). Finally, *1 Clem.* 55.1 talks of how kings in the past have averted disaster by consulting oracles "when a time of plague has arisen" (λοιμικοῦ τινος ἐνστάντος καιροῦ). Except for this last case, all the instances are perfect participles of ἐνίστημι, and all have a present sense.

1.4. Philo

Philo employs the verb on a number of occasions (28x). There are ten or eleven cases in the present tense,[17] five in the aorist,[18] one in the

2009), 239. Probably also, though with slightly less clarity, J. Lust, E. Eynikel and K. Hauspie, *A Greek-English Lexicon of the Septuagint, Part I: A - I* (Stuttgart: Deutsche Bibelgesellschaft, 1992), 153. Cf. Walter Bauer, *Griechisch-deutsches Wörterbuch zu den Schriften des Neuen Testaments und der frühchristlichen Literatur*, edited by Kurt Aland and Barbara Aland (Berlin: De Gruyter, [6]1988), 538; similarly ibid., ([5]1958), 528.

[15] E.g. Bauer, *Griechisch-deutsches Wörterbuch* ([6]1988), 538.

[16] Cf. Rom. 8.38; 1 Cor. 3.22; SVF 3.94 §388.

[17] Philo, *Leg.* 1.6; *Mut.* 109; *Mos.* 1.115; *Spec.* 1.183; 2.84; 2.179: 2.210; 2.220; *Legat.* 30; *Aet.* 10 (a conjectural emendation); *Flacc.* 83.

[18] Philo, *Agr.* 59; *Ios.* 158; *Ios.* 260; *Spec.* 1.186; *Virt.* 47.

pluperfect,[19] and eleven in the perfect. Notably, every one of these eleven instances in the perfect is a participle:

> *Leg.* 2.42: "Sense perception by nature *is present* (νῦν ἐστι), *existing solely in present time* (κατὰ τὸν ἐνεστῶτα χρόνον ὑφισταμένη μόνον)."
>
> *Sacr.* 47: "Time is tripartite – *consisting of the past, the present and the future* (ἐκ παρεληλυθότος καὶ ἐνεστῶτος καὶ μέλλοντος συνεστώς)."
>
> *Plant.* 114: "Tripartite time... which is naturally *divided into the past, the present, and the future*" (εἰς τὸν παρεληλυθότα καὶ ἐνεστῶτα καὶ μέλλοντα τέμνεσθαι).
>
> *Migr.* 43: "*not the present time but the future*" (οὐ τὸν ἐνεστῶτα, ἀλλὰ τὸν μέλλοντα)
>
> *Somn.* 2.209: "Pleasure ... consists of the memory of past delights, *of the enjoyment of those present* (ἐξ ἀπολαύσεως τῶν ἐνεστηκότων), and of the hope of those in the future."
>
> *Somn.* 2.210: "the three parts of time... the memories of past delights, *the enjoyments of those present* (ἐνεστηκότων μετουσίαις), and the expectations of thôse in the future"
>
> *Praem.* 71: "Because there are four affections in the soul, two conversant with good, *either present or future* (ἐνεστὸς ἢ μέλλον), i.e. pleasure and desire; and two with evil, *either present or expected* (παρὸν ἢ προσδοκώμενον), i.e. sorrow and fear...."
>
> *Legat.* 158: "*when the sacred sabbath was being held*" (τῆς ἱερᾶς ἑβδόμης ἐνεστώσης)
>
> *Legat.* 275: "*about the present circumstances*" (περὶ τῶν ἐνεστώτων)
>
> *QG* 2.72a: "Just as what is later comes after what is earlier, *so also the future comes after the present*" (οὕτω καὶ τὰ μέλλοντα τῶν ἐνεστώτων).
>
> *QG* 2.72b: "Therefore every wise person, who is not a man but an intellect, looking behind him and seeing all around, is protected *against circumstances which occur* (πρὸς τὰ ἐνεστῶτα) and storms which break out unexpectedly."

As elsewhere, we also see the present participle of ἐνίστημι being used to refer to times or seasons *beginning* (*Leg.* 1.6; *Mos.* 1.115; *Spec.* 2.220). Conversely, when a feast is already underway and in progress, the perfect participle is used (*Legat.* 158). The meaning "be imminent" is particularly obviously impossible in cases when Philo says that something is about to happen (i.e. is anticipated in the imminent future), using μέλλω as an auxiliary verb with ἐνίστασθαι (*Spec.* 2.84: *Flacc.* 1.83).[20] This is

[19] Philo, *Mos.* 1.220.

[20] *Spec.* 2.84: "when the most holy number, the seventh year, *is about to arrive*" (ἐνίστασθαι μέλλῃ); *Flacc.* 83: "I know of cases of men who had been crucified when such a holiday *was about to be held* (μελλούσης ἐνίστασθαι)...".

of course different from those cases where μέλλω and ἐνίστημι are contrasted: Philo is interested in what he calls "tripartite" time, "consisting of past, present and future" (*Sacr.* 47).[21] Again, the clear conclusion is that there is a consistent meaning of ἐνίστημι in the perfect tense in Philo as well.

1.5. Josephus

There are a number of occurences of ἐνίστημι in Josephus (58 in all): 26 cases appear in the aorist,[22] 6 in the present,[23] along with 1 future and 1 pluperfect.[24] Of those instances in the perfect (24), all but two are participles. The exceptions are a perfect indicative and a perfect infinitive:

[21] See further Philo, *Plant.* 1.114; *Migr.* 1.43; *Somn.* 2.209-210; *Praem.* 1.71; *QG* 2.72a. Cf. also Apollodorus of Seleucia (*SVF* 3.260 §8) (ii BCE): τὸ μὲν γάρ ἐστιν αὐτοῦ παρεληλυθός, τὸ δὲ ἐνεστηκός, τὸ δὲ μέλλον. Similarly among grammarians, e.g. Dionysius Thrax, *Ars Grammatica* 53 (ii-i BCE): Χρόνοι τρεῖς, ἐνεστώς, παρεληλυθώς, μέλλων. "There are three tenses: present, past and future."; additionally, *IGLSyr* 3,1 801.1-2 (end ii CE): Χρόνοι. Αἰών. Μέλλων. Ἐνεστώς. Παρῳχημένος. See LSJ, ἐνίστημι III.2.

[22] Almost all of these cases of the aorist are references to the arrival of a date or festival, with the aor. ptcp. in the genitive absolute ("When the time X came..."): *Ant.* 2.312; 3.283; 4.209; 4.273; 5.172; 8.230; 9.223; 9.271; 11.109; 12.175; 12.217; 13.46; 13.304; 14.285; 14.338; 17.213; 17.254; 20.106; *War* 1.253; 2.10; 2.42; 2.280; 5.99; 5.349; 6.423. The only exception is of the arrival of a time in the indicative (*Ant.* 13.252). *Contra* Bretschneider, *Lexicon Manuale Graeco-Latinum*, 142, and the various editions of Bauer/ BDAG, citing Josephus, *Ant.* 4.209 (4.8.12) as an example: the phrase τῆς σκηνοπηγίας ἑορτῆς ἐνστάσης, however, simply means "at the season of the feast of tabernacles" (H.St-J. Thackeray, *Josephus*, vol. 6 (LCL; Cambridge, MA: Harvard University Press, 1930), 209]), or "at the Feast of Tabernacles" (Whiston).

[23] Again, all but one of the present-tense examples are instances of particular times coming or beginning. See *Ant.* 8.225: "when the Feast of Tabernacles was about to take place" (τῆς σκηνοπηγίας ἑορτῆς ἐνίστασθαι μελλούσης); *Ant.* 12.201: "when the appointed day came, when taxes had to be paid to the king" (τῆς προθεσμίας ἐνισταμένης, καθ' ἣν ἔδει τῷ βασιλεῖ τοὺς φόρους ἀπαριθμεῖν); *Ant.* 13.234: "the year arrived on which it was incumbent on the Jews to do no work" (ἐνίσταται τὸ ἔτος ἐκεῖνο, καθ' ὃ συμβαίνει τοὺς Ἰουδαίους ἀργεῖν); *Ant.* 14.38: "at the beginning of spring" (ἐνισταμένου τοῦ ἔαρος); *Ant.* 17.166: "the day on which the fast takes place" (ἡμέραν, ᾗ ἡ νηστεία ἐνίστατο). The exception, in *War* 4.21, is a reference to the Jewish defenders of Gamala at first blocking the initial entrances of the Romans and preventing them from advancing further (οἱ δὲ τέως μὲν κατὰ τὰς πρώτας εἰσόδους ἐνιστάμενοι προσωτέρω χωρεῖν ἐκώλυον). This is a spatial use of the verb, not a temporal one.

[24] The sole future example (*Ant.* 11.170) comes in Nehemiah's address to the people about the building of the temple; he warns them that, when their neighbours hear about the building, "they will come (ἐνστήσονται) and devise many obstacles against us to stop it". Alternatively, the verb may mean "they will oppose (it)". The pluperfect instance (*Ant.* 8.62) comes in a statement that the year the temple began to be built was when "Hiram was already in the eleventh year of his reign at Tyre" (ἤδη τῆς ἐν Τύρῳ βασιλείας ἑνδέκατον ἐνειστήκει Εἰρώμῳ).

Ant. 15.7: "There was no end to these ills, for the greed of the prince who was 'in need' brought them, and the land had to remain uncultivated because of the sabbatical year, *for it was still continuing at that time* (ἐνεστήκει γὰρ τότε)."

Ant. 17.353: "I did not consider these histories irrelevant to the present work, *because it is about kings* (διὰ τὸ περὶ τῶν βασιλέων αὐτὸν ἐνεστηκέναι)."

There are then 22 instances of ἐνίστημι in the perfect participle:

Ant. 3.24: "rescue *in connection with the present distresses* (περὶ τῶν ἐνεστηκότων ἀπόρων)"
Ant. 3.224: "for it happens that my account *is about sacrifices* (περὶ τῶν θυσιῶν ἐνεστάναι)"
Ant. 7.391: "*concerning both what is to come* (καὶ περὶ τῶν μελλόντων) and *the organisation of present affairs* (καὶ τῆς τῶν ἐνεστηκότων οἰκονομίας)"
Ant. 11.219: "on the fourteenth day of the twelfth month *of this present year* (τοῦ ἐνεστῶτος ἔτους)"
Ant. 13.428: "*about the present state of affairs*" (περὶ τῶν ἐνεστώτων)
Ant. 14.58: "*about the present state of affairs*" (περὶ τῶν ἐνεστώτων)
Ant. 16.162: "*not only in the present, but also in the past*" (οὐ μόνον ἐν τῷ ἐνεστῶτι καιρῷ ἀλλὰ καὶ ἐν τῷ προγεγενημένῳ). Oddly, Wahl appears to provide this as an example of the sense "immineo" or "proxime instans",[25] but this is untenable, given the consistent usage in Josephus: compare especially *Ant.* 7.391 above.
Ant. 17.89: "*about the present state of affairs*" (περὶ τῶν ἐνεστηκότων)
Ant. 17.185: "as though *his present difficulty* (τοῦ ἀγῶνος ἐνεστηκότος) was concerned with such matters"[26]
Ant. 17.212: "*while some were there* (τῶν τε ἐνεστώτων) at his instigation"
Ant. 17.215: "*the violence of those present*" (τὴν ὁρμὴν τῶν ἐνεστηκότων)[27]
Ant. 17.229: "*about the present state of affairs*" (περὶ τῶν ἐνεστηκότων)
Ant. 17.237: "since this had taken place *during the festival* (ὡς ἑορτῆς τε ἐνεστηκυίας)"

[25] Christian Abraham Wahl, *Clavis Novi Testamenti Philologica* (Leipzig: Barth, 1843), 176.

[26] The Greek is slightly obscure here. Whiston has "as if that were the only thing now in question"; the Loeb has "as though the time had come for him to exert himself about such matters": Ralph Marcus & Allen Wikgren, tr. *Josephus. Jewish Antiquities, Volume VII: Books 16-17* (LCL; Cambridge, MA: Harvard University Press, 1963).

[27] The manuscripts proper read τὴν ὁρμὴν τῶν ἐνεστηκότων; the reading τὴν ὁρμὴν τῶν στασιαζόντων (printed in e.g. the Loeb) is attested only in the Epitome. See the note *ad loc.* in LCL.

Ant. 17.353: "because my account *is about kings* (περὶ τῶν βασιλέων ... ἐνεστηκέναι)"
Ant. 18.122: "*while the traditional Jewish festival was taking place*" (ἑορτῆς πατρίου τοῖς Ἰουδαίοις ἐνεστηκυίας)
Ant. 18.178: "to be an alleviation *of the present ills* (τῶν ἐνεστηκότων κακῶν)"
Ant. 18.320: "to bring us clear news *about the present state of affairs* (τῶν ἐνεστηκότων)"
Ant. 19.272: "*when the sacrifices to the dead were being offered*" (ἐναγισμῶν ἐνεστηκότων)
Ant. 20.267: "*until this present day*" (μέχρι τῆς νῦν ἐνεστώσης ἡμέρας)
War 2.280: "*while the Feast of Unleavened Bread was taking place*" (τῆς τῶν ἀζύμων ἑορτῆς ἐνεστώσης)
War 6.109: "*the oracle that is already coming to pass*" (χρησμὸν ἤδη ἐνεστῶτα)

The usage here is unremarkable. There is calendrical usage, referring to the "present year" or "the present day" (*Ant.* 11.219; 20.267), and usages in descriptions of a festival in progress (*Ant.* 17.237; 18.122; 19.272; *War* 2.280). As in 1 Cor. 7, Josephus in a few places refers to present *woes*: "the present distresses", "the present difficulty" and "the present ills" (*Ant.* 3.24; 17.185; 18.178). There is a clear contrast with both the past (τῷ ἐνεστῶτι *versus* τῷ προγεγενημένῳ in *Ant.* 16.162), and with the future (τῶν μελλόντων *versus* τῶν ἐνεστηκότων in *Ant.* 7.391). In none of these cases above does the verb mean "be imminent".

1.6 Jewish Documentary Papyri

Apart from a reference to the present tense of ἐνίστημι in the *Testaments of the Twelve Patriarchs* which is not relevant here,[28] the references in other Jewish texts are confined – as far as I know – to documentary papyri. Apart from one special case which will be discussed later, they are all straightforward.

The archive of the Jewish community in Herakleopolis from the second century BCE[29] contains two instances of the calendrical use, in

[28] *T. Gad.* 6.7: ἐὰν δὲ ἀναιδὴς ἐστι καὶ ἐνίσταται τῇ κακίᾳ... ("If he is shameless and set in evil..."). The sense of ἐνίστημι is spatial, rather than temporal here. I leave aside here the question of to what extent the *Testaments* are Christian or not.

[29] For the texts, see James M.S. Cowey & Klaus Maresch, *Urkunden des Politeuma der Juden von Herakleopolis (144/3-133/2 v. Chr.) (P. Polit. Iud.): Papyri aus den Sammlungen von Heidelberg, Köln, München und Wien* (Wiesbaden: Westdeutscher Verlag, 2001).

which the participle means the "present" year or the "present" month (cf. the old-fashioned English "inst."):[30]

> "*On the 12th of the present month* (τῆι ιβ τοῦ ἐνεστῶτος μηνός), Nicarchus, a member of the harbour residents, deliberately started a fight in the street." (*P.Polit.Jud.* 1,5-11; 135 BCE)
>
> "*In the present year* (ἐν τῶι ἐνεστῶτι ἔτει), I was betrothed to Nicaea, the daughter of Lysimachus..." (*P.Polit.Jud.* 4,5-7; 134 BCE)

Since these are all reports of past incidents, it is clear enough that these first two instances, with perfect participles, are referring to the present month and year respectively. This is an entirely standard usage, noted in all substantial dictionaries.

From the Babatha archive, *P.Yadin* 1.22 (11 Sept. 130 CE) deals with the sale or lease of the date-palm crop of the current year (line 12: εἰς τὸ ἐνεστῶτος ἔτους) from three orchards near Maoza.[31] The year is the 14th year of Hadrian's principate. Scholars agree that the reference is to the "current year" rather than that following;[32] Radzyner comments: "the contract was dated just before harvest time, usually around September-October-November".[33] Another manuscript from the Babatha archive refers to something happening τῇ ἐνεσ[τ]ώσῃ ἡμ[έρ̣α̣]; there is no illuminating context but it is clearly an instance of the general usage.[34]

There are many other instances of the calendrical formula in papyri which are Jewish or which relate to Jews. These can simply be presented in list form:[35]

> *C.Pap.Jud.* 1.131,2 = *P.Tebt.* 3.1.730 (178 or 167 BCE): "*On the 5th of the present month* (τῆι ε τοῦ ἐνεστῶτος μη(νός)) when patrolling the fields I found an effusion of blood."

[30] Abbreviations for papyri follow those in the "Checklist of Editions of Greek, Latin, Demotic, and Coptic Papyri, Ostraca, and Tablets" at https://papyri.info/docs/checklist.

[31] On the difficulty of determining the nature of the financial transaction, see Amihai Radzyner, "P.Yadin 21–22: Sale or Lease?", in Ranon Katzoff & David Schaps, eds. *Law in the Documents of the Judaean Desert* (Leiden: Brill, 2005), 145-164, where intermediate stages between sales and leases are also discussed.

[32] Dorota Hartman, *Archivio di Babatha I* (Brescia: Paideia, 2016), 126 ("questo anno"); Michael Zellmann-Rohrer, "A Trilingual Sales Contract on Papyrus from Roman Arabia (P.Yadin I 22)", *Manuscript and Text Cultures* 2.1 (2023). https://mtc-journal.org/index.php/mtc/article/view/25

[33] Radzyner, "P.Yadin 21–22: Sale or Lease?", 148.

[34] *P.Yadin* 24 frr. b-c, line 13; cf. *P.Yadin* 24 fr. a, line 2.

[35] Translations here are from the *Corpus Papyrorum Judaicarum* volumes I-V. Tcherikover, the editor of *C.Pap.Jud.* 3.473,12 (*P.Oxy.* 9.1205), supplies [τῆς ἐνεστώσης ἡμέρας] in the restoration of a lacuna.

C.Pap.Jud. 2.143,10 = *BGU* 4.1151 (13 BCE): "the 100 drachmai which he owes (?) 17 months *from the present month Pharmouthi* (ἀπὸ [.] τοῦ ἐνε(στῶτος) μη(νὸς) Φαρμ(οῦθι))"

C.Pap.Jud. 2.144,30 = *BGU* 4.1102 (13 BCE): "... or from any other matter arising *up to the present day* (ἕως τῆς ἐν[ε]στώσης ἡ[μ]έρας)"

C.Pap.Jud. 2.145,6 = *BGU* 4.1129 (13 BCE): "Since an agreement validated by the same court *in the present 17th year of* Caesar (τῶι ἐνε(στῶτι) ιζ (ἔτει) Καίσαρος)..."

C.Pap.Jud. 2.146,9 = *BGU* 4.1106 (13 BCE): "With regard to this matter, Theodote agrees that she will for 18 months *from Phamenoth of the present 17th year of Caesar* ([ἀπὸ Φα]μενὼθ τοῦ ἐνεστῶτος ιζ (ἔτους) Καί[σαρος]) bring up and suckle in her own house in the city with her own milk pure and uncontaminated the foundling..."

C.Pap.Jud. 2.147,6 = *BGU* 4.1153 (14 BCE): "... nor on the basis of any other agreement, written or unwritten, made from that time *to the present day* ([μέχρι] τῆ(ς) ἐνε(στώσης) ἡμέρα(ς))."

C.Pap.Jud.2.148,7 = *BGU* 4.1155 (10 BCE): "Whereas Apollonios presented to the archidikastes Artemidoros *in the present 20th year of Caesar* (τῷ ἐνεστῶτι κ (ἔτει) Καίσα[ρ]ος) in the month Hathyr a petition..."

C.Pap.Jud. 2.148,31-32 (*ibid.*): "nor to any other loan or demand whatsoever, written or unwritten, arising from that time *to the present day* ([μέχρι τῆς ἐνεσ]τώσης ἡμ[έρας]). . ."

C.Pap.Jud. 2.411,14 = *SB* 4.7341 (3 CE): "And the borrower shall repay this loan, six artabai of barley, to Herakles or his representatives in the month Payni *of the present thirty-third year of Caesar* (τοῦ ἐνεστῶτος τρίτου καὶ τριακοστοῦ ἔτους Καίσαρος)..."

C.Pap.Jud. 2.411,37 (ibid.): "I shall repay these in the month Payni *of the present thirty-third year of Caesar* ([τ]οῦ ἐνεστῶτος τρίτου καὶ {καὶ} τριακοστοῦ ἔτους Καίσαρος), as has been written above."

C.Pap.Jud. 2.417,12 = *P.Hamb.* 1.2 (59 CE): "600 drachmai, which we will repay to you before the thirtieth of Tybi *of the present sixth year of Nero Claudius Caesar Augustus Germanicus the Emperor* (τοῦ ἐνεστῶ[το]ς ἕκτου ἔτους Νέρωνος Κλαυ[δί]ου Καίσαρος Σεβαστοῦ [Γε]ρμανικοῦ Αὐτοκράτορος), without interest..."

C.Pap.Jud. 2.420a,4 = *P.Ryl.* 2.166 (26 CE): "I desire to lease for 6 years *from the present 13th year of Tiberius Caesar Augustus* (ἀπὸ τοῦ ἐνεστῶτος τ[ρ]ισκαιδεκάτου ἔτους Τιβέριου Καίσαρος Σεβαστοῦ) of the lands... "

C.Pap.Jud. 2.420b,9 = *P.Ryl.* 2.126 (28-29 CE): "*In the present month* (τῶι [ἐ] νεστῶτι μηνί) ... of the 15th year of Tiberius Caesar Augustus..."

C.Pap.Jud. 2.427,9-10 = *BGU* 4.1068 (101 CE): "Iosepos died *in the month of Tybi of the present fourth year of our lord Trajan Caesar* (τῷ Τῦβι μηνὶ τοῦ ἐνεστῶτος τετάρτου ἔτους Τραιανοῦ Καίσαρος τ[ο]ῦ κυρίου)."

C.Pap.Jud. 2.430,14 = *P.Lond.* 3.1119a (105 CE): "And so I make my return *in the present 8th year of our lord Trajan Caesar* ([ἐν] τῶι ἐνεστῶτι η (ἔτει) Τραιανοῦ [Καίσαρος τοῦ κυρίου])."

C.Pap.Jud. 2.432 col. I, 14 = *P.Lond.* 3.1177 (113 CE): "Account of receipts and expenditures on the water-supply *from Pachon of the past 16th year of the Emperor and Lord Trajan Caesar till Phaophi 30 of the current 17th year* (ἀπὸ Παχὼν τοῦ διεληλυθότος ις (ἔτους) Τραιανο[ῦ] Καίσαρος τοῦ κυρίου ἕως Φαῶφι λ του ἐνεστῶτο(ς) ιζ (ἔτους))."

C.Pap.Jud. 3.453,5 = *P.Würzb.* 1.14 (132 CE): "We wish of our own free will to lease from you, for two years *from the present 17th year of Hadrianus Caesar the lord* (ἀπὸ το[ῦ] ἐνεστῶτος ιζ (ἔτους) Ἁδριανοῦ Καίσαρος τοῦ κυρίου), the thirteen fixed arourai ..."

C.Pap.Jud. 3.471 col. I, 6 = *BGU* 2.585 (iii CE): "... those who pay us from their produce in the month of Pachon *of the present year* (τοῦ ἐνοστῶτος (*sic*) ἔ[το]υς)"

C.Pap.Jud. 3.482,4-5 = *P.Oxy.* 2.353 (27/28 CE): "I declare, *for the present 13th year of Tiberius Caesar Augustus* (εἰς τὸ ἐνεστὸς ιγ (ἔτος) Τιβερίου Καίσαρος Σεβαστοῦ), the thirty sheep, two goats in my possession..."

C.Pap.Jud. 3.483,4 = *BGU* 3.854 (45 CE): "And I have forthwith received, in cash on the spot, the whole agreed price in full, and I will guarantee the transaction with every form of guarantee *from the present day* ([ἀπὸ τῆς] ἐνεσ[τώ]σ[ης ἡμ]έλας (*sic*)) for all time..."

C.Pap.Jud. 3.487,9-10 = *SB* 4.7359 (112 CE): "Pakysis died in the month Hathyr *of the present 15th year of Imperator Caesar Nerva Traianus Augustus Germanicus Dacicus* (τοῦ ἐνεστῶτος ιε (ἔτους) Αὐτοκράτορος Καίσαρος Νερούας Τραιανοῦ Σεβαστοῦ Γερμανικοῦ Δακικοῦ."

C.Pap.Jud. 3.517,6 = *P.Ant.* 2.89 (early iv): "We wish of our own free will and choice to lease from you *for the present year only* (πρὸς μ[όνον τ]ὸ ἐνεστὸς ἔτος) of the twelfth happy indiction the arourai..."

C.Pap.Jud. 3.518a,14 (65 CE): "Charixeinos... leased... one aroura of vineyard... *from the present twelfth year of Nero Claudius Caesar Augustus Germanicus* (ἀπὸ τοῦ ἐνεστῶτος δωδεκάτου ἔτους Νέρωνος Κλαυδίου Καίσαρος Σεβαστοῦ Γερμανικοῦ)..."

C.Pap.Jud. 4.583,2-11 = *BGU* 20.2847 (49 BCE): "*On the 27th of the current month of Epeiph, which was a day before Sabbath* (τῆι κζ τοῦ ἐνεστῶτος μηνὸς Ἐπειφ, ἥ ἐστιν προσάμβατον), we came [...] few so that [...] beating us [...] and on the field [they made] an attack."

C.Pap.Jud. 5.640,4-9 = *P.IFAO* 3.43 (20/21 CE): "I declare, *for the present 7th year of Tiberius Caesar Augustus* (εἰς τὸ ἐνεστὸς ζ (ἔτους) Τιβερίου Καίσαρος Σεβαστοῦ) sheep and cattle, twenty-five ..."

C.Pap.Jud. 5.649,7-10 = *SB* 16.13012 (42 CE): "We wish to rent... the olive fruits which have ripened *in the present 3rd year of Tiberius Claudius*

Caesar Augustus Germanicus Imperator (εἰς τὸ ἐνεστὸς γ (ἔτος) Τιβερίου Κλαυδίου Καίσαρος Σεβασ[τοῦ Γ]ερμανικοῦ Αὐτοκράτορος)."

C.Pap.Jud. 5.670,10-13 = *P.Köln* 2.97 (119-120, 140-141 or 163-164 CE): "*Tybi of the present 4th year* (Τῦβι τοῦ ἐνεστῶτος δ (ἔτους)) ... total: 5442 drachmai 2 chalkoi..."

The usage in Jewish documentary papyri, then, is consistent: in the common calendrical use, the perfect participle of ἐνίστημι has a present sense. We will see this also in the legal context of *P.Polit.Jud.* 6, discussed in §2.4 below.

1.7 Conclusion on §1

On the basis of the dozens of examples discussed or noted here (83x in the perf.), there is consistency in a present reference in cases of the perfect tense of ἐνίστημι. In addition to the perfect examples, we have also discussed some cases, especially those alleged by Conzelmann and Fitzmyer, where ἐνίστημι in another tense in the corpora above are taken as meaning "be imminent"; these have also been found unconvincing. Given the quantity of references to the perfect tense of ἐνίστημι meaning "be present" or "to have come", there is a strong *prima facie* case for this being the meaning in cases where temporality is to the fore, rather than any of these examples giving evidence for a reference to the immediate future.

With this *prima facie* case made, we can proceed to examine other examples cited in lexica where this sense has been alleged.

2. A Critical Analysis of "Imminent" Ἐνίστημι in Lexica

This section does not attempt any comprehensive coverage of uses of ἐνίστημι, but focuses on examples adduced in dictionaries as evidence for glosses like "be imminent" or "be impending". It is also chronologically selective, with a recentist bias towards those dictionaries currently most influential, and with some notes initially also on the earliest definitions of ἐνίστημι.

2.1 Beginnings: The Fifteenth and Sixteenth Centuries

The background to much Greek lexicography lies in the Vulgate, where the most common "translational equivalent" for ἐνίστημι is *insto.*[36]

[36] See 1 Esdr. 5.47; 1 Macc. 8.24, Rom. 8.38; 1 Cor. 7.26; 2 Thess. 2.2; 2 Tim. 3.1; Heb. 9.9. 1 Macc. 12.44 has *sum*; 2 Macc. 4.43 has *coepi*; 1 Cor. 3.22 and Gal. 1.4 have *praesum*/ *praesens*.

In some ways this is an unsurprising choice because *in-sto* obviously functions as a calque of ἐν-ίστημι. It is no surprise, then, that the first printed Greek-Latin dictionary, Crastonus's *Lexicon* (1478), provides *insto* as its gloss for ἐνίστημι.[37] Similarly, the Greek vocabulary list of the Complutensian Polyglot (1514) gives the following glosses for some of the verb's various inflections:[38]

> ἐνέστηκα. *institi. instavi*
> ἐνεστηκώς. οτος. ὁ. *postq(ua)m instauit. institit.*
> ἐνεστώς. τος. ὁ. *praesens.*
> ...
> ἐνίσταμαι. μ. ησομαι. π. μαι. *insurgo*
> ἐνίστημι. μ. ησω. π. ηκα. *insto. as*

One difficulty raised by the Vulgate's rendering, however, is that the lexicography of *insto* is far from simple, given its ambiguities.[39]

An important development in lexicography was the provision of illustrative parallels, which we see in Budé's *Commentarii Graecae Linguae* (1st ed., 1528-29).[40] In one part, Budé renders ἐνίστημι with another gloss which will become influential: *immineo.*[41] (This word also has some complexity to it.[42]) He cites as an illustration Plutarch, *Lucullus* 13.1:

> "Having done this, Lucullus hastened in his pursuit of the king. He was hoping to find Mithridates still in Bithynia guarded by Voconius whom he had sent to Nicomedia with a fleet of ships *in order to intercept his flight* (ἐνστησόμενον τῇ φυγῇ)."

[37] Johannes Crastonus, *Lexicon Graeco-Latinum* (Milan: Bonus Accursius, ca. 1478), no page.

[38] *Nouum testamentum grece et latine in academia complutensi nouiter impressum*, vol. 5 of the Complutensian Polyglot (Complutense University in Alcalá, 1517), no page. On this word-list, see most recently John A.L. Lee, "Bartolomé de Castro, the Author of the Complutensian Lexicon of the New Testament", *FilNeot* 36 (2023), 65-93.

[39] See P.G.W. Glare, ed. *Oxford Latin Dictionary* (Oxford: Clarendon, 1982), 930.

[40] Guillaume Budé, *Commentarii lingvae Graecae, Gvlielmo Bvdeao, consiliario Regio, svpplicvmqve libellorvm in Regia magistro, avctore* (Paris: Venundantur Iodoco Badio Ascensio, 1529).

[41] Budé, *Commentarii lingvae Graecae*, 94.

[42] See *OLD*, p. 835: e.g. "**4** (of pursuers, attackers, etc.) To press closely on, be almost on. **b** (of soldiers in ambush, etc.) to be ready to fall (on); (of other mil. forces) to be in a threatening position" to threaten (cf. *mineo*), or "**5** to be a threat or menace to" or "**6** (of dangers, unpleasant events or conditions, etc.) To impend, threaten, be imminent. **b** (w. little or no idea of menace) to be close at hand."

The current edition of LSJ uses the Plutarch passage to illustrate ἐνίστημι B IV.1: "stand in the way, resist, block". But the key point here is that Budé starts the tradition of glossing ἐνίστημι with *immineo*. Budé became very influential because his work formed the basis of Stephanus' *Thesaurus Graecae Linguae* (first edition, 1572).[43]

Budé adds, as a different sub-entry, a legal sense of the perfect of ἐνίστασθαι, meaning "*Lis contestata est*" ("a law-suit has been issued for a legal decision"), illustrated by two examples:[44]

> "On my side, the estate left by Hagnias is not yet secured to me; *for trials for perjury are still pending/ have been instituted* (δίκαι γὰρ ἐνεστήκασι ψευδομαρτυρίων), and the law ordains that, if there is any conviction for perjury, the action claiming an estate must be heard over again." (Isaeus, *On Hagnias's Legacy* [*Or.* 11] 45)

> "Well, our opponent says that Archiades had no son of the body, but in the affidavit he has sworn to the words 'since there are lawfully born children,' thus making a sworn statement that is contrary to the truth. He admits that he is an adopted son, yet it is manifest that he was not adopted by the dead man himself; so how can you claim that this status is 'rightfully established according to the statute'? Because, he will say, he was registered as the son of Archiades. Yes, by the arbitrary act of these men, and that only the other day, *when the suit for the estate had already been instituted/ was already pending* (ἤδη τῆς τοῦ κλήρου διαδικασίας ἐνεστηκυίας). Surely it is not right for a man to regard as evidence his own illegal act." (Demosthenes, *Against Leochares* [*Or.* 44] 49-50)

I have cited these examples at some length because the possible gloss "be pending" (cf. "be imminent") will be important later.[45]

2.2 Nineteenth-Century Lexica

For those accustomed to using Liddell & Scott, it is surprising that many dictionaries do not provide any illustrative quotations from Greek authors. The first nineteenth-century lexicon I have seen providing some fresh parallels is Schleusner (1814). Schleusner states that the perfect of

[43] Henricus Stephanus, *Thesaurus Graecae Linguae* (France: Stephanus, 1572), col. 1758.

[44] Budé, *Commentarii lingvae Graecae*, 93.

[45] K.J. Dover, *Aristophanes, Clouds* (Oxford: Clarendon, 1968), 195 gives Isaeus 11.45 as an example of this sense.

ἐνίστημι is used "et de *tempore praesente* et *futuro* ac *imminente*, monente Hesychio", and he then lists 1 Macc. 12.44; 2 Macc. 3.17; Pindar, *Olymp.* 9.8; Sextus Empiricus, *Phys.* 2.193, and Josephus, *Ant.* 16.6.2 as illustrations. Here we encounter a difficulty which arises elsewhere: when providing parallels Schleusner does not specify which meaning he thinks applies in each case. The Jewish examples, from 1 and 2 Maccabees, we have already examined in §1 above. The instance from Sextus Empiricus is about the present (διαιρεῖται εἴς τε τὸν παρῳχημένον καὶ τὸν ἐνεστῶτα καὶ εἰς τὸν μέλλοντα), resembling Philo's statements distinguishing past, present and future time. The others are curious. There is no instance of ἐνίστημι in *Olympian Odes* 9.8, or indeed anywhere in Pindar at all.[46] As for "monente Hesychio", none of Hesychius's glosses suggest such an ambiguity according to the most recent editions of the text.[47]

Shortly after Schleusner, the *Thesaurus Graecae Linguae* was republished (1816-), first as an *editio nova auctior et emendatior*, though it is not *auctior* as far as ἐνίστημι is concerned. The subsequent edition of Hase and Dindorf, however (vol. 4 on *epsilon* published in 1829), does add two parallels from Polybius and Aesop to illustrate ἐνίστημι in the sense of "*immineo*".[48] Both, however, are in the present tense:

> "The members of the Senate... thinking it was profitable – indeed, necessary – not to ignore the Spanish problem but *to resist the Carthaginians* (ἐνίστασθαι τοῖς Καρχηδονίοις) and step up the war effort...". (Polybius, 3.97.1)

> "Now when mistletoe was growing, a swallow saw *danger beginning for the birds* (τὸν ἐνιστάμενον τοῖς πτηνοῖς κίνδυνον) and assembled them all and advised them to cut off the oaks bearing mistletoe – or if this proved impossible, to flee to the humans and beg them not to use the application of the mistletoe and catch them." (Aesop 39a[49])

In the former, the meaning is probably sense "IV" in LSJ: "resist", "block" (cf. Plutarch, *Lucullus* above). In the Aesop case, we have ἐνίστημι

[46] Neither Rumpel's *Lexicon Pindaricum* nor the *Dammii Lexicon Pindaricum*, nor William J. Slater's *Lexicon to Pindar*, attest the use of ἐνίστημι.

[47] See Kurt Latte, ed. *Hesychii Alexandrini Lexicon*, vol. 2: Ε - Ο (Hauniae: E. Munksgaard, 1953), 97, 102; Ian Cunningham, ed. *Hesychii Alexandrini Lexicon*, vol. 2: Ε - Ο (Berlin: De Gruyter, 2020), 122, 129.

[48] Karl Hase, Wilhelm Dindorf & Ludwig Dindorf, ed. *Thesaurus Graecae linguae ab Henrico Stephano constructus* (Graz: Akademische Druck - U. Verlagsanstalt, 1954 [1829]), 1106.

[49] A. Hausrath & H. Hunger, *Corpus fabularum Aesopicarum*, vol. 1.1 (Berlin: De Gruyter, ²1970), 54.

in the sense of "begin" (LSJ I A 3). Neither of these passages in Polybius or Aesop, then, provides a good parallel for ἐνίστημι in the perfect.

A surge of new information comes in the 1840s, with the first edition of Liddell & Scott, and the new editions of Passow. Liddell & Scott and Passow add parallels to Budé's examples of legal usage. We can begin with Passow's examples:

> "Was it not you and your ancestors who made no allowance for Timotheus, though he had sailed round the Peloponnese and beaten the Spartans in the sea-fight at Corcyra? ... You did not take this record into consideration at all, or allow such services to outweigh *the case before you at that time* (τῆς τότε ἐνεστώσης κρίσεως) or the oaths which you swear before giving your verdict, but fined him a hundred talents, because Aristophon said he had been bribed by the Chians and Rhodians." (Dinarchus, *Against Philocles* 17; tr. LCL adapted)

> "You should consider all public trials to be significant, but particularly this one in which you are now about to vote. For when you adjudicate on proposals contrary to law, you merely set right that case alone and you prevent single error, and in preventing the intended measure your scope depends upon the extent to which the decree in question will harm the city. *But the present case* (ὁ δὲ νῦν ἐνεστηκὼς ἀγών) deals with no mere particle of the city's affairs, nor with only ephemera, but with our ancestral city in its entirety..." (Lycurgus, *Leocrat.* 7; tr. LCL)

These examples are significant precisely because they raise significant problems for the "pending" gloss. In the former, Dinarchus reminds the Athenian jury that they did not take Timotheus's merits into account in the case *at that time before them*, but found him guilty. In the latter example, the trial is *in progress*, and Lycurgus is urging the jury who are just about to vote.

Liddell & Scott's examples from Aristophanes' *Clouds* and from Aeschines may be more promising. In the Aristophanes example, Socrates challenges Strepsiades to consider how to avoid a lawsuit he was going to lose; the latter gives his ingenious reply:

> "This is what I'd do. *If there was still one case instituted beforehand, in advance of mine being called* (εἰ πρόσθεν ἔτι μιᾶς ἐνεστώσης δίκης πρὶν τὴν ἐμὴν καλεῖσθ'), I could run off and hang myself!" (Aristophanes, *Clouds* 779).

Despite this being used as an example of the sense "pending" or "left on the docket",[50] it may well be that we have the same meaning as in the previous two examples. Could Strepsiades not run off and hang himself while the case previous to his own *was in process*? This appears likely, given the following example.

Assuming that "Aeschin.35.27" in the earlier editions of Liddell & Scott corresponds to the Aeschines 2.58 cited in later editions, it is no more help to the "pending" view:

> "For in the public archives you have the record of the dates when you chose the several embassies which you sent out into Hellas, *when the war between you and Philip was still in progress* (ἔτι τοῦ πολέμου τοῦ πρὸς Φίλιππον ὑμῖν ἐνεστηκότος), and also the names of the ambassadors; and the men themselves are not in Macedonia, but here in Athens." (Aeschines, *On the Embassy* 58; tr. LCL)

Here the sense is of a war under way, as is clear from the ἔτι. The Brill Dictionary glosses ἔτι τοῦ πολέμου ... ὑμῖν ἐνεστηκότος correctly here as "while the war was still going on for you".

The first edition of Liddell & Scott was also the earliest lexicon, to my knowledge, to introduce epigraphic evidence, citing "*impending, immediate, instant, present,* μεἰς Böckh Inscr. 2, p. 476", i.e. a reference to ὁ ἐνεστὼς μείς in *I. Mylasa* 87 / *CIG* 2693c/e, line 12 (ii-i BCE). Böckh, in a complex reconstruction of the timings of events in the inscription, interprets ἐνεστώς here as meaning "proximus instans s(eu) insequens", i.e. "immediately impending or following on". However, subsequent scholarship took issue with Böckh's reconstruction of the scenario in the inscription, partly a result of a faulty transcription earlier in the text.[51] Later editions of Liddell & Scott dropped the reference to this inscrip-

[50] Wilhelm Pape, *Handwörterbuch der griechischen sprache* (Braunschweig, F. Vieweg & Sohn, 1849), 741 ("anhängig"); Dover, *Aristophanes, Clouds*, 195: "779 ἐνεστώσης: 'Still to be heard', 'pending'; a technical term. Cf. Is(aeus) xi. 45 δίκαι ἐνεστήκασι ψευδομαρτυριῶν." The Loeb translation has for εἰ πρόσθεν ἔτι μιᾶς ἐνεστώσης δίκης πρὶν τὴν ἐμὴν καλεῖσθ' the English "If only one case was left on the docket before mine was called...". Similarly, S. Douglas Olson, *Aristophanes' Clouds: A Commentary* (Ann Arbor: University of Michigan Press, 2021), 164: "here used as a technical term – 'be on the docket', 'be pending'", referring to the Demosthenes parallel (and also commenting that in the same place καλέω is used in a technical sense). For the Demosthenes passage, cf. Charles Rann Kennedy, tr. *The Orations of Demosthenes* (London: George Bell, 1877), 163: "While both their actions were pending...".

[51] Marcel Dubois & Amédée Hauvette-Besnault, "Antiquités de Mylasa", *Bulletin de Correspondance Hellénique* 5 (1881), 95-119 (117): "cette faute de texte, corrigée, comme beaucoup d'autres, par M. Waddington, explique aisément la difficulté que Boeckh éprouvait à concilier les dates inscrites dans le contrat."

tion,[52] and the *DGE* cites it to illustrate the present sense.[53] This is not surprising, given that – as we saw in §1.6 above – ἐνεστώς etc. are used very frequently to refer to the present year, the present month or the present day. As Preisigke says, for this sense there are "Belege überall".[54]

The second edition of Liddell & Scott introduced another parallel which has endured, from Herodotus:

> "*All this had befallen the Spartans* (τοιούτων δὲ τοῖσι Σπαρτιήτῃσι ἐνεστεώτων πρηγμάτων) when the Sardian herald came to entreat their help for Croesus, now besieged." (Herodotus 1.83; LCL)

The immediate context is that the Spartans were engaged in a feud with the Argives, and the last survivor of the 300 Spartans who had fought the initial battle against them had killed himself; many Spartans also died in the subsequent battle as well (1.82). Hence *Hist.* 1.83 begins: "When these things had happened to the Spartans...". Here the idea is not "threaten" or "impend": the tragedies had already taken place (Loeb: "had befallen").

More important introductions from Passow are two historical passages. The first, from Polybius (ii BCE), concerns the Carthaginian troubles in their civil war with the Libyan rebels:

> "For they (the Carthaginians) had been much worn by the long continued war for Sicily, and had hoped that the peace would procure them some rest and a grateful period of tranquillity, but what happened was just the reverse, *as they were now threatened by the outbreak of a greater and more formidable war* (μείζονος γὰρ ἐνίστατο πολέμου καταρχὴ καὶ φοβερωτέρου)." (Polybius 1.71.3-4; tr. LCL)

This passage has long been understood as providing evidence for the meaning "be imminent". Passow gives it as an instance where ἐνίστημι could be glossed as "bevorstehen, drohen, imminere", and it is similarly cited by the Brill Dictionary with the sense of "threaten". However, while "drohen" / "threaten" might be legitimate glosses, the threat is not something in the future: the καταρχή of the war is not projected in the imminent future, because the Libyans had already revolted, laying siege to the loyal Carthaginians cities of Utica and Hippou Acra (1.70.9). ἐνίστατο ...

[52] It survives in the 1873 edition, but is gone by 1883.

[53] http://dge.cchs.csic.es/xdge/ἐνίστημι.

[54] Friedrich Preisigke, *Wörterbuch der griechische Papyrusurkunden mit Einschluss der griechischen Inschriften, Aufschriften, Ostraka, Mumienschilder usw. aus Ägypten*, vol. 1: E–K (Berlin: Self-published by Preisigke's heirs, 1925), 800.

καταρχή does not itself refer to future danger but to the present outbreak of war.[55] ἐνίστατο is also in the present tense.

Still under the heading of "bevorstehen, drohen, *imminere*", Passow provides another, potentially more promising, instance from Dionysius of Halicarnassus (i BCE):

> "But we have decided for many reasons to take a moderate view towards them [sc. the families in the cities which Rome had conquered], *both because we fear the retribution of the gods, which threatens/opposes all the proud* (θεῶν τε νέμεσιν ὑφορώμενοι τὴν ἅπασι τοῖς ὑπερόγκοις ἐνισταμένην), and because we dread the hatred of men..." (*AR* 2.35.3)

This is an example in the present tense, and so not strictly relevant to our investigation; additionally, we have here not the absolute sense of "be imminent" but a transitive usage (ἐνίστημι + dat.). To use this passage to illustrate the dictionary gloss of "be imminent" is to confuse reference and lexical meaning; rather than the "totality transfer" or importing the context of the situation into the word, *DGE*'s well-attested "llegar" (B III 1-2), or "oponerse" (B I 4) may be more appropriate.

2.3 The Twentieth Century

One of the major developments in the twentieth century was the incorporation of papyrological evidence. The later revisions of Liddell & Scott themselves (i.e. up to ⁷1890 and ⁸1897) contained only few references to papyri, and none in the definitions of ἐνίστημι.[56] In the 1920s, however, in advance of the major revision of Liddell & Scott in 1940, both Moulton & Milligan's and Preisigke's lexica based on papyrological evidence appeared. Preisigke, amidst a number of cases attesting the present sense of the perfect tense, also supplies one alleged instance with a future meaning:[57]

> *Inscribed by Peteësis the hieroglypher, about King Nectanebo:*
> "In the sixteenth year, on the 21st to the 22nd of Pharmouthi, in the divine reckoning by the full moon, Nectanebo the king was in Memphis. He carried

[55] Robinson, *A Greek and English Lexicon*, 254, also adduces Polybius, 2.28.9, for the sense "to be at hand, to impend". But cf. the Loeb translation: "*At first the battle was confined to the hill* (τὸ μὲν οὖν πρῶτον αὐτὸς ὁ κατὰ τὸν λόφον ἐνειστήκει κίνδυνος), all the armies gazing on it, so great were the numbers of cavalry from each host combating there pell-mell." The sense of ἐνίστημι here is clearly spatial, rather than temporal.

[56] Scott died in 1887 and Liddell in 1898.

[57] Preisigke, *Wörterbuch der griechische Papyrusurkunden*, 800.

out a sacrifice, and asked the gods to show him τὰ ἐνεστηκότα. In a dream he saw a boat made of papyrus..." (*UPZ* 1.81 col. I,8—col. II,6 [mid-second century BCE])

In *The Dream of Nectanebo* here, it seems natural to render τὰ ἐνεστηκότα as what is "bevorstehend" (Preisigke) or "the impending future" (Lewis) because of the visionary setting.[58] But even such an apparently clear case is not so. The dream vision reported here is not about the future, as the narrative goes on to make clear. Nectanebo sees a vision of the gods' *present* verdict of his reign: he has generally ruled well, but the temple of Onouris has been neglected. Nectanebo has been given a revelation of the divine realm and of the gods' present thoughts, but not of the future. Hence, the gods showed Nectanebo what is happening now.[59]

Later editions of LSJ also supply an example from a text edited by Preisigke:

> "On the 5th leap day of the year 31, one of us named Harmiysis was washing the linen garments of the ibis and falcon statues of the temple, when - *although we had no lawsuit instituted against them* (οὐδενὸς ἡμεῖν ἐνεστῶτος πρὸ[ς] αὐτούς)[60] - the son of Phanesis, and Siueris son of Siueris, and his son came along, beat him, and stole the linen cloths of the gods and his own linen clothes... ." (*P.Stras.* 2.91,5-17; 86 BCE)

Understandably, LSJ sees this as an example of the legal meaning of a case being pending. The formulaic language in the Greek above, as we will see below, is common in legal documents. The complainants' point is that, although Harmiysis and his companions institute a case against the miscreants later in the document, at the time there was no legal quarrel between the two parties; the assumption is presumably that violence might be expected from an accused party in the middle of a legal process (as in *BGU* 6.1244 or *P.Enteux.* 86 discussed below).

The same can be said of one of Conzelmann's proposed parallels, which comes from a well-known document announcing a census in

[58] Naphtali Lewis, *The Interpretation of Dreams & Portents in Antiquity* (Wauconda, IL: Bolchazy-Carducci, 1996), 51.

[59] Ludwig Koenen, "The Dream of Nektanebos", *BASP* 22 (1985), 171-194 (185): "King Nektanebos had a dream in a temple at Memphis. He saw Isis as she was sitting on the throne of her boat, surrounded by the gods of Egypt. Ares/Onuris, in superhuman size, stepped forward, prayed, performed his prostration, and complained about the king, because he had not completed the construction of a particular adyton in the god's temple."

[60] Cf. the non-legal rendering of Friedrich Preisigke, *Griechische Papyrus der Kaiserlichen Universitäts- und Landesbibliothek zu Strassburg 1856-1924*, vol. 2 (81-125) (Leipzig: J. C. Hinrichs, 1912), 33: "ohne daß wir den Übeltätern irgendeinen Anlaß gegeben hätten".

Egypt and that residents should return to their homes (cf. Lk. 2.1-5).[61] There is an initial attraction to seeing *P.Lond.* 3.904 as providing evidence for the "imminent" sense of ἐνίστημι in the perfect. There went out a decree from Gaius Vibius Maximus, the prefect of Egypt, as follows, according to one translation: "*As a house-to-house registration is impending* (τῆς κατ' οἰ[κίαν ἀπογραφῆς ἐ]νεστώ[σης]), it is necessary to announce to all those absent from their nomes for any cause whatsoever to return home...." (ll. 20-24).[62] Another option is possible, however: Lewis and Sherk both take the genitive absolute to mean "the house-to-house census having begun" or "since the house-to-house census has begun".[63] On this reading, the perfect refers to a previous event. Perhaps better still would be the translation in the *Ancient Roman Statutes* collection: "As a house-to-house registration has been authorized...".[64] This fits well with the possible sense "instituted" noted already for the literary examples (Isaeus, Demosthenes, Aristophanes) as well as *P.Stras.* 2.91 above, and which we will see in other examples below.[65]

Kiessling's supplement to Preisigke provides a greatly expanded entry for ἐνίστημι.[66] There persists the difficulty of illustrative citations which are provided for multiple senses. The fourth sub-entry provides the somewhat different glosses "herankommen, bevorstehen (zeitlich)". Leaving aside *UPZ* I 81.22 already discussed, and the examples translated by Kiesling as clearly illustrating the past/present sense, there are five other cases:

P.Tebt. 3.1.787 (ca 138 BCE). Here Apollonius is trying to force farmers to supply grain which was not forthcoming "given the present harvest of produce" (τῆς δὲ συν[κομιδῆς τ]ῶν γενημάτων ἐνεστηκυίας, ll. 18-19).

[61] Conzelmann, *1 Corinthians*, 132 n. 14.

[62] Tr. Allan Chester Johnson, *Roman Egypt: To the Reign of Diocletian* (Baltimore: Johns Hopkins Press, 1936), 250 (§143).

[63] Naphtali Lewis, *Life in Egypt under Roman Rule* (Oxford: Clarendon, 1983), 156, and Robert K. Sherk, *The Roman Empire: Augustus to Hadrian* (Cambridge: Cambridge University Press, 1988), 157 (§114), respectively.

[64] Allan Chester Johnson, Paul Coleman-Norton & Frank Card Bourne, *Ancient Roman Statutes* (Austin, TX: University of Austin Press, 1961), 167 (§208).

[65] Similarly also A.S. Hunt & C.C. Edgar, *Select Papyri*, vol. 2 (LCL; Cambridge, Mass; Harvard University Press, 1934), 109: "The house-to-house census having started"; Horst Braunert, *Die Binnenwanderung: Studien zur Sozialgeschichte Ägyptens in der Ptolemäer- und Kaiserzeit* (Bonn: Röhrscheid, 1964), 168: "Während der derzeitig laufenden Arbeiten zum Provinzialzensus." I am especially grateful to Peter-Arzt Grabner for his help with this document.

[66] Emil Kießling, et al. *Wörterbuch der griechischen Papyrusurkunden, mit Einschluß der griechischen Inschriften, Aufschriften, Ostraka, Mumienschilder usw. aus Ägypten. Begründet von Friedrich Preisigke* (Marburg: Selbstverlag des Verfassers, 1944-1993), IV/4:799-800. The relevant *epsilon* fascicle (IV/4) was published in 1971.

P.Tebt. 3.1.789 (ca 140 BCE). Similarly here, farmers had appealed against oppression, including the seizure of corn. The reference to "the time for sowing which had come" has the verb in the aorist and so clearly cannot have an imminent sense (τὸν καιρὸν τῆς κατασπορᾶς ἐνστάντα, l. 26).

P.Mich. 1.60 = PSI 6.619 (248 or 247 BCE). Pais is requesting permission from Zenon to repair a boat which is so old that no-one will hire it; there is, however, an opportunity now to repair it because the shipbuilders do not have work (ἐνέστηκεν γὰρ ὁ καιρὸς καὶ οἱ ναυπηγο[ὶ ἀ] σχολάζουσιν, ll. 6-7).[67]

P.Paris 64 = UPZ 1.146 (ii BCE). The anonymous author concludes his letter by asking that the recipient have consideration "given the present circumstances" (διὰ δὲ τὸν ἐνεστηκότα καιρόν, l. 39), or as Wilcken translates, "wegen der jetzigen schlimmen Zeiten".[68]

BGU 8.1756 (58 BCE). The background to this document is a vexatious litigation. The *dioiketes* informs the *strategos* that he should protect the two applicants until the end of the harvest. The two applicants have an opponent who has obtained a summons against them out of malice to remove them "when the present season is at its peak bloom" (τοῦ ἀκμαιοτάτου καιροῦ ἐνεστῶτος, l. 13), i.e. ready for harvesting. These examples illustrate well the present sense of ἐνίστημι in the perfect.

Still in the papyrological field, Bauer's Lexicon – perhaps the most influential upon New Testament scholarship – cites an illustration from the Greek Magical Papyri for the gloss "bevorstehen":[69]

> "Protect me from every fear, *from any danger which threatens me* (ἀπὸ παντὸς κινδύνου τοῦ ἐνεστῶτός μοι) *on this day, at this present hour* (ἐν τῇ σήμερον ἡμέρᾳ, ἐν τῇ ἄρτι ὥρᾳ)." (*PGM* 1.13,1045-1050).

Rather than "threaten", however, a more cautious sense like "get in the way", "intervene", "oppose" (Cambridge Lexicon **6**) or "stand in the way" (LSJ **IV**), might be appropriate, or *DGE*'s well-attested "llegar" (B III 1-2), or "oponerse" (B I 4). There is probably nothing intrinsically negative about ἐνίστημι, although of course it may have a negative referent in particular contexts.

[67] See Fik Meijer & Onno van Nijf, *Trade, Transport and Society in the Ancient World: A Sourcebook* (London: Routledge, 1992), 66 (§91): "for the opportunity has come and the boat builders are free".

[68] Ulrich Wilcken, *Urkunden der Ptolemäerzeit (ältere Funde)*, vol. 1 (Berlin: De Gruyter, 1927), 633.

[69] Bauer, *Griechisch-deutsches Wörterbuch* ([6]1988), 538.

2.4 The Twenty-First Century

Recent years have seen a series of excellent new dictionaries: the *Diccionario Griego-Español* (2009-), the *Brill Dictionary of Ancient Greek* (2015-) which is a translation of Montanari's Greek-Italian lexicon, and the *Cambridge Greek Lexicon* (2021). The latter two do not provide new parallels, but the *DGE* provides the most extensive list thus far.[70]

Several different examples are noted to illustrate the sense "estar pendiente" both in a section on general usage, and in a different part with the legal examples. To take the general first:

> **2** c. suj. abstr., fig. *estar en pie, estar pendiente, mantenerse* c. o sin dat. pers. τοιούτων τοῖσι Σπαρτιήτησι ἐνεστεώτων πρηγμάτων *siendo tales los asuntos de los que los espartanos estaban pendientes* Hdt.1.83, ἔτι ἐνέστηκεν ὃ νυνδὴ Κέβης ἔλεγε *todavía está en pie lo que Cebes decía hace un momento* Pl.*Phd*.77b, ἡ ἐνεστῶσα ἀνάγκη 1*Ep.Cor*.7.26, τὰ ἔργα τὰ ἐνεστηκότα *PPetr*.2.4.6.6 (III a.C.)

Leaving aside 1 Cor. 7.26, which is itself "pending" in this article, and the Herodotus example which has been treated above, we can note first that the Plato case is evidence for the first gloss: *estar en pie.* The *Phaedo* reference states, "what Cebes said just now still stands" (ἔτι ἐνέστηκεν, *todavía está en pie*)", i.e. stands as a problem or objection (cf. LSJ ἐνίστημι IV: "stand in the way", citing this passage).[71] It is not intended as an illustration of the gloss *estar pendiente.* The last cited Petrie papyrus is not a very helpful illustration of any particular view of ἐνίστημι, since the phrase τὰ ἔργα τὰ ἐνεστηκότα has a half-line lacuna before it and another immediately after it.[72]

The legal examples in *DGE* consist first of the known cases from Aristophanes, Isaeus, Demosthenes, Aeschines and Lycurgus. *DGE* also lists, as examples of "*estar abierto, estar en curso, estar pendiente* " which come "en cont. jur.", a number of papyri:

> "*SB* 12722.5, cf. *PAmh*.33.6 (II a.C.) en *BL* 1.1, οὐδενὸς ἡμῖν ἐνεστῶτος πρὸς αὐτοὺς *PStras*.91.21 (I a.C.), cf. *POxy*.1195.8 (II d.C.), τὰ ἐπ' αὐτῶν ἐνεστηκότα *los procesos en curso*, *PTeb*.7.7 (II a.C.), δ[ιαδι]κα[σί]ας περὶ κληρονομίας μοι ἐν[σ]τάσης Mitteis *Chr*.89.10 (II d.C.), cf. *SB* 4416.6."

[70] The *DGE* does not yet extend to every initial letter of the alphabet, but has been done for ἐνίστημι.

[71] In fact, the *Phaedo* example goes back to Pape, *Handwörterbuch*, 741.

[72] See J.P. Mahaffy, ed. *The Flinders Petrie papyri*, Part II (Dublin: Academy House, 1893), IV, 6.

Here again we have the difficulty of the two senses *estar en curso* and *estar pendiente* being combined in a single paragraph with illustrative quotations for both at the same time. In fact, whether any of them attests the sense *estar pendiente* is highly questionable. *P.Stras.* 2.91 has already been discussed above; here we treat the other *DGE* examples.

P.Tebt. 1.7 = C.Ord.Ptol. 61 (114 BCE).[73] This decree of Soter II and Cleopatra III orders that any cases against certain financial officials cannot be decided by ordinary judges: instead, "one is to send the complaints lodged against them and τὰ ἐπ᾽ αὐτῶν ἐνεστηκότα" directly to the *dioiketes* (ll. 5-8).[74] This has nothing to do with the timing of the cases being pending; the Grenfell-Hunt translation "the state of the matter concerning them" is vague but possible, because τὰ ἐνεστηκότα does often mean "the current circumstances".[75] Conversely, Lenger takes it to mean "leurs procès en cours", i.e. their ongoing trials.[76] This seems more likely in the legal context, and so the reference is to the progress of cases in a very general sense – i.e. where the legal processes have reached.

P.Amh. 2.33 (ca. 157 BCE).[77] This Amherst Papyrus records that "*we have a plea* ([ἐ]νεστηκυίας ἡμῖν καταστάσεως) *before Zopyros* (ἐπὶ [Ζω]πύρου) the epimeletes and Petearpsenesis the royal scribe... *against Tesenouphis* (πρὸς Τεσενοῦφιν)", who has been accused of various misdemeanours (περί τινων ἀδικημάτω[ν]) (ll. 6-13). In this papyrus, a minor issue is that the reading ἐνεστηκυίας is uncertain, though it is probably correct.[78] Secondly, and more importantly, the rest of the papyrus shows that the trial has clearly started, because the author of the petition is complaining that the defendant has been pleading with the help of advocates, which was unlawful.[79] Here we encounter our first

[73] Bernard P. Grenfell, Arthur S. Hunt, & J. Gilbart Smyly, eds. *The Tebtunis Papyri*, Part I (London: Frowde, 1902), 65-66.

[74] Grenfell, Hunt, & Smyly, *Tebtunis Papyri*, 65.

[75] Cf. e.g. 3 Macc. 1.16; Philo, *Legat.* 275 above; also Polybius, *Hist.* 2.26.3.

[76] Marie-Thérèse Lenger, *Corpus des Ordonnances des Ptolémées (C. Ord. Ptol.)* (Brussels: Académie royale de Belgique, 1964), 180.

[77] Bernard P. Grenfell & Arthur S. Hunt, *The Amherst Papyri*, Part II (London: Frowde, 1901), 38-41.

[78] [ἐ]νεστηκυίας is printed in Friedrich Preisigke, *Berichtigungsliste der griechischen Papyrusurkunden aus Ägypten* (Berlin: Walter de Gruyter, 1922), 1 (what *DGE* means by the reference to *BL* 1.1); Grenfell & Hunt give [σ]υνεστηκυίας in *Amherst Papyri*, Part II, 39. The *upsilon* is not secure, as Plate IX printed in the Grenfell & Hunt edition shows.

[79] Grenfell & Hunt, *Amherst Papyri*, Part II, 40: "A trial *has been* arranged before Zopyrus the *epimeletes* and Petearpsenesis the royal scribe, there being also on the bench the *chrematistae* who judge cases concerning the Crown, the revenues or private affairs in the aforesaid nome and whose clerk is Dexios, in which we accuse Tesenouphis the ex-komarch of the aforesaid village by written declarations previously handed in to them of certain misdeeds and peculations of both corn and money. *Just as our side is already coming into court we hear* that the defendant Tesenouphis is pleading with the assistance of advocates,

instance of what we will see is an established legal formula, in a fairly complete form:

> naming of the suit: e.g. κατάστασις, διαδικασία, ἀμφισβήτησις, etc. +
> use of perf. (usually ptcp.) ἐνίστασθαι +
> complainant: pronoun or proper noun in the dative +
> opponent: πρός + proper noun in the accusative +
> the presiding judge: ἐπί + name in the genitive +
> the subject matter of the suit: περί + genitive

In this particular instance, the formula indicates that the case about Tesenouphis's financial misdemeanours is in progress, but has been interrupted by this plea accusing Tesenouphis of legal impropriety in the case as well.

SB.1.4416 (ca. 157/ 158-159 CE).[80] This plea to Theodoros contains a variation on this formula. The document is a complaint of land-superintendants against two assistants of the overseers, who had made inaccurate reports.[81] Here Ptolemaios and Harpalos *inter alios* lodge the complaint: "*We have a claim against* (ἐνεστώσης ἡμεῖν ἀμφισβητήσεως πρός) Herakles and Herodes..." (ll. 6-8) because of their false declarations about the harvest.[82] This is not a reference to a trial pending or current, but about a claim being initially lodged, which Ptolemaios and Harpalos hope will be resolved by a judge: "For this reason we request that a copy of this indictment be given to them by one of your aides that they may have a written copy of it and may appear before his most sacred tribunal whenever he holds his circuit court in the nome and dispenses justice."[83]

Chrest.Mitt. 89 = BGU 2.613 (161 CE?).[84] This plea comes before the same Theodoros as in *SB* I 4416 just discussed. It contains another

although your ancestors ordained by the decree appended that advocates who take up revenue cases to the detriment of the revenues should have to pay to the Crown twice the sum (of the damage) increased by one tenth and should not be allowed to be advocates any longer. We entreat you, the great gods, if it please you, to send this our petition to the aforesaid chrematistae in order that when the examination of petitions is held they may give instructions to Tesenouphis forbidding him to appear in court with the help of an advocate. For if this is done your interests will not suffer damage. Farewell."

[80] Friedrich Preisigke, ed. *Sammelbuch Griechischer Urkunden aus Ägypten*, vol. I (Strassburg: K.J. Trübner, 1915), 347.

[81] Edgar J. Goodspeed, "A Group of Greek Papyrus Texts", *Classical Philology* 1 (1906), 167-175 (170-171).

[82] Tr. Johnson, *Roman Egypt*, 138-139: "Since a dispute has arisen between us and Heracles and Herodes...".

[83] Tr. Johnson, *Roman Egypt*, 139.

[84] 89.14, not 89.10 as in *DGE*. Ludwig Mitteis & Ulrich Wilcken, eds. *Grundzüge und Chrestomathie der Papyruskunde* (Hildesheim: G. Olms, 1963 [1912]), 100-103.

variant of the formula, this time specifying the process as a διαδικασία. Here Tiberinus is contesting an inheritance, and states: "*when a hearing about my inheritance had been instituted by me* (δ[ιαδι]κα[σί]ας περὶ κληρονομίας μοι ἐν[σ]τάσης), I brought it before Theodoros..." (ll. 14-15). Here we have an instance of the formula with the aorist, so the focus is on the event that has brought the suit about.

SB 16.12722 (ca. 143/142 BCE).[85] In this text, the official Pankrates states that he is sending a copy of the petition lodged with him from a certain Ptolemaios; the petition is περὶ ὧν προφέρεται ἐνεστάναι αὑτῶι πρὸς Πετοσίριν (ll. 5-6).[86] Casanova takes this phrase to mean "riguardo alla causa che dichiara di avere contro Petosiris", i.e. about the case which he claims to have against Petosiris.[87] This appears to be an elliptical version of the formula noted above, with ἐνίστασθαι + [Person A (dat.)] + πρός + Person B (acc.) but without a particular noun. The document harks back to when Ptolemy first lodged the complaint.

P.Oxy. 9.1195 (135 CE).[88] Here Hermaios also called Anoubion promises to come to court the following day, "*in explanation of my case against Hermaios* (ἐκβιβάζων τὰ ἐνεστῶτ[ά μοι π]ρὸς Ἑρμ[α]ῖον, ll. 8-9)". Here again we have ἐνίστασθαι + Person A (dat.) + πρός + Person B (acc.) in the elliptical form, without a particular noun. Evidently, the formula is so stereotyped that in documents such as *SB* 16.12722 and *P.Oxy.* 9.1195, phrases like τὰ ἐνεστῶτα can on their own refer to a case in progress.

The same formula can be seen in other papyri as well. I provide them, to avoid prejudice, in the standard translations:

> *P.Polit.Jud. 6 = C.Pap.Jud. 4.562* (134 BCE). In the archive of the Jewish community in Herakleopolis from the second century BCE already noted in §1.6 above, I mentioned a special case where a papyrus does not follow a merely calendrical convention. It too is an instance of ἐνίστημι in the perfect: ἐνέστηκεν ἐμοί τε καὶ τοῖς ὀρφανοῖς ἐφ᾽ ὑμῶν κατάστασις πρὸς Τιμόθεον (ll. 5-7). Cowey & Maresch translate: "Es hat vor Euch stattgefunden mir und

[85] Gerardo Casanova, "Lettera d'ufficio", *Aegyptus* 63 (1983), 24-27, part of O. Montevecchi et al., "Papiri documentari dell'Università Cattolica di Milano", *Aegyptus* 63 (1983), 3-102.

[86] "Pankrates to Petesouchos, greetings. We have sent you a copy of the *hypomnema* lodged with us by Ptolemaios son of Ptolemaios [...], one of the residents of Oxyrhynchus in the district of Polemon, *concerning the case he claims to have against Petosiris* (Casanova: *riguardo alla causa che dichiara di avere contro Petosiris*) a.k.a. Dionysios the former *komogrammateus* of the same village."

[87] Casanova, "Lettera d'ufficio", 27.

[88] Arthur S. Hunt, *The Oxyrhynchus Papyri*, Part IX (London: Egypt Exploration Fund, 1912), 216.

den Waisen eine Verhandlung gegen Timotheos ..."[89] In the *Corpus Papyrorum Judaicarum* edition, Kugler translates: "You had before you a pleading by me and the orphans against Timotheos....".[90] These scholars therefore understand the trial as having already taken place. This is not a conventional sense of the formula, but the legal situation here is unclear, because of a lacuna at a key point.[91] What is absolutely clear is that the sense cannot be of a trial pending. The complainant Theodotos, a Jew, is petitioning for the case to be reopened, perhaps after it was dismissed at the first hearing when Timotheos had subverted the process in some way, or alternatively after the trial.

BGU 6.1244 (225 BCE). "I had a trial (ἐνεστηκυίας [μ]οι κρίσεως) *against Pasis* (πρ[ὸς] Πᾶσιν) and ...-thea, their mother, *before* (ἐπί) the chrematistai who adjudicate in matters that concern the (royal) revenues, concerning the baseless charge of the murder of a slave fifteen days ago, (a charge) which they levelled against me and my agents. On account of this, the accused broke into my house..." (ll. 7-19).[92] Here the timing of ἐνεστηκυίας is immaterial to the document, as the murder case is completely in the background, and so we have no information about its progress. Perhaps it has been resolved, as Bauschatz's translation above presupposes (and it is official that the φόνου was ἀγενήτου). It seems that, in revenge (διὰ τούτ[ο]υ), the family of Pasis have seized ownership of Tkollousis's house.

P.Enteux. 86 (221 BCE). "To King Ptolemy, greeting from Tetosiris. I have a lawsuit pending (κρίσις μοι ἐνέ[στηκ]αν) before ... (ἐπ[ὶ] [...]) against Apollodoros ([πρὸς Ἀ]πολλόδωρον) over a house (περὶ οἰκίας) located in Berenike Thesmophorou..." (*recto* ll. 1-2).[93] Here the case is in process but has not yet come to trial.

P.Yale 4.148 (138/137 BCE). "Weil uns vor dem Strategen Euphranor ein Prozess über ein Haus anhängig ist gegen den Athleten Heliodoros ... (ἐνεστώ[σης ...] ἡμῖν καταστάσεως ἐπ᾽ Εὐφράνορος τοῦ στρατη[γ]οῦ πρὸς Ἡλιόδωρον ἀθλητὴν)" (ll. 4-6). This is a petition to the *epistrategos* Boethos

[89] Cowey & Maresch, *Urkunden des Politeuma der Juden*, 84.

[90] Tr. R. Kugler, in Noah Hacham & Tal Ilan, eds. *Corpus Papyrorum Judaicarum. Volume 4: The Ptolemaic Period (323 BCE–30 BCE)* (Berlin: De Gruyter, 2020), 106.

[91] The issue concerns Timotheos's alleged misdemeanour. Cowey & Maresch, *Urkunden des Politeuma*, 84, restore the sense as follows: "Timotheos [hintertrieb?] das Urteil mit der Begründung, dass wir vor den Dorfältesten bereits ein Urteil und eine Subscriptio erlangt hätten. Wir haben aber überhaupt kein Urteil erlangt, noch haben sie sich der Mühe unterzogen, eine Subscriptio zu schreiben."

[92] Tr. John Bauschatz, *Law and Enforcement in Ptolemaic Egypt* (Cambridge: Cambridge University Press, 2013), 86–87.

[93] Tr. Naphtali Lewis, *Greeks in Ptolemaic Egypt: Case Studies in the Social History of the Hellenistic World* (Oxford: Clarendon, 1986), 60-61.

with the request to speed up a trial before the *strategos*. It is very similar to *SB*.5.7870 above. The request to expedite the process (ll. 20-26; n.b. ἐνίστημι in line 21) has the desired effect, as the *epistrategos* instructs Euphranor to deal with case immediately (ll. 27-30). A first hearing before the *strategos* (ἐπ' Εὐφράνορος) has taken place, but the case is not concluded.[94]

PSI 3.173 (ca. 118 BCE). In this fragmentary submission, a *cleruch* complains that his opponent has made an unlawful claim on the *kleros* he manages.[95] The *cleruch* pleads: "I ask you to arrange for the settlement of *the affairs relating to the present suit before you, which I have against him* (τὰ κα[τὰ τὴν ἐ]νεστῶσάν μοι πρὸς [αὐτὸν] ἐπὶ σοῦ κρίσιν)." (ll. 15-17). Here, the author is requesting that a process which has not yet started be expedited. All that had happened was that the complaint had been lodged.

UPZ 2.162 col. IV (117 BCE). "... da habe auch der Apollonios mit ihm eine Vergleichsurkunde eingereicht, indem er zurücktrat von dem Grundstück, und durch diesen Prozeßausgang, sagte er, werde ein wichtiges Zeugnis *für den jetzt gegen Horos und seine Leute um das Haus geführten Prozeß* (πρὸς τὴν ἐνεσκτηκυῖαν αὐτῶι πρὸς τοὺς περὶ τὸν Ὦρον κρίσιν περὶ τῆς οἰκίας) gewonnen." (ll. 9-14; tr. Wilcken).[96] Wilcken thus reconstructs this section of the very complex and lengthy papyrus document (spanning ten columns and more than 250 lines) as saying that this particular legal process is currently going on. Similarly Bagnall: "Apollonios gave him a deed of cession, surrendering the land; he (the attorney) said that in accordance with this decision an important piece of evidence was contributed *to the case being pursued at present against Horos and his associates about the house* (πρὸς τὴν ἐνεσκτηκυῖαν αὐτῶι πρὸς τοὺς περὶ τὸν Ὦρον κρίσιν περὶ τῆς οἰκίας)."[97]

SB 5.7870 (103-107 CE). "À Apollonios, stratège du district de Polemon dans l'Arsinoïte, de la part de Theophilos, fils de Cronion, de la metropole, inscrit au quartier des Greniers. *Comme j'ai une contestation non sans importance avec Cronion, fils de Cronion, ainsi que je montrerai dans tous les details au moment fixé...* (ἐνεστώσης ἀμφισβητήσεως οὐ<κ> ὀλίγης πρὸς Κρονίωνα Κρονίωνος, καθὼς καὶ ἐπὶ τοῦ ῥητοῦ ἅπαντα δηλώσω{ι})."

[94] Hélène Cuvigny, Ruth Duttenhoefer & Ann Ellis Hanson, eds. *Yale Papyri in the Beinecke Rare Book and Manuscript Library*, vol. 4 (Michigan: University of Michigan Press, 2021), 77 (§148).

[95] Charikleia Armoni et al., "Bemerkungen zu Papyri XVI (Korr. Tyche 490-504)", *Tyche* 18 (2003), 255-260 (259-260).

[96] Cf. also ἐνίστασθαι in VIII 7 and VIII 29.

[97] Roger S. Bagnall & Peter Derow, *The Hellenistic Period: Historical Sources in Translation* (Oxford: Wiley, 2003), §132.

(ll. 1-7).[98] Here the legal process has not yet begun when Theophilus was writing. The case was certainly not pending, but Theophilus still had a dispute with Cronion: the dispute had begun but the case had not. When Theophilos's petition was received, it was then dealt with, and an official added a note to say that it had been processed (ll. 22-23).

SB 6.9314 (135 CE). "To Kallistrates, *strategos* of the Arsinoite nome, in the Polemon district. From Sabinus also known as Ninnos Ptolemaios. I and my household, along with Posis and Cronion (who became managers of the property of Patrōn Geminus when he died), as well as the managers and slaves of Paulinus the Shore Warden) *currently have a claim* (ἀ̣μφι<ζ>βητήσεως ἐν[εστώ]σ̣ης) before Gellius Bassus the most honoured *epistrategos*, along with the deferred case (τοῦ πράγματος ὑπερτεθέντος) before the most excellent governor Petronius Mamertinus..." (ll. 1-10).[99] As in the previous text, here we have again an ἀμφισβήτησις, and Sabinus, the author of this plea, is petitioning the magistrate to send the defendant a copy of the the summons (ll. 11-17).

The same pattern is seen in these examples as in the cases discussed from *DGE*, but also in Aristophanes (§2.2) and *P.Stras.* 2.91 (§2.3).

The Legal Usage of ἐνίστημι: Concluding Analysis

We have surveyed here a number of instances of the legal use, which occurs in a highly formulaic pattern: Person A (in the dative) has a suit (e.g. κατάστασις) current (perf. of ἐνίστημι) against Person B (πρός + acc.), with the more optional supplements of the designation of the presiding official (ἐπί + gen.) and the subject matter of the case (περί + gen.). There have been various translations of the perfect participle of ἐνίστημι published, broadly boiling down to two main options: present (i.e. highlighting that the case is running or current) or pending (i.e. the case has not yet received a verdict). Because of the highly standardised nature of the language, we can probably assume a consistent meaning to the legalese throughout. Three main factors point clearly in the direction of a *present* sense.

[98] Tr. P. Collart, "Demande d'assignation à la session du préfet adressée au stratège", *Mélanges Bidez* (Annuaire de l'Institut de Philologie et d'Histoire orientales 2; Bruxelles: Secretariat de l'Institut, 1934), 91-98 (94: text; 95: tr.).

[99] For text and discussion see Achille Vogliano, Amalia Cinotti & Anna Maria Colombo, "Papyrologica", in *Studi in onore di Vincenzo Arangio-Ruiz nel XLV anno del suo insegnamento* (Naples: Jovene, 1953), 497-525.

(1) A variant on this formula, in place of the usual perfect form, has the aorist instead. We saw this in 2 Macc. 4.43 (περὶ δὲ τούτων ἐνέστη κρίσις πρὸς τὸν Μενέλαον) and *Chrest.Mitt.* 89 = *BGU* 2.613 (διαδικασίας περὶ κληρονομίας μοι ἐνστάσης). In these cases it is obvious that an event, i.e. the beginning of the case (or institution of a suit), is in view. The distinction between the aorist and the perfect makes clear the difference of focus: while the aorist highlights the action in the narrative, the perfect tense form refers to a situation of being current or ongoing: a case ἐνέστη (highlighting event), therefore it ἐνέστηκεν (highlighting state). Additionally, however, the option of the aorist usage indicates that the instances in the perfect may not be entirely suppressing the prior event of instituting the suit.

(2) In his edition of *SB* 5.7870, Collart draws attention to an interesting parallel in *BGU* 1.226 (= *Chrest.Mitt.* 50). In this document, Tabous daughter of Teses has a serious dispute with her brother. She states: "*I have a significant claim* (πολλῆς μοι ἀμφισβητήσεως οὔσης) *against my full-brother Satabous* (πρὸς τὸν ὁμοπάτριον καὶ ὁμομήτριόν μου ἀδελφὸν Σαταβοῦς)" (ll. 6-8). What this indicates is that – with apparently no difference in sense – the present participle of the verb εἰμί (οὔσης) can stand in for the perfect participle of ἐνίστημι. Both simply refer to present existence. In both cases the dative is functioning as a dative of possession.

(3) Finally, these are cases described with the perfect tense usage at various stages – not all are "pending". Some are at the very beginning of the process, when a complaint is first lodged (*SB* 1.4416; *SB* 5.7870.1-21), and so it would be inappropriate to say at this point that a trial was already pending. This initial complaint often requests that the opponent be summoned (e.g. *SB* 6.9314,11-17). Therefore, when the relevant official processes the petition (e.g. *SB* 5.7870, 22-23; *P.Yale* 4.148.27-30), the summons is issued. One document is a response to such a summons (*P.Oxy.* 9.1195). In others, such as *P.Yale* 4.148, a first hearing has taken place, but the case is not concluded; this is probably the case also with *P.Enteux.* 86. The case may also have gone to trial, but could be interrupted because of legal misdemeanours (*P.Amh.* 2.33). In others, the trial may have taken place but aspects of the dispute rumble on (*BGU* 6.1244; *P.Polit.Jud.* 6).

Some of these cases are difficult to reconstruct, but the main point about ἐνίστημι is clear. As already noted, given the stereotyped formula across these documents, it makes sense to interpret them as using the ἐνίστημι language with a high degree of consistency. As a result, we should *not* assign the perfect of ἐνίστημι a technical meaning of "be pending": to deduce a lexical meaning from (for example) Lewis's translation of *P.Enteux.* 86 would be to import the context of this particular case into the dictionary. The point of the ἐνίστημι language is, rather, that a case is in a general sense "going" or "running" or "current". In these cases, as Collart implies in his translation of *SB* 5.7870, ἐνίστασθαι + μοι means little more than "I have". In all these papyri with this formula, the contribution of ἐνίστημι is neither that a case is *currently* in the middle of a trial (as is the timing in *P.Amh.* 2.33) nor about a case being pending *for the future*.

The fact that the formula can be used in reference to cases at various stages indicates that ἐνίστημι may mean, in the broadest sense, *to begin*; hence, the perfect participle refers to a legal dispute having begun (if there is an emphasis on the event) or to be "going" or "current" (if the emphasis is on state). In other words, it – entirely unsurprisingly – refers to the case having in some sense begun, as the verb does in many other contexts: compare the discussions of the outbreak of war or the beginnings of periods of time above, and the lexical definitions "begin" (LSJ I A 3) or "comenzar" (*DGE* B I 2). As a result, such a case can be at any stage. On the other hand, the emphasis in most cases of the perfect participle of ἐνίστημι that we have examined seems to be upon state.[100]

The comment of Casanova, the editor of *SB* 16.12722 discussed above, is instructive:

> "Il verbo ἐνίστημι si trova spesso usato, in epoca tolemaica e romana per indicare l'esistenzia di controversie, cause, processi in corso: cfr. *e.g.* P.Oxy. IX 1195,8 (135[p]): τὰ ἐνεστῶτά μοι πρὸς Ἑρμ[α]ῖον; P.Amh. II, 33,6 (157[a]): ἐνεστηκυίας (BL I) ἡμῖν καταστάσεως ἐπὶ Ζωπύρου; SB I, 4416,6 (ca. 157[p]): ἐνεστώσης ἡμεῖν ἀμφισβητήσεως πρὸς Ἡρακλῆν; P.Tebt. I, 7,7 (114[a]): τὰ ἐπ' αὐτῶν ἐνεστηκότα; inoltre *WB.* I, IV, e *Suppl. s.v.*"[101]

2.5 Conclusion

As a result of this evidence, two unnecessary or erroneous senses can be retired.

[100] This is not because the perf. intrinsically has stative aspect, but because of the stereotyped expression; the aspect is largely lexically determined. See Robert S. D. Crellin, "The Perfect System in Ancient Greek", in idem & Thomas Jügel (eds.), *Perfects in Indo-European Languages and Beyond* (Amsterdam: John Benjamins, 2020), 436–481 (437) for the point about lexical determination. As Crellin also remarks: "the transitivity of a given perfect appears to be linked to its temporal denotation: where intransitive or passive senses are present, there is often little felt reference to any event taking place prior to reference time." See idem, *The Syntax and Semantics of the Perfect Active in Literary Koine Greek* (Publications of the Philological Society 113; Chichester: Wiley-Blackwell, 2016), 4.

[101] Casanova, "Lettera d'ufficio", 27.

First, the narrower sense of a legal case being "pending", even though championed by giants such as Dover and major lexica, can be dropped. We saw that both in literary works with legal reference (e.g. Aristophanes' *Clouds*), and legal speeches such as those of Isaeus or Pseudo-Demosthenes, as well as in the legal documentary papyri, the "pending" sense is highly dubious or, at best, unnecessary.

Secondly, and more significantly, we have seen that the illustrations for glosses such as *immineo*, "be impending" or "bevorstehen" are not in fact correctly given. There has been a problem of the mixing of examples for the present and future senses, which afflicts works such as Preisigke-Kiessling ("*herankommen, bevorstehen*"), the current LSJ ("pending, present") and DGE ("*estar en curso, estar pendiente*"). But even when one disentangles those cases which are supposed to support the future meaning, they prove to be nothing of the sort.

Some scholars have already recognised this. Carrez's Greek-French lexicon, for example, only gives the glosses "être présent" and "être là" for the perfect of ἐνίστημι.[102] Moulton & Milligan took the view that the papyri offered no support whatever for a future sense of ἐνίστημι in the perfect tense: "Contemporary usage makes it clear that in 2 Th 2[2] ὡς ὅτι ἐνέστηκεν ἡ ἡμέρα τοῦ Κυρίου, ἐνέστηκεν should be rendered as pointing to strictly *present* time."[103] Similarly Oepke in the *TWNT*: "Die B(e)d(eu)t(un)g ‚drohend bevorstehen' ist jedoch nicht nachzuweisen, auf keinen Fall für das Perfekt."[104] We can proceed to apply these findings to our remaining New Testament examples.

3. 1 Corinthians 7.26

> "Now concerning virgins, I have no commandment from the Lord, but I give my opinion as one who by the Lord's mercy is faithful. Therefore I consider this to be good διὰ τὴν ἐνεστῶσαν ἀνάγκην: it is good that a person remain as he is." (1 Cor. 7.25-26)

In this passage in 1 Corinthians 7 the ἐνεστῶσα ἀνάγκη is Paul's reason for stating that it is better for people to remain unmarried. In

[102] Maurice Carrez, *Dictionnaire grec-français du Nouveau Testament* (Genève: Labor et Fides, 1985), 92.

[103] J.H. Moulton & G. Milligan, *The Vocabulary of the Greek Testament: Illustrated from the Papyri and Other Non-Literary Sources* (London: Hodder and Stoughton, 1929), 215.

[104] A. Oepke, "ἐνίστημι", *TWNT* 2:540.

broad terms, the interpretations of διὰ τὴν ἐνεστῶσαν ἀνάγκην in 1 Cor. 7.26 can be classified into three groups.

First, there are those for whom τὴν ἐνεστῶσαν ἀνάγκην refers to "the coming crisis", i.e. the imminent parousia. The most influential modern representatives of this view are Conzelmann ([1]1969, [2]1981; ET 1975) and Fitzmyer (2008).[105] Their predecessors arguing for this position included Lightfoot, Wendland, Moffatt, Gould and Héring. More recently, Lang, Keener and Gardner have opted for this view.[106] Several Bible translations also adopt readings such as "the impending distress" (Amplified Bible; Lexham Bible; RSV Catholic) or "the impending crisis" (NET; NRSVUE).

Secondly, there are a number who favour the *present* meaning.[107] Unfortunately, scholars rarely refer to primary sources in this case, except for the New Testament usages.[108] An exception, notable for its introduction of new evidence (i.e. not simply copied from New Testament dictionaries), is Ruth Elizabeth Kritzer's commentary in the 1 Corinthians volume in the Papyrologische Kommentare zum Neuen Testament series.[109] She notes: "In den Papyri bezeichnet das Partizip einen gegenwärtigen Zustand oder eine ‚laufende' Zeit..." supplying a large number of parallels from close to Paul's time.

Thirdly, there are various hybrid combinations of the two views.[110] For

[105] Conzelmann, *1 Corinthians*, 132 n. 14; Fitzmyer, *First Corinthians*, 315.

[106] Friedrich Lang, *Die Briefe an die Korinther* (NTD; Göttingen: Vandenhoeck & Ruprecht, [16]1986), 99; Craig S. Keener, *1-2 Corinthians* (NCBC; Cambridge: Cambridge University Press, 2005), 68, and Paul D. Gardner, *1 Corinthians* (ZECNT; Grand Rapids: Zondervan, 2018), 344.

[107] E.g. Martin Luther, "Commentary on 1 Corinthians 7 [1523]", *LW* 28.47-48 = WA 12.133-135; John Calvin, *The First Epistle of Paul the Apostle to the Corinthians* (Grand Rapids: Eerdmans, 1960), 156-157; Adolf Schlatter, *Die Korintherbriefe* (SENT; Stuttgart: Calwer, 1950), 87; Ben Witherington III, *Conflict and Community in Corinth: A Socio-Rhetorical Commentary on 1 and 2 Corinthians* (Grand Rapids: Eerdmans, 1995), 176; David E. Garland, *1 Corinthians* (BECNT; Grand Rapids: Baker, 2003), 323; Peter Arzt-Grabner, Ruth Elisabeth Kritzer, et al. *1. Korinther* (PKNT; Göttingen: Vandenhoeck & Ruprecht, 2006), 291; Florian Wilk, *Der erste Brief an die Korinther* (Göttingen: Vandenhoeck & Ruprecht, 2023), 99.

[108] E.g. Gordon Fee, *The First Epistle to the Corinthians* (NICNT; Grand Rapids: Eerdmans, 1987), 328-329; Roy Ciampa & Brian Rosner, *The First Letter to the Corinthians* (Grand Rapids: Eerdmans, 2010), 336; John Barclay, "Apocalyptic Allegiance and Disinvestment in the World: A Reading of 1 Corinthians 7:25-35", in B. Blackwell, J. Goodrich & J. Maston, eds. *Paul and the Apocalyptic Imagination* (Minneapolis: Fortress, 2016), 257-274.

[109] Arzt-Grabner & Kritzer, *1. Korinther*, 291-292. Useful new material is also supplied in the 2 Thessalonians volume (on 2.2): see Christine Kreinecker, *2. Thessalonicher* (PKNT; Göttingen: Vandenhoeck & Ruprecht, 2010), 158.

[110] Several commentators, such as A.C. Thiselton, *The First Epistle to the Corinthians* (NIGTC; Eerdmans: Grand Rapids, 2000), 572 note that the perfect of ἐνίστημι can refer either to the present or to the future; similarly Longenecker & Brookins, *1 Corinthians 1-9*, 179.

Fascher, the "*present* crisis" is that the parousia is *imminent*: Paul argues "um des gegenwärtigen Notzustandes der bevorstehenden Enderwartung willen" – "because of the present state of emergency with its imminent expectation of the end".[111] Or again, for Evans, "The present distress... is the approaching end of the world".[112] This retains the translation of the second view. Schrage also wants to combine elements of the two when he writes of "nicht nur ... eine zukünftig drohende Anagke" but also a present one.[113]

As we have seen, the *present* meaning is the only really tenable position. The usage in 1 Cor. 7.26 is not particularly surprising as an instance of this meaning, given that there are a number of similar phrases that other Greek authors and documents have used:

- διὰ τὴν ἐν[εστ]ῶσαν κακίαν – "in view of the terrible present situation" (*P.Petr.* 2.19(2),5; iii BCE)[114]
- δι' ἄλλα ἐνεστηκότα ἀναγκαῖα – "because of other present constraints" (*PSI* 4.392,4; 240 BCE)[115]
- διὰ τὸν ἐνεστῶτα χειμῶνα – "because of the present bad weather" (1 Esdras 9.6)
- τὴν ἐνεστῶσαν ταλαιπωρίαν – "the present misery" (2 Macc. 6.9)
- περὶ τῶν ἐνεστηκότων ἀπόρων – "in connection with the present distresses" (Josephus, *Ant.* 3.24)
- τοῦ ἀγῶνος ἐνεστηκότος – "his present difficulty" (Josephus, *Ant.* 17.185)
- τῶν ἐνεστηκότων κακῶν – "the present ills" (Josephus, *Ant.* 18.178)
- μετὰ τὴν ἐνεστῶσαν καὶ σφόδρα κατεπείγουσαν με χρείαν – "after the present and very pressing need" (*PGM* 1.4,503)

The phrase δι' ἄλλα ἐνεστηκότα ἀναγκαῖα from the Zeno papyrus noted above is a particularly striking parallel. Therefore Paul's justification for advocating singleness διὰ τὴν ἐνεστῶσαν ἀνάγκην must mean

[111] Erich Fascher, *Der erste Brief des Paulus an die Korinther*, vol. 1 (THkNT; Berlin: Evangelische Verlagsanstalt, [4]1988), 196.

[112] Ernest Evans, *The Epistles of Paul the Apostle to the Corinthians* (Clarendon Bible; Oxford: Clarendon, 1930), 99.

[113] Wolfgang Schrage, *Der erste Brief an die Korinther* (EKK; Neukirchen-Vluyn: Neukirchener, 1991-2001), 2:157; similarly C.K. Barrett, *A Commentary on the First Epistle to the Corinthians* (London: A. & C. Black, 1968), 174-175: "Paul is thinking ... of the eschatological woes that are impending over the world, and are already anticipated in the sufferings of Christians."

[114] Mahaffy, ed. *The Flinders Petrie papyri* (Part II), 60.

[115] Società italiana per la ricerca dei papiri greci e latini in Egitto, *Papiri greci e latini*, vol. 4 (nos. 280-445) (Florence: Le Monnier, 1917), 121-123, as noted by Kritzer in Arzt-Grabner & Kritzer, *1. Korinther* (PKNT; Göttingen: Vandenhoeck & Ruprecht, 2006), 291-292.

"because of the present constraint" or "the present crisis". There have been various explanations of what this present situation is. Some have argued, retaining an eschatological tinge, that the reference is to the messianic woes.[116] Others have posited a particular social crisis, such as famine or the prospect of famine.[117] Barclay has recently taken the reference here to "the present constraint" as an intrinsic feature of the present evil age, namely "the inevitable mortality and decay of all things in 'this age'", an unwilling slavery to corruptibility: "In other words, the present is marked by the limitation and constraint of decay."[118] A theological sense like that of Barclay is probably more plausible than the interpretation in terms of a particular famine, because Paul seems to be referring to a general policy he has, rather than one contingent upon particular social circumstances in Corinth.

4. 2 Thessalonians 2.2

> Concerning the coming of our Lord Jesus Christ and our being gathered to him, we ask you, brothers and sisters, not to become quickly unsettled or alarmed by the opinion allegedly from us – whether by a spirit or word of mouth or by letter – ὡς ὅτι ἐνέστηκεν ἡ ἡμέρα τοῦ κυρίου. (2 Thess. 2.1-2)

The principal question here is whether the Thessalonians have been misinformed that the day of the Lord is imminent (ἐνέστηκεν in the alleged future sense), or that the day of the Lord is already present (ἐνέστηκεν as 'has come' or 'is present'). A minority of scholars argues for the "imminent" view.

The imminent view has had a long history in the English-speaking world because of the KJV's translation "as that the day of Christ is at hand". Warfield, for example, is incredulous at the alternative, referring to "the almost ludicrous inappropriateness of the contention of some that the error of the Thessalonians was not feverish expectancy of the Lord's coming, but the belief that the day of the Lord had already come"![119]

[116] E.g. Barrett, *First Epistle*, 174.

[117] E.g. Bruce W. Winter, 'Secular and Christian Responses to Corinthian Famines', *TynB* 40 (1989), 86-106.

[118] John Barclay, "Apocalyptic Allegiance and Disinvestment in the World: A Reading of 1 Corinthians 7:25-35", in B. Blackwell, J. Goodrich & J. Maston, eds. *Paul and the Apocalyptic Imagination* (Minneapolis: Fortress, 2016), 257-274 (263).

[119] B.B. Warfield, "The Prophecies of St. Paul. I: 1 and 2 Thessalonians", *The Expositor* 4 (1886), 30-44 (37). The substantial discussion in A.M.G. Stephenson ("On the Meaning of ἐνέστηκεν ἡ ἡμέρα τοῦ κυρίου in 2 Thessalonians 2.2", in F.L. Cross, ed. *Studia Evangelica*

Arguments have also been made in two major German commentaries in recent times. Trilling states: "Once the issues are established for understanding the whole document, the translation of the verb (ἐνέστηκεν) becomes a secondary question."[120] Trillling argues for the sense that the end is on the way. Marxsen similarly says that the verb clearly has a present meaning, but then asks if this makes sense. He answers his own question: "Das scheint nicht der Fall zu sein."[121] Rigaux takes a similar line. "On a adopté «imminent », non pour des raisons de lexique ou de grammaire, mais parce que les Thessaloniciens ne pouvaient vraiment pas penser que le jour du Seigneur était réellement déjà arrivé."[122] He also notes, as further representatives of the imminent view, Schmiedel, von Dobschütz, Buzy, Amiot, Osty. One could also add Lightfoot.

More recently Peerbolte starts from a different assumption, viz.: "The perfect tense ἐνέστηκεν can elicit one of two meanings: either the Day of the Lord 'has already come' or it 'is about to come.' There are no grammatical considerations that urge a decision in favour of either direction."[123] Even judging by most dictionaries, however, the idea that it is an equal bet either way is wrong. He then makes several objections to the "present" view: such a view is implausible because the reference to the day of the Lord entails final judgment and the general resurrection, because of the contents of 2 Thess. 2.3-12, and in view of the fact that 2 Thessalonians is intended as a later correction of the eschatology of 1 Thessalonians and so must be opposed to *Naherwartung*.[124] He concludes: "Therefore, the meaning 'is about to come' is preferable. The attitude which the author of 2 Thessalonians combats is not that of realised eschatology, but that of

(TU 102; Berlin: Akademie Verlag, 1968), 442-451) begins with a long and wistful remembrance of better times in which the verb was translated "to be at hand", and is essentially an argument from antiquity. He also notes that the translation "is imminent" is "logically" possible for 1 Cor. 7.26 and 2 Tim. 3.1, but does not supply any positive linguistic reason why one would actually adopt this translation. As we have seen, it is nonsensical for 2 Tim. 3.1 ("in the last days, difficult times will be imminent"!).

120 Wolfgang Trilling, *Der Zweite Brief an die Thessalonicher* (EKK; Neukirchen: Neukirchener Verlag, 1980), 79: "Sind die Weichen zum Verstehen des ganzen Dokuments so gestellt, wird die Übersetzung des Verbums (ἐνέστηκεν) zu einer zweitrangigen Frage."

121 Willi Marxsen, *Der zweite Thessalonicherbrief* (ZBK; Zürich: Theologische Verlag, 1982), 43: "Im Griechischen steht es im Perfekt, das präsentische Bedeutung hat: Der (erwartete) Tag ist gekommen — und nun eben da. Diese sprachlich ohne Zweifel richtige Übersetzung wirft indes die Frage auf, ob die damit gemachte Aussage überhaupt Sinn gibt. Das scheint nicht der Fall zu sein."

122 Béda Rigaux, *Saint Paul: Les épitres aux Thessaloniciens* (Éb; Paris: Gabalda, 1956), 653.

123 L.J. Lietaert Peerbolte, *The Antecedents of Antichrist: A Traditio-Historical Study of the Earliest Christian Views on Eschatological Opponents* (Leiden: Brill, 1996), 73.

124 Lietaert Peerbolte, *Antecedents of Antichrist*, 73-74.

a vivid expection of the coming of the end."[125] Schreiber notes, as other representatives of the imminentist view, Dibelius, Lindemann, Laub, Börschel, Green, Röcker, Shogren (2012), Ehrman (2013) and Nicklas/ Sommer (2015). This illustrates the persistence of this position.

It is certainly the case, however, that the majority of scholars accept the *present* sense of ἐνέστηκεν.[126] (There are also some hybrid options here as well.[127]) As we have seen, linguistically this is really the only option. The detailed treatment of John Lillie in 1860 has been quite influential.[128] The question of how the Thessalonians could have been persuaded that the day of the Lord had arrived depends, of course, on what conception of the day of the Lord they had. If the Thessalonians thought that the day of the Lord was the occasion of Jesus' glorious return and resurrection of the dead, accompanied by cosmic collapse and the end of the world, then it would indeed be completely implausible that the Thessalonians

[125] Lietaert Peerbolte, *Antecedents of Antichrist*, 74.

[126] For comments on the scholarly majority, see e.g. I. Howard Marshall, *1 and 2 Thessalonians* (NCB; London: Marshall, Morgan & Scott, 1983), 186, and, more recently, Maria-Irma Seewann, *"Tag des Herrn" und "Parusie": 2 Thess 2 in der Kontroverse* (Würzburg: Echter Verlag, 2013), 335; similarly F.F. Bruce, *1 & 2 Thessalonians* (WBC; Waco: Word, 1982), 165: "It cannot be seriously disputed that 'is present' is the natural sense of ἐνέστηκεν." In fairly recent scholarship, see e.g. Maarten J.J. Menken, *2 Thessalonians* (London: Routledge, 1994), 97; Bonnie Bowman Thurston, *Reading Colossians, Ephesians, and 2 Thessalonians: A Literary and Theological Commentary* (New York: Crossroad, 1995), 175; Beverly Roberts Gaventa, *First and Second Thessalonians* (Interpretation; Louisville: John Knox Press, 1998), 109; Abraham Malherbe, *The Letters to the Thessalonians* (Anchor; New York: Doubleday, 2000), 417; Colin R. Nicholl, *From Hope to Despair in Thessalonica: Situating 1 and 2 Thessalonians* (Cambridge: Cambridge University Press, 2004), 185; Gordon D. Fee, *The First and Second Letters to the Thessalonians* (NICNT; Grand Rapids: Eerdmans, 2009), 273; Yann Redalié, *Deuxième épître aux Thessaloniciens* (Genève: Labor et Fides, 2011), 95-99; Seewann, *"Tag des Herrn" und "Parusie"*, 335; Andy Johnson, *1 and 2 Thessalonians* (Two Horizons; Grand Rapids: Eerdmans, 2016), 156; Mary-Ann Beavis and HyeRan Kim-Cragg, "2 Thessalonians", in Linda Maloney, ed. *1—2 Thessalonians* (Wisdom; Collegeville: Liturgical Press, 2016), 141; Stefan Schreiber, *Der zweite Brief an die Thessalonicher* (ÖTkNT; Gütersloh: Gütersloher Verlagshaus, 2017), 142; Marlene Crüsemann, *The Pseudepigraphal Letters to the Thessalonians* (London: T&T Clark, 2019), 261; Sydney Tooth, *Suddenness and Signs: The Eschatologies of 1 and 2 Thessalonians* (Tübingen: Mohr Siebeck, 2024), 71.

[127] E.g. Simon Légasse, *Les épîtres de Paul aux Thessaloniciens* (Lectio Divina; Paris: Cerf, 1999), 384: 'l'expression hyperbolique d'une imminence'; M. Eugene Boring, *I & II Thessalonians: A Commentary* (NTL; Louisville: Westminster John Knox Press, 2015, 268: 259-260: ἐνέστηκεν is linguistically "be present", but means "the apocalyptic countdown has already been triggered", because "such language... is often used when something expected is seen to be arriving, even if not yet literally present." Possibly also Linda McKinnish Bridges, *1 & 2 Thessalonians* (Macon: Smyth & Helwys, 2008), 231, who seems to suggest both views.

[128] Lillie, *Lectures on the Epistle of Paul to the Thessalonians*, 497-502. See also the lesser known but equally powerful discussion in John Eadie, *A Commentary on the Greek Text of the Epistles of Paul to the Thessalonians* (London: Macmillan, 1877) 259-264.

thought that this had already happened. As many note, however, the "day" is not a single twenty-four hour date but a period.[129] Moreover, it is obviously not a phrase that has a straightforward meaning for gentiles such as those in Thessalonica. They could have understood it as historical circumstances viewed in an apocalyptic light, or as a spiritual event in the community.[130] As many scholars note, however, our information about the situation is very limited, and our only source for what is meant by "the day of the Lord has come" is the response in verses 3-12.[131] But to rely on these verses to establish a reading of 2 Thess. 2.2 would be to interpret *obscurum per obscurius.*

Conclusion

To summarise, the linguistic evidence is fairly unambiguous. Out of the hundred or so examples above, none give any real evidence that ἐνίστημι can mean "be imminent" or "*bevorstehen*". Unfortunately, the trend in lexica has been to try to supply more and more evidence for this futurist sense of ἐνίστημι in the perfect; the example of the *DGE* is telling here. New Testament scholars, if they are going to write a commentary, are inevitably compelled to take short-cuts and trust what dictionaries say, despite the many warnings about their reliability.[132] A common problem in some (especially New Testament) lexica is an unrecognised dependence on the Vulgate.[133] This is true in our case as well, where the gloss *insto* is the most common translation equivalent even though *insto* has its own ambiguities, as to some extent does Budé's gloss of *immineo.* A particular difficulty in the case of the perfect of ἐνίστημι has been the tendency, as we have seen, to lump together illustrations of both the present and supposed future senses of the perfect tense form, which leads to unclarity in what exactly the parallels are intended to show. Conversely, present and aorist tense forms of ἐνίστημι are also adduced alongside perfects to support the English definitions "be pending" or "be imminent". Another difficulty has been the confusion of lexical meaning and reference.[134] The most egregious example of this is where the use of ἐνίστημι in 2 Timo-

[129] Boring, *I & II Thessalonians*, 259-260.

[130] E.g. for the former, Gaventa, *First and Second Thessalonians* 109 (intense sufferings); for the latter, Seewann, *"Tag des Herrn" und "Parusie"*, 335.

[131] Bruce, *1 & 2 Thessalonians*, 165; Mary-Ann Beavis & HyeRan Kim-Cragg, "2 Thessalonians", 143-144.

[132] The most salutary warning is John A.L. Lee, *A History of New Testament Lexicography* (New York: Peter Lang, 2003).

[133] Lee, *History of New Testament Lexicography*, 290.

[134] See e.g. Lee, *History of New Testament Lexicography*, 197 on the phenomenon in the lexicography of ἀγαπητός.

thy is taken to be evidence for the "imminent" sense, because the woes come in the future. But this is because the verb is in the future tense, not because there is some latent futurist sense in the semantics of ἐνίστημι itself. (Cf. also 1 Macc. 8.23-25 and 3 Macc. 3.24, which envisage scenarios in the future.) There has also been an enduring and authoritatively supported claim for a technical legal sense of "be pending", which adds further weight to the idea that the perfect of ἐνίστημι could mean "be *im*-pending". Additionally, Cremer points out that confusion may arise from the fact that ἐνίστημι can mean both "begin" and also "oppose", and so secondarily imply "threaten", and thereby imply a future danger.[135]

Despite the situation in lexica, there has been some independent work done, especially in the Papyrologische Kommentare zum Neuen Testament. As we have seen, there has increasingly been a realization that the present meaning must be correct for 2 Thessalonians 2.2. Perhaps strangely, however, there has not been a similar discernible shift in the interpretation of 1 Corinthians 7.26. The hold which the imminent eschatological interpretation has on the chapter as a whole has clearly influenced a number of interpreters to cling to the "imminent" or "bevorstehend" interpretation of τὴν ἐνεστῶσαν ἀνάγκην.

As Samuel Johnson famously remarked, the work of compiling dictionaries is a drudgery, which must make articles like the present one – seeking to correct dictionaries – even more so. While I certainly do not intend to disparage the monumental work involved in lexica, there is the inevitable problem that they often default to the work of their predecessors, and incorporate their shortcomings alongside their positive linguistic achievements.[136]

Simon GATHERCOLE
Faculty of Divinity
West Road
Cambridge CB3 9BS
UNITED KINGDOM
sjg1007@cam.ac.uk

[135] J. Kögel, ed. *Hermann Cremers Biblisch-theologisches Wörterbuch des neutestamentlichen Griechisch* (Stuttgart: Perthes, [11]1923), 531: "Die für d. Gebrauch d. Wortes im zeitl. Sinne angenommene Bedeutung „bevorstehen" ist **teils** auf d. Bedeutung d. Präs. Med. „sich einstellen, eintreten, beginnen" zurückzuführen u. danach zu berichtigen, z. B. ἐνιστάμενου θέρους, mit Eintritt d. Sommers (1 Esr. 5, 47: ἐνστάντος δὲ τοῦ ἑβδόμου μηνὸς. 1 Mcc. 8, 24: ἐὰν δὲ ἐνστῇ πόλεμος. 2 Mcc. 4, 13. 3 Mcc. 3, 24), **teils** auf d. missverstandenen Gebrauch d. Wortes im Sinne feindl. Auftretens = sich drohend hinstellen, auftreten, drohen, resp. entgegenstehen, z. B. bei Polyb. u. Plut. von d. Interzession d. Volkstribunen."

[136] I am very grateful to Peter Arzt-Grabner, Robert Crellin, Jamie Davies, John Lee and Peter Williams for their help with this article.

The Meaning of Σώφρων in the Pastoral Epistles: A Lexical Semantic Analysis

YAN MA

The Greek word σώφρων occurs four times in the New Testament, all of which are in the Pastoral Epistles, namely 1 Tim 3:2, Titus 1:8, 2:2, and 2:5. Appropriately defining the meaning of σώφρων must have significance to the interpretation of the Pastoral Epistles. However, different English versions render this word differently in the four verses. In this paper, I argue that the meaning of σώφρων should be restraining sensual desires, with possible stress on sexual desire, and the gloss "temperate" captures the lexical meaning of σώφρων by conducting a lexical semantic analysis based on Systemic Functional Linguistics (SFL).

Keywords: Σώφρων, Pastoral Epistles, Lexical Semantic Analysis, Lexicography, Systemic Functional Linguistics

Introduction

The Greek word σώφρων occurs four times in the New Testament, all of which are in the Pastoral Epistles, namely 1 Tim 3:2, Titus 1:8, 2:2, and 2:5. The word group of σωφρο-, which is not frequently used in the New Testament, occurs ten times in the Pastoral Epistles.[1] Appropriately defining the meaning of σώφρων must have significance to the interpretation of the Pastoral Epistles. However, different English versions render this word differently in the four verses. In 1 Tim 3:2, σώφρων is translated as sensible (NRSV, RSV), self-controlled (ESV, NASB, NIV), sober-minded (NKJV), or sober (KJV). In Titus 1:8, σώφρων is translated as prudent (NRSV), master of himself (RSV), self-controlled (ESV, NASB, NIV), sober-minded (NKJV), or sober (KJV). In Titus 2:2, σώφρων is translated as prudent (NRSV), sensible (RSV), self-controlled (ESV, NASB, NIV), or temperate (NKJV, KJV). In Titus 2:5, σώφρων is translated as self-controlled (NRSV, ESV, NIV), sensible (RSV, NASB), or discreet (NKJV, KJV). That is to say, the translation of this Greek adjective demonstrates neither consistency in different verses nor consensus among different English versions.

[1] Total occurrences of the words with stem σωφρο- are sixteen times in the New Testament, of which ten occurrences are in the Pastoral Epistles, namely σώφρων in 1 Tim 3:2, Titus 1:8, 2:2, and 2:5, σωφροσύνη in 1 Tim 2:9 and 2:15, σωφρονέω in Titus 2:6, σωφρονίζω in Titus 2:4, σωφρονισμός in 2 Tim 1:7, and σωφρόνως in Titus 2:12.

In this paper, I argue that the meaning of σώφρων should be defined as restraining sensual desires, with possible stress on sexual desire, and the gloss "temperate" captures the lexical meaning of σώφρων by conducting a lexical semantic analysis based on Systemic Functional Linguistics (SFL). According to the theory of SFL, the co-text serves as the primary constraint on the meaning of the text in discourse since the interpretation of any text, except for the first fragment of the discourse, is forcibly constrained by the preceding text. Co-text is the linguistic units, involving words, clauses, and clause complexes, within a specific discourse that surround a particular point in the discourse.[2] Hence the meaning of a word can be determined by examining its co-text. A word is generally related to other words in its co-text, the lexical and/or semantic relationships of which can be perceived from the collocation of these words. Collocation refers to the tendency of words to occur together, which reflects an association between individual words. Semantic relationships can be expected among the words regularly collocated because they tend to share the same lexical environment.[3] Although the words in collocation with one another may or may not share the same meaning, exploring the related words in the co-text provides evidence for figuring out the meaning of a word.

Since 1 Tim 3:2, Titus 1:8, 2:2, and 2:5 act as the co-text of the word σώφρων in each occurrence and the respective discourse unit acts as the co-text of each verse, I study the meaning of σώφρων by observing the collocation within each verse and also considering the co-text of each verse. The same word occurs in four different locations, each corresponding to a different context of use. The lexical semantic analysis in this paper thus not only defines the meaning of σώφρων but also accounts for the variability of meaning from context to context. First, I survey the extant lexical resources to assess how σώφρων has been interpreted.

[2] Christian M. I. M. Matthiessen, et al., *Key Terms in Systemic Functional Linguistics*, Key Terms Series (London: Continuum, 2010), 74; Stanley E. Porter, "Dialect and Register in the Greek of the New Testament: Theory," in *Rethinking Contexts, Rereading Texts: Contributions from the Social Sciences to Biblical Interpretation*, ed. M. Daniel Carroll R., Journal for the Study of the Old Testament, Supplement Series 299 (Sheffield: Sheffield Academic, 2000), 198; Jeffrey T. Reed, *A Discourse Analysis of Philippians: Method and Rhetoric in the Debate over Literary Integrity*, Journal for the Study of the New Testament, Supplement Series 136 (Sheffield: Sheffield Academic, 1997), 42; Cynthia Long Westfall, "A Discourse Analysis of Romans 7.7–25: The Pauline Autobiography?" in *The Linguist as Pedagogue: Trends in the Teaching and Linguistic Analysis of the Greek New Testament*, ed. Stanley E. Porter and Matthew Brook O'Donnell, NTM 11 (Sheffield: Sheffield Phoenix, 2009), 148–49.

[3] M. A. K. Halliday and Colin Yallop, *Lexicology: A Short Introduction* (London: Continuum, 2007), 15; M. A. K. Halliday and Ruqaiya Hasan, *Cohesion in English*, English Language Series 9 (London: Longman, 1976), 284–87.

Second, I examine the co-text of σώφρων within 1 Tim 3:2, Titus 1:8, 2:2, and 2:5 to determine its meaning, taking into account the co-text of each verse. Third, σώφρων is used in ten verses of the Septuagint, which are Wis 9:11, 4 Macc 1:35, 2:2, 2:16, 2:18, 2:23, 3:17, 3:19, 7:23, and 15:10. There is no occurrence of σώφρων in any book of the Hebrew Bible, thus no Hebrew counterpart helps to discern the meaning of this Greek word. I consult the uses of σώφρων in Wis 9:11, 4 Macc 1:35, 2:2, 2:16, 2:18, 2:23, 3:17, 3:19, 7:23, and 15:10 to verify its meaning.[4]

Surveying Lexical Resources

In this section, I survey six major Greek–English lexicons, which are *A Greek–English Lexicon* (LSJ), *A Greek and English Lexicon to the New Testament* (PRM), *A Greek–English Lexicon of the New Testament* (GELNT), *The Concise Greek–English Lexicon of the New Testament* (CGELNT), *A Greek-English Lexicon of the New Testament and Other Early Christian Literature* (BDAG), and *Greek-English Lexicon of the New Testament* (Louw–Nida),[5] to assess how the Greek word σώφρων has been interpreted in the extant lexical resources.[6]

[4] The meaning of σώφρων is determined in the Pastoral Epistles through a synchronic study, the conclusion of which is confirmed by the uses of this word in the Septuagint. Following the principle of modern linguistics, the lexical semantic analysis in this paper emphasizes the priority of synchronic over diachronic data. This principle is originally from the theory of Ferdinand de Saussure (1857–1913), a Swiss linguist widely acknowledged as the founder of modern linguistics. See Stanley E. Porter, "Studying Ancient Languages from a Modern Linguistic Perspective," *Filología Neotestamentaria* 2 (1989), 153.

[5] Henry George Liddell and Robert Scott, *Greek–English Lexicon*, rev. and augm. Henry Stuart Jones and Roderick McKenzie (Oxford: Clarendon, 1996); John Parkhurst, *A Greek and English Lexicon to the New Testament*, rev. Hugh James Rose and J. R. Major (London: Longman, 1845); Joseph Henry Thayer, *A Greek–English Lexicon of the New Testament*, 2nd ed. (New York: American Book, 1889); Frederick William Danker, *The Concise Greek–English Lexicon of the New Testament* (Chicago: University of Chicago Press, 2009); Walter Bauer, *A Greek-English Lexicon of the New Testament and Other Early Christian Literature*, rev. and ed. Frederick W. Danker, 3rd ed. (Chicago: University of Chicago Press, 2000); Johannes P. Louw and Eugene A. Nida, eds., *Greek-English Lexicon of the New Testament: Based on Semantic Domains*, 2 vols., 2nd ed. (New York: United Bible, 1989). For a comprehensive list of Greek lexicons, see John A. L. Lee, *A History of New Testament Lexicography*, Studies in Biblical Greek 8 (New York: Peter Lang, 2003), 321–26.

[6] It is worth mentioning that I did not include *Theological Dictionary of the New Testament* (TDNT) in this survey due to its many fallacies, although many biblical scholars still rely heavily on this dictionary to compose their commentaries. One example is I. Howard Marshall's *A Critical and Exegetical Commentary on the Pastoral Epistles*, in which σώφρων is explained as "a suitable restraint in every respect" that leads to thoughtful, prudent, and self-controlled behavior, a characteristic of the Christian life that is made possible by faith in Christ. Another example is William D. Mounce's *Pastoral Epistles*, in which σώφρων is explained as "self-controlled," "moderate," "restraint," and "chastity" with the

LSJ is regarded as the most comprehensive and authoritative lexicon of ancient Greek by many scholars. This lexicon provides a reference for all important Greek texts discovered up to 1940 from the eleventh century BC to the Byzantine period, including the early Greek work, the classical Greek literature, the Greek Old Testament, and the New Testament. In LSJ, each entry lists a word's etymology, definition, and quotations from a full range of sources to demonstrate its usage.[7] As for σώφρων, LSJ identifies σῶς and φρήν as its etymology normally used in the Epic dialect and poet, which means "of sound mind." The glosses listed under this category are "discreet" and "prudent." Moreover, LSJ also defines the meaning of σώφρων used in the Attic dialect, namely "having control over the sensual desires." Under this category, the glosses listed are "temperate," "self-controlled," and "chaste," with 1 Tim 3:2 as a source.[8]

PRM, GELNT, and CGELNT are heavily dependent on the etymology of a word to ascertain its meaning and employ the gloss method by listing the gloss of a word without further explanation. True etymology of a word may contribute to the understanding of its meaning, whereas this might not be the case for the Greek language.[9] The problem with the gloss method is that glosses do not define the meaning of a word but just

possible nuance of sexual fidelity in 1 Tim 3:2 and Titus 2:5. However, TDNT cannot be counted as a qualified lexical resource. As TDNT indicates, the word σώφρων is contracted from σαόφρων which originally means "of sound mind" and the word group of σώφρων, σωφρονέω, and σωφροσύνη denotes "the rational," "rational," "discretion," "modesty," and "wisdom" in Greek literature. This discussion is very confusing since it is the meaning of the word group rather than the meaning of each individual word that is under consideration. The lexical meaning of σώφρων is thus hard to be discerned. TDNT was criticized for its questionable assumptions and lacking linguistic methods first by James Barr and then by many scholars, such as Stanley E. Porter and Moisés Silva. First, TDNT regards New Testament Greek as Semiticized Greek distinct from nonbiblical Greek. Second, TDNT expects direct correspondence between language and mentality. Third, TDNT organizes the theological thought of the New Testament instead of the lexical meaning under each word. Fourth, TDNT uses the etymology rather than the context of a word to determine its meaning. For commentaries that rely on TDNT, see I. Howard Marshall, *A Critical and Exegetical Commentary on the Pastoral Epistles*, International Critical Commentary (Edinburgh: T. & T. Clark, 1999), 182–84; William D. Mounce, *Pastoral Epistles*, Word Biblical Commentary (Nashville: Thomas Nelson, 2000), 173. For TDNT's interpretation of σώφρων, see Ulrich Luck, "Σώφρων, Σωφρονέω, Σωφρονίζω, Σωφρονισμός, Σωφροσύνη," in *Theological Dictionary of the New Testament*, ed. Gerhard Kittel, et al., 10 vols. (Grand Rapids: Eerdmans, 1964–1976), 7:1097–98. For scholars' criticism of TDNT, see James Barr, *The Semantics of Biblical Language* (Oxford: Oxford University Press, 1961), 216–46; Stanley E. Porter, *Studies in the Greek New Testament: Theory and Practice*, Studies in Biblical Greek 6 (New York: Peter Lang, 1996), 60–63; Moisés Silva, *Biblical Words and Their Meaning: An Introduction to Lexical Semantics*, 2nd ed. (Grand Rapids: Zondervan, 1994), 18–19.

[7] Liddell and Scott, *A Greek-English Lexicon*, iii– xiv.

[8] Liddell and Scott, *A Greek-English Lexicon*, 1751–52.

[9] Porter, *Studies in the Greek New Testament*, 58.

act as equivalents or translation equivalents of the word.[10] In PRM, σόος and σῶς which mean "sound" and φρήν which means "the mind" are considered to be the etymology of σώφρων. The meaning of this word offered by PRM is "of a sound mind, as opposed to folly or madness." PRM lists the glosses "sober, modest, recollected, regular, discreet, as opposed to intemperate, indecent, light, irregular, or foolish in behavior" and the sources 1 Tim 3:2, Titus 1:8, 2:2, and 2:5.[11] GELNT suggests that σώφρων is developed from the etymology σάος with contract form σῶς and φρήν. Two groups of glosses are provided in GELNT. The first group lists "of sound mind," "sane," and "in one's senses." The second group lists "curbing one's desires and impulses," "temperate," and "self-controlled," with 1 Tim 3:2, Titus 1:8, 2:2, and 2:5 as the sources.[12] In CGELNT, σώφρων is explained as "marked by serious awareness of responsibility," with the etymology σᾶος (σῶς), namely "free from harm," and φρήν. CGELNT lists the glosses "prudent" and "self-controlled" as well as the sources 1 Tim 3:2, Titus 1:8, 2:2, and 2:5.[13]

BDAG advances New Testament lexicography by differentiating the meaning or functional usage (bold text), gloss (bold italic text), and translation equivalent (italic text) of each word. The discussions of individual words are clearly organized and presented.[14] However, as an English version of a German lexicon produced in the nineteenth century, BDAG depends on the previous lexicon and still follows the methods and framework of traditional lexicography in many ways, such as arranging the words according to their alphabetical order and listing etymology of each word as reference.[15] In addition, BDAG uses the Greek grammar monographs which are probably inherited from the previous edition with no update as its reference, such as *Grammatik des neutestamentlichen Sprachidioms* and *Accidence and Word-Formation with an Appendix on Semitisms in the New Testament.*[16] Without employing appropriate

[10] Lee, *A History of New Testament Lexicography*, 15–29.

[11] Parkhurst, *A Greek and English Lexicon to the New Testament*, 608.

[12] Thayer, *A Greek-English Lexicon of the New Testament*, 613.

[13] Danker, *The Concise Greek-English Lexicon of the New Testament*, 346.

[14] Stanley E. Porter, "Greek Linguistics and Lexicography," in *Understanding the Times: New Testament Studies in the 21st Century; Essays in Honor of D. A. Carson on the Occasion of His 65th Birthday*, ed. Andreas J. Köstenberger and Robert W. Yarbrough (Wheaton: Crossway, 2011), 21; Stanley E. Porter, *Linguistic Analysis of the Greek New Testament: Studies in Theory, Method, and Practice* (Grand Rapids: Baker, 2015), 62.

[15] Lee, *A History of New Testament Lexicography*, 166–71; Porter, "Greek Linguistics and Lexicography," 21.

[16] G. Winer, *Grammatik des neutestamentlichen Sprachidioms* (Göttingen: Verlag nicht ermittelbar, 1867); J. Moulton and W. Howard, *Accidence and Word-Formation with an Appendix on Semitisms in the New Testament*, vol. 2 of *A Grammar of New Testament Greek* (Edinburgh: T. & T. Clark, 1919–29).

modern linguistic methodology, BDAG provides unclear meanings of some words and categorizes the meaning of each word inconsistently.[17] In BDAG, the meaning of σώφρων is defined as "to being in control of oneself" according to the Hellenic model "avoidance of extremes and careful consideration for responsible action," with three glosses "prudent," "thoughtful," and "self-controlled." BDAG distinguishes the contextual usage of σώφρων in the Pastoral Epistles, namely intent on a moderate lifestyle in Titus 2:2, characteristic of the person to be qualified as a bishop in 1 Tim 3:2 and Titus 1:8, and chaste, decent, modest especially for women in Titus 2:5.[18]

Louw-Nida, the first lexicon based on semantic domains, makes a significant improvement to New Testament lexicography in organizing individual words according to their semantic domains rather than their alphabetic orders. Within each semantic domain and subdomain, the semantic relations of words in the same group are ready to be perceived. Furthermore, Louw-Nida distinguishes between the meaning (generic meaning) and gloss (specific meaning) of each word. However, the polysemous approach to lexical meaning adopted in Louw-Nida generates some difficulties in the placement of words within different semantic domains and subdomains.[19] Louw-Nida classifies σώφρων in 1 Tim 3:2, Titus 1:8, 2:2, and 2:5 into domain 88 "moral and ethical qualities and related behavior" and subdomain "sensible behavior, senseless behavior." The generic meaning of σώφρων is "pertaining to being sensible and moderate in one's behavior," with specific meanings "sensible," "sensibly," "moderate," and "moderately." As a derivative of the stem σωφρο- "to behave in a sensible manner," σώφρων may also be rendered as "to have right thoughts about what one should do" or "to let one's mind guide one's body."[20]

As this survey demonstrates, most major Greek-English lexicons follow the meaning of σώφρων in the Attic dialect rather than the Epic dialect to interpret this word used in the Pastoral Epistles. The Epic dialect represents the earliest literary Greek, a literary dialect based primarily upon a form of Ionic dialect with influence from other dialects. Instead of a spoken language, the Epic dialect is a poetic form of language that impacted all Greek poets to a greater or lesser degree. The Attic dialect, often called classical Greek, was the prestige dialect of the Greek world

[17] Porter, "Greek Linguistics and Lexicography," 21–22; Porter, *Linguistic Analysis of the Greek New Testament*, 67–68; Silva, *Biblical Words and Their Meaning*, 172–75.

[18] Bauer, *A Greek-English Lexicon of the New Testament and Other Early Christian Literature*, 987.

[19] Porter, "Greek Linguistics and Lexicography," 22–23; Porter, *Linguistic Analysis of the Greek New Testament*, 48–55.

[20] Louw and Nida, eds., *Greek-English Lexicon of the New Testament*, 752.

for centuries and the base of the Hellenistic Koine Greek. This Koine Greek is the Greek language in the New Testament, the language used as both a spoken and written language in the Greco-Roman world of the first century.[21] In this case, major Greek–English lexicons are correct to follow the meaning of σώφρων in the Attic dialect. Therefore, "having control over the sensual desires," "curbing one's desires and impulses," "to being in control of oneself," and "pertaining to being sensible and moderate in one's behavior" are possible meanings of σώφρων. Accordingly, "temperate," "self-controlled," "chaste," "sensible," and "moderate" are possible glosses of σώφρων in 1 Tim 3:2, Titus 1:8, 2:2, and 2:5.

Determining the Meaning of Σώφρων

To determine the appropriate meaning of σώφρων in the Pastoral Epistles, I conduct a synchronic analysis from a monosemous perspective in this section. As indicated in the above survey, the polysemous approach may have inherent theoretical difficulties in lexical semantic studies since this approach counts the meaning resulting from contextual factors as the lexical meaning of a word. I thus follow the theory of monosemy, which assumes that "a word has a single meaning" and "if a word has more than one meaning, its meanings are related by general rules." In other words, each individual word has one unitary meaning and can have specific functional meanings when it is used in various contexts. The word that has two distinct meanings is actually two different lexemes with the same written form, which is named homographs.[22] In the following lexical semantic analysis, I examine both the co-text of σώφρων within 1 Tim 3:2, Titus 1:8, 2:2, and 2:5 and the co-text of each verse to determine the unitary meaning of this word, paying particular attention to the words that occur in collocation with and have the same semantic domain as σώφρων.[23]

[21] Stanley E. Porter, "The Greek Language of the New Testament," in *Handbook to Exegesis of the New Testament*, ed. Stanley E. Porter, New Testament Tools and Studies 25 (Leiden: Brill, 1997), 99–110; Stanley E. Porter, "Greek of the New Testament," in *Dictionary of New Testament Background*, ed. Craig A. Evans and Stanley E. Porter (Downers Grove: InterVarsity, 2000), 426–31.

[22] Charles Ruhl, *On Monosemy: A Study in Linguistic Semantics*, SUNY Series in Linguistics (New York: State University of New York Press, 1989), 4–6; Porter, "Greek Linguistics and Lexicography," 32; Porter, *Linguistic Analysis of the Greek New Testament*, 50–52.

[23] I have to use Louw–Nida for the assessment of the semantic relations between different words. In addition, I have to use Greek–English lexicons for the meanings of the words that occur in collocation with and have the same semantic domain as σώφρων. I realize that the accuracy of the semantic domains of these words assigned in Louw–Nida and the meanings of these words explained in Greek–English lexicons affect the result of my lexical

1 Tim 3:1–7 presents Paul's instructions on the qualifications for bishops. Within this discourse unit, the word νηφάλιος has the same semantic domain as σώφρων to elucidate the qualifications for a bishop in 1 Tim 3:2. It is worth noticing that νηφάλιος occurs only in the Pastoral Epistles as well, namely 1 Tim 3:2, 3:11, and Titus 2:2. Among these three occurrences, νηφάλιος occurs in collocation with σώφρων in 1 Tim 3:2 and Titus 2:2. Although νηφάλιος and σώφρων both refer to moral and ethical qualities that will lead to related behaviors and both bear the sense of self-control, the two words seem to emphasize different aspects. As the co-text of 1 Tim 3:2 testifies, the meaning of νηφάλιος is related to behaving in a sober manner due to being moderate in drinking alcoholic beverages.[24] In 1 Tim 3:3, the first mentioned characteristic that makes a person unqualified for a bishop is πάροινος, a word that means habitually drinking too much and has the same semantic domain as νηφάλιος.[25] Paul probably contrasts πάροινος with νηφάλιος to clarify the qualifications for a bishop. The co-text of σώφρων within 1 Tim 3:2 indicates that the meaning of this word is concerned with restraining sensual desires. Paul might imply stress on sexual desire since he requests a bishop to be the husband of one woman in the same verse. Moreover, σώφρων has been used to depict the chaste and decent of women in non-biblical literature. The gloss of σώφρων is most likely "temperate" which captures the lexical meaning of this word. The other glosses "chaste," "sensible," and "moderate" listed in extant Greek–English lexicons convey the contextual meanings of σώφρων because these three glosses can be viewed as the result of "temperate."

Titus 1:5–9 outlines Paul's instructions on the qualifications for elders and bishops. Within this discourse unit, the word ἐγκρατής has the same semantic domain as σώφρων appearing in the list of qualifications for a bishop in Titus 1:8. This is the only occurrence of ἐγκρατής in the New Testament, which is in collocation with σώφρων. Again ἐγκρατής and σώφρων both refer to moral and ethical qualities that will lead to related behaviors and both bear the sense of self-control, but the nuance of the two words can be perceived from the co-text of Titus 1:8. The meaning of ἐγκρατής probably concentrates on possessing the power to

semantic analysis regarding the meaning of σώφρων in the Pastoral Epistles. However, due to the scope of this paper, it is impossible to verify the semantic domains and the meanings of the words that occur in collocation with σώφρων.

[24] Liddell and Scott, *A Greek-English Lexicon*, 1175; Bauer, *A Greek-English Lexicon of the New Testament and Other Early Christian Literature*, 672; Louw and Nida, eds., *Greek-English Lexicon of the New Testament*, 751.

[25] Liddell and Scott, *A Greek-English Lexicon*, 1342; Bauer, *A Greek-English Lexicon of the New Testament and Other Early Christian Literature*, 780; Louw and Nida, eds., *Greek-English Lexicon of the New Testament*, 772.

have emotions, impulses, or desires under control.[26] Titus 1:7 lists four characteristics of the person not to be qualified as a bishop, namely αὐθάδης which means being arrogant due to self-will and stubbornness, ὀργίλος which means being inclined to anger, πάροινος which means habitually drinking too much, and πλήκτης which means being pugnacious and demanding.[27] All these words have the same semantic domain as ἐγκρατής and indicate the lack of self-control. It seems that Paul uses these four words αὐθάδης, ὀργίλος, πάροινος, and πλήκτης to contrast with ἐγκρατής in order to underline the qualifications for a bishop. The meaning of σώφρων focuses on restraining sensual desires, with possible stress on sexual desire. As the co-text of Titus 1:8 evidences, Paul commands that the person being the husband of one woman is qualified to be appointed as an elder in Titus 1:5–6. This qualification is also applicable to a bishop as stated in 1 Tim 3:2. The gloss "temperate" can express the lexical meaning of σώφρων.

Titus 2:1–10 states Paul's instructions on the characteristics of different groups of believers. Within this discourse unit, two words νηφάλιος and σεμνός have the same semantic domain as σώφρων to describe the characteristics required for the older men in the church in Titus 2:2. In addition to 1 Tim 3:2, Titus 2:2 is the other instance that νηφάλιος occurs in collocation with σώφρων in the New Testament. The co-text of Titus 2:2 once more affirms that νηφάλιος means behaving in a sober manner because of being moderate in drinking alcoholic beverages.[28] In Titus 2:3, the older women are instructed likewise not to be slaves of wine, which might be counted as an explanation of νηφάλιος. The meaning of σεμνός is probably worthy of respect as the result of appropriate behavior.[29] With respect to σώφρων, the meaning of restraining sensual desires and the gloss of "temperate" are proper in Titus 2:2 as well. Paul's stress on sexual desire with this word is suggested in his encouraging the young women to love and be submissive to their husbands in Titus 2:4–5 which can be counted as part of the co-text of Titus 2:2.

[26] Liddell and Scott, *A Greek–English Lexicon*, 473; Bauer, *A Greek-English Lexicon of the New Testament and Other Early Christian Literature*, 274; Louw and Nida, eds., *Greek-English Lexicon of the New Testament*, 751.

[27] Liddell and Scott, *A Greek–English Lexicon*, 275, 1246, 1342, 1418; Bauer, *A Greek-English Lexicon of the New Testament and Other Early Christian Literature*, 150, 721, 780, 826; Louw and Nida, eds., *Greek-English Lexicon of the New Testament*, 756, 760, 763, 772.

[28] Liddell and Scott, *A Greek–English Lexicon*, 1175; Bauer, *A Greek-English Lexicon of the New Testament and Other Early Christian Literature*, 672; Louw and Nida, eds., *Greek-English Lexicon of the New Testament*, 751.

[29] Liddell and Scott, *A Greek–English Lexicon*, 1591; Bauer, *A Greek-English Lexicon of the New Testament and Other Early Christian Literature*, 919; Louw and Nida, eds., *Greek-English Lexicon of the New Testament*, 747.

Again Titus 2:1–10 is Paul's instructions on the characteristics of different groups of believers. Within this discourse unit, two words ἁγνός and ἀγαθός have the same semantic domain as σώφρων to depict the characteristics required for the young women in the church in Titus 2:5. Both ἁγνός and ἀγαθός denote good qualities in moral and ethical sense. The former means pure without moral and ethical defect or blemish, while the latter means positive moral and ethical characters of the most general nature.[30] The co-text of σώφρων within Titus 2:5 and the co-text of Titus 2:5 both confirm that the meaning of this word should be restraining sensual desires, which probably hints at stress on sexual desire. In the same verse, Paul exhorts the young women to be submissive to their husbands. Paul also urges the young women to love their husbands in Titus 2:4. The lexical meaning of σώφρων can be rendered by the gloss "temperate."

Verifying the Meaning of Σώφρων

Since there is no Hebrew counterpart of σώφρων that helps to discern its meaning, I verify the meaning of this Greek word by consulting its uses in the Septuagint. Two extant major Greek–English lexicons of the Septuagint, namely *A Greek-English Lexicon of the Septuagint* (GELS) and *Greek-English Lexicon of the Septuagint* (LEH LXX Lexicon),[31] define the meaning and list glosses of σώφρων. GELS explicates the meaning of σώφρων as "capable of controlling excesses and deviations from the right path."[32] LEH LXX Lexicon offers two glosses "temperate" and "wise" of σώφρων without further explanation.[33] However, GELS and LEH LXX Lexicon both adopt the methods and framework of traditional lexicography. By arranging the words according to their alphabetical order rather than their semantic domain and by generating the meanings and glosses of each word almost exclusively with reference to TDNT and other theological lexicons, these two lexicons might be misleading. In addition, LEH LXX Lexicon provides each word with only glosses, which are translation equivalents rather than lexical meanings. As a lexicon, nevertheless, it is supposed to define the meaning

[30] Liddell and Scott, *A Greek-English Lexicon*, 4, 12; Bauer, *A Greek-English Lexicon of the New Testament and Other Early Christian Literature*, 3, 13; Louw and Nida, eds., *Greek-English Lexicon of the New Testament*, 742, 745.

[31] T. Muraoka, *A Greek-English Lexicon of the Septuagint*, rev. ed. (Louvain, MA: Peeters, 2009); Johan Lust, et al., *Greek-English Lexicon of the Septuagint*, 2 vols, rev. ed. (Stuttgart: Deutsche Bibelgesellschaft, 2003).

[32] Muraoka, *A Greek-English Lexicon of the Septuagint*, 668.

[33] Lust, *Greek-English Lexicon of the Septuagint*, 603.

of each word. The translation equivalents can be misleading, especially when they are misunderstood as the lexical meaning of a word.[34] Due to the problems that the two extant major Greek-English lexicons of the Septuagint demonstrate, the uses of σώφρων in the Septuagint must be understood by examining its co-text within Wis 9:11, 4 Macc 1:35, 2:2, 2:16, 2:18, 2:23, 3:17, 3:19, 7:23, and 15:10 and taking into consideration the co-text of each verse.

Wis 9:1–18 recounts Solomon's prayer for wisdom, in which Solomon praises God and petitions God to give his wisdom. Within this discourse unit, Solomon declares that wisdom will guide and guard him because of her all-encompassing knowledge in Wis 9:11. In this verse, σώφρων is used to delineate how wisdom will guide Solomon in his actions. Given the co-text of Wis 9:11, the gloss of "temperate" conveys the lexical meaning of σώφρων. As Solomon explains in Wis 9:12, only with the aid of wisdom that his works will be acceptable to God, he can judge God's people justly, and he shall be worthy of his father's throne. In the light of Jewish tradition which is reflected in 4 Macc 1:30b–31, "rational judgment is sovereign over the emotions by virtue of the restraining power of self-control" and "self-control is dominance over the desires." Hence Solomon needs self-control in his actions during his reign in order to judge God's people justly. In Wis 9:12, σώφρων probably means restraining sensual desires.

4 Macc 1:30b–2:2 elaborates that submission to the Torah enables reason to master the passions and thus cultivates self-control and justice. Within this discourse unit, 4 Macc 1:35 uses σώφρων together with mind and 4 Macc 2:2 uses σώφρων to modify Joseph, the lexical meaning of which in both verses can be captured by the gloss "temperate." In 4 Macc 1:35, the author contends that all the impulses of the body are restrained by the "temperate" mind. In 4 Macc 2:2, the author mentions the "temperate" Joseph, who resisted the temptation of his master's wife, as the exemplar of overcoming sexual desire by mental effort. In 4 Macc 1:35 and 2:2, the meaning of σώφρων must be defined as restraining sensual desires. The former generally deals with sensual desires, whereas the latter specifically refers to sexual desire.

4 Macc 2:24–3:18 clarifies reason's ability to master the passions of the body and soul by discussing whether reason is able to completely eradicate or merely restrain the passions. Within this discourse unit, 4 Macc 2:16, 2:18, and 3:17 all use σώφρων together with mind, while 4 Macc 2:23 uses σώφρων to modify the person who submits to the Torah. The gloss of "temperate" expresses the lexical meaning of this word in

[34] Porter, *Studies in the Greek New Testament*, 53.

these four verses. The author asserts the power of the "temperate" mind to repel all malicious emotions in 4 Macc 2:16, to get the better of the emotions by correcting some and rendering others powerless in 4 Macc 2:18, and to conquer the drives of the emotions and quench the flames of frenzied desires in 4 Macc 3:17. 4 Macc 2:23 is the author's statement that the person who lives subject to the Torah given by God to the mind is "temperate" and can rule a just, good, and courageous kingdom. In 4 Macc 2:16, 2:18, 2:23, and 3:17, σώφρων is employed to mean restraining sensual desires in the general term.

4 Macc 3:19–4:26 narrates historical precedents to demonstrate that observing the Torah enables reason to master the passions. Within this discourse unit, 4 Macc 3:19 uses σώφρων to modify reason, the lexical meaning of which is properly rendered by the gloss "temperate." This verse invites the readers to a narrative demonstration of "temperate" reason. In 4 Macc 3:19, restraining sensual desires rightly defines the meaning of σώφρων, which denotes the desires of the body and soul in general.

4 Macc 6:31–7:23 reiterates reason's ability to master the passions and commends Eleazar. Within this discourse unit, 4 Macc 7:23 uses σώφρων to modify the person who can master the emotions, with the gloss "temperate" reflecting its lexical meaning. The author claims in this verse that only the wise, "temperate," and courageous people are masters of their emotions. In 4 Macc 7:23, the meaning of σώφρων should be restraining sensual desires, with no particular emphasis.

4 Macc 14:11–15:32 expounds that reason is able to master parental affection utilizing the example of the mother of the seven sons. Within this discourse unit, 4 Macc 15:10 uses σώφρων to modify the seven sons. The lexical meaning of this word can be conveyed by the gloss "temperate." In this verse, the author explains the reason for the seven sons' obeying their mother even to death in keeping the ordinances is that they were righteous, "temperate," self-controlled, brave, and magnanimous as well as loved their brothers and their mother. In 4 Macc 15:10, σώφρων most likely means restraining sensual desires and refers to any desire in the general sense.

Conclusion

Based on the lexical semantic analysis above, I conclude that the meaning of σώφρων in the Pastoral Epistles should be defined as restraining sensual desires, with possible stress on sexual desire. The gloss "temperate" captures the lexical meaning of σώφρων. According to the examination of both the co-text of σώφρων within 1 Tim 3:2, Titus 1:8, 2:2, and 2:5 and the co-text of each verse, which pays particular attention to the words that occur in collocation with and have the same semantic domain as this word, the meaning and gloss of σώφρων proposed in this paper are appropriate in the context of all four occurrences. In both 1 Tim 3:2 and Titus 1:8, σώφρων is used to elucidate the qualifications for a bishop, with the former alongside νηφάλιος and the latter alongside ἐγκρατής. In Titus 2:2, σώφρων is used together with νηφάλιος and σεμνός to describe the characteristics required for the older men in the church. In Titus 2:5, σώφρων is used together with ἁγνός and ἀγαθός to depict the characteristics required for the young women in the church. Furthermore, the meaning and gloss of σώφρων proposed in this paper are verified by the uses of this word in the Septuagint. Wis 9:11, 4 Macc 1:35, 2:2, 2:16, 2:18, 2:23, 3:17, 3:19, 7:23, and 15:10 all use σώφρων to mean restraining sensual desires. It is worth noticing that 4 Macc 2:2 specifically refers to sexual desire. In the Pastoral Epistles, σώφρων signifies a moral and ethical quality not only for church leaders particularly but also for the congregation generally. This word represents a fundamental characteristic of the Christian life and a distinctive feature of the Pastoral Epistles.

Yan MA
Canadian Chinese School of Theology
Tyndale University
3377 Bayview Ave
Toronto, ON M2M 3S4
CANADA
yma.ccst@tyndale.ca

RECENSIONES Y PRESENTACIÓN DE LIBROS

Recensiones

Marc Grønbech-Dam, *Jesus as the Son of 1–2 Samuel's David: An Intertextual Reading of the Gospel of Matthew*, Biblical Interpretation Series 222 (Leiden/Boston: Brill, 2024). ISBN 978-9004693883.

In this important monograph, Marc Grønbech-Dam, who currently works as Assistant Professor of New Testament at Vanguard University in California, conducts an intertextual reading of David's role as shepherd-ruler of Israel as depicted in 1–2 Samuel in the Gospel of Matthew (p. 2) to consider Matthew's portrayal of Jesus "as a new type of Davidic shepherd-ruler (Matt 2:6)". Grønbech-Dam is surprised that such a study has not yet been conducted, especially because Jesus is depicted as υἱοῦ Δανίδ ("David's son") in Matt 1:1, which invites readers to consider the relation of this Gospel and 1–2 Samuel (p. 2). Therefore, Grønbech-Dam "systematically explore[s] all potential intertextual links between 1–2 Samuel and Matthew" (p. 15). Particular attention is paid to the Davidic commission in 2 Sam 5:2 and its reuse in Matt 2:6 "and their coupling of shepherding and the term נגיד/ἡγούμενος" (p. 15). Grønbech-Dam identifies this as a composite citation that he rightly treats as programmatic for Matthew's portrayal of Jesus.

To accomplish the goal of this study, Grønbech-Dam structures his monograph in nine chapters, beginning with "The Question of 1–2 Samuel in Matthew" (ch. 1, pp. 1–20) in which the reason for this study is explained, recent history of Matthean research is provided, the plan of this study is stated, and its assumptions and limitations are explained. This is followed by chapter 2, "Methodology" (pp. 21–49) in which the genre of this Gospel is examined, the methodological tools of narrative criticism and intertextually of this study are explained, which are informed among others by the works of Richard B. Hays, Dale C. Allison, and Ulrich Luz. Because Matt 2:6/2 Sam 5:2 contains imagery of David shepherding the people Israel, chapter 3 (pp. 50–59) explains what it means for a ruler to be called a shepherd in both an Ancient Near East context as well as in the Jewish Scriptures (p. 15). Chapter 4, "The Shepherd-Ruler in 1–2 Samuel" (pp. 60–82), explores how the image of shepherd-ruler relates to kingship in these Jewish texts as well as to the ways that David as king secures justice and righteousness. Chapter 5 next examines how the Davidic shepherd-ruler emerged in the prophets, extra-canonical writings, and other texts that were roughly contemporaneous with the Gospel of Matthew (pp. 83–99).

The chapters thereafter make a textual analysis of Matthean passages in which intertextual links are shared between Matthew and 1–2 Samuel, thus of "1–2 Samuel in Matthew 1–4" in ch. 6 (pp. 100–142), of "1–2 Samuel in Matthew 5–20" in ch. 7 (pp. 143–179), and of "1–2 Samuel in Matt 21–28" in ch. 8 (pp. 180–230). Finally, conclusions about the occurrences of 1–2 Samuel in Matthew are summarized and their effect on Matthew's story are examined in ch. 9 (pp. 231–248). Here, the author suggests that Matthew often highlights the themes of mercy, justice, and righteousness, which are crucial to kingship in 1–2 Samuel and are evoked in Matthew to depict Jesus not as "militaristic" (p. 234), but instead "as a merciful and righteous ruler who is greater than David of old" (p. 16). The book closes with an appendix (pp. 249–260) listing possible but not unquestionable intertexts shared between 1–2 Sam and Matthew, before concluding with a bibliography (pp. 261–317).

Grønbech-Dam's work is significant for several reasons. First, his monograph reframes Matthew's "son of David" designation not as a militaristic figure who exerts territorial rule and triumph (as argued by some scholars like Joel Willitts; cf. pp. 233–234), but as a just and merciful ruler—a shepherd in the tradition of David as portrayed in 1–2 Samuel, as suggested by the studies of Konradt and Blumenthal (p. 234). Additionally, Grønbech-Dam's study enhances the understanding of how New Testament authors re-read and re-frame the Hebrew Scriptures not just through explicit quotations but through more subtle allusions that shape theological messaging and narrative coherence. Throughout his work, the author interacts with Davidic shepherd-ruler motif in numerous ancient and modern languages, including Hebrew and rabbinic texts (cf. e.g., pp. 60–81), Second Temple Jewish literature, including Qumran texts, pseudepigrapha, and Hellenistic Jewish writings (cf. e.g., pp. 83–97), Latin writings (cf. e.g., p. 127), French literature (cf. e.g., p. 119), and with German texts (cf. e.g., pp. 75, 92, 110, 111). By situating the Davidic shepherd-ruler motif in this broad literary context, the author provides a historically plausible and extensively researched thesis in which Matthew's allusions would have resonated with his intended audience.

The methodological framework of Grønbech-Dam's text is especially noteworthy. Drawing on and refining the criteria developed by Ziva Ben-Porat, Dale Allison, Richard B. Hays, and Ulrich Luz (pp. 39–45), the author establishes a nuanced spectrum of intertextual relationships, from explicit citations to more subtle echoes and thematic correspondences. Chapters 2 and 3 outline this methodology with clarity, integrating insights from literary, narratological, and socio-historical approaches. Particularly compelling is the sustained focus on the term נָגִיד and its Greek counterpart ἡγούμενος, which Grønbech-Dam traces through both the Hebrew Scriptures and the Matthean narrative to underscore a conception of Davidic kingship centered on justice and shepherding rather than militarism.

In light of these strengths, Grønbech-Dam's monograph makes a significant contribution to biblical studies, particularly for Matthean scholars and for those interested in intertextuality and Second Temple Judaism. It combines exegetical precision with theological depth, offering a new lens – namely an intertextual analysis of Matthew's use of use of the Davidic shepherd-ruler image of 1–2 Samual – for understanding Matthew's Gospel. New Testament scholars and graduate students in biblical studies, particularly those interested in intertextuality, Matthean Christology, or the Davidic tradition, will profit greatly from Grønbech-Dam's insightful text.

While the monograph is technical in places and presumes a level of familiarity with biblical languages and intertextual methodology, it remains accessible to a wide variety of fields and interests.

Andrew Bowden
abowden@uni-mainz.de

Martin M. Culy - Mikeal C. Parsons, - Josiah D. Hall, *Acts 1-14, vol I; Acts 15-28, vol. II. A Handbook on the Greek Text.* Second Edition. Revised and Expanded. (Waco, Texas: Baylor University Press, 2022). Volume I: ISBN 978-1481313247, Volume II: ISBN 978-1481313254.

The two volumes under review, *Acts 1–14* and *Acts 15–28: A Handbook on the Greek Text*, constitute a thoroughly revised and expanded version of the earlier one-volume edition by Mikeal C. Parsons and Martin M. Culy (*Acts: A Handbook on the Greek Text* BHGNT Series, 2003), and are edited by the same editors, now together with Josiah D. Hall. They are part of the *Baylor Handbook on the Greek New Testament* series—a series dedicated to providing a grammatical analysis of books of the New Testament. The series already includes the Gospels (Matthew 1–14; 15–28 [2019]; Mark [2 vols., 2014]; Luke [2010]; John [2 vols., 2020]), Pauline Epistles (Romans [2023]; 1 Corinthians [2 vols, 2016]; 2 Corinthians [2015]; Galatians [2014]; Ephesians [2009]; Philippians [2020]; Colossians and Philemon [2013]), General Epistles (James [2013]; 1 Peter [2010]; 2 Peter and Jude [2011]; 1-3 John [2004]), Pastoral Epistles (1 & 2 Timothy, Titus [2017]), and Revelation ([2016]).

The re-issue in two parts follows the natural division of the Acts narrative (chapters 1–14 and 15–28) and provides a verse-by-verse grammatical analysis of the Greek text, making it especially useful for students and readers seeking close linguistic engagement with a book that contains approximately 2,000 non-classical vocabulary items and poses significant syntactic challenges.

Each of the two volumes begins with a substantial introduction, duplicated in each—a defensible editorial decision for readers consulting a single volume, though somewhat redundant for those engaging with the full set. This introduction opens with a five-page note by the series editors (Martin Culy and Lidija Novakovic), followed by a two-page acknowledgements section and a list of grammatical abbreviations. It is followed by a 15-page essay introducing the two-volume work (pp. xxi–xxxv). The main content presents the English text in segments (e.g., Acts 1:1–14, 1:15–26, etc.), followed by the Greek text arranged verse by verse and, accompanied by a full grammatical analysis of virtually every word. The volume concludes with several helpful reference tools: a glossary of grammatical terms (pp. 379–387), a works cited list (pp. 389–404), an author index (pp. 405–411), and a comprehensive and remarkably detailed grammar index (pp. 413–438).

The primary aim of the volumes is to provide a comprehensive grammatical guide to the Greek of Acts. Although decidedly not a commentary, the work offers essential linguistic insights that can substantially assist in the composition of exegetical or interpretive work. In most instances, the analyses reiterate information available through standard morphologically tagged digital tools such as www.stepbible.com. Nevertheless, the authors add value through their attention to the distinctive characteristics of Lukan style and Greek grammar, particularly those related conjunctions, discourse markers, and syntactic functions.

A key feature of the handbook is its detailed explanation of the base text adopted. The Acts of the Apostles, as is well known, presents significant textual-critical challenges due to its complex transmission history. The longer, so-called 'Western' text (also referred to as the D-text) and the shorter Alexandrian text (or B-text) have long been the focus of competing reconstructions. The authors adopt the *Editio Critica Maior* (ECM)—available for Acts since 2017—as their base text, which makes use of the computer-assisted Coherence-Based Genealogical Method (CBGM) for evaluating variant readings.

This is of particular interest since the ECM will serve as a foundational reference for the forthcoming NA29 (p. xxi). While the text largely aligns with NA28, the handbook highlights 52 textual divergences (p. xxii), notably where the ECM removes NA28's square brackets—often inserted to mark editorial uncertainty—because CBGM focuses on genealogical relationships between readings and witnesses, rather than attempting to weigh internal and external evidence in the traditional sense.

The introduction provides helpful clarifications on CBGM-specific terminology such as 'text', 'witness', 'ancestor', 'descendant', 'coherence', 'textual flow', and 'transcriptional probability' and the like. Additionally, it explains the ECM's distinctive category of 'A-related witnesses', referring to manuscripts that are genealogically close to the presumed initial text of Acts. These include the majuscules A, B, C, D, and '08' (oddly referred to by its Gregory-Aland number rather than the usual siglum 'E' for Codex Laudianus), as well as the papyri P45 and P74 and key minuscules (33, 81, 181, 307, 623, 1175, 1409, 1642, 1739). Although the CBGM offers innovative ways to visualise textual relationships, its atomistic method—focusing on readings in isolation, often at the level of single words—remains a significant limitation: the global context of discourse and sentence-level coherence tends to be lost, which highlights a broader methodological tension between traditional textual criticism and algorithmic models.

On the grammatical level, the handbook places considerable emphasis on a pedagogically effective functional approach. Technical terms such as 'dative of advantage' (where the action benefits the dative noun) and 'subjective genitive' (where the genitive noun functions as the subject of an implied verbal idea) are used informatively but without unnecessary formalism. The authors also draw significantly on Stephen Levinsohn's work on discourse analysis, offering comments on phenomena such as the pragmatic use of δέ as a marker of further development in the discourse, rather than merely as an alternative to καί, the importance of pre-verbal position for emphasis, and other discourse structuring devices. This grammatical sensitivity represents a notable strength of the volume, as it moves beyond the mechanical repetition of morphological data to foreground features such as word order, conjunctions and verbal aspect—elements often overlooked in discussions of the Greek text of New Testament books.

This two-volume edition stands out as a valuable tool for engaging directly with the Greek text of Acts. Its strength lies not merely in the accumulation of grammatical data, but in the way it draws attention to the distinctive linguistic texture of Luke's writing according to the eclectic edition of his text. The editors succeed in balancing detailed morphological analysis with functional grammar and discourse features—such as word order, connective usage, and pragmatic structuring—offering readers insight into how meaning is shaped at both the sentence and discourse levels. Their sensitivity to stylistic nuance, combined with a clear pedagogical orientation, makes the work especially useful for those seeking to move beyond surface-level parsing. Furthermore, by grounding their textual base in the *Editio Critica Maior* and incorporating the CBGM, they provide students and scholars with access to the most up-to-date textual foundation for studying Acts critically and contextually. In this respect, the handbook could also serve as a useful companion to works that foreground the D-text, such as the four-volume *The Message of Acts in Codex Bezae: A Comparison with the Alexandrian Tradition*, edited by Jenny Read-Heimerdinger and Josep Rius-Camps (LNTS 236, 257, 302, 365; London - New York: T. & T. Clark, 2004–2009), previously reviewed in *Filología Neotestamentaria* 25 (2012) 164–184, which offers an alternative perspective rooted in the Bezan text of Acts.

Laurent Pinchard
lpinchard@uco.fr

Stanley E. Porter and Ron C. Fay (eds). *The Gospel of John in Modern Interpretation.* Milestones in New Testament Scholarship (Grand Rapids: Kregel Academic, 2018). ISBN 978-0825445101.

Stanley E. Porter (McMaster Divinity College) and Ron C. Fay (Liberty University) serves as editors of the Milestones in New Testament Scholarship series published by Kregel Academic. At present two volumes are available: *The Gospel of John in Modern Interpretation* (2018), reviewed here, and *Luke-Acts in Modern Interpretation* (2021). The editors have chosen to highlight the scholarship of a number of key thinkers for each text. In *The Gospel of John in Modern Interpretation* eight scholars were selected spanning from 1825 to the present:

- B. F. Westcott (1825–1901) – English theologian, biblical scholar, and Bishop of Durham, author of *The Gospel According to St. John: The Authorized Version with Introduction and Notes* (1881) and *Introduction to the Study of the Gospels* (1860)
- Adolf Schlatter (1852–1938) – Swiss-German Protestant theologian and New Testament scholar, author of *Der Evangelist Johannes: Wie er spricht, denkt und glaubt* (trans. "John the Evangelist: How He Speaks, Thinks, and Believes"; 1930) and *Die Theologie des Neuen Testaments* (trans. "The Theology of the New Testament"; 1909)
- C. H. Dodd (1884–1973) – Welsh New Testament scholar known for his work on the parables of Jesus and early Christian eschatology, author of *The Interpretation of the Fourth Gospel* (1953) and *Historical Tradition in the Fourth Gospel* (1963)
- Rudolph Bultmann (1884–1976) – German Lutheran theologian and biblical scholar, famous for his work on demythologization and form criticism, author of *Das Evangelium des Johannes* (1941; *The Gospel of John: A Commentary*, trans. 1971) and *The History of the Synoptic Tradition* (1921)
- John A. T. Robinson (1919–1983) – Anglican bishop and scholar, most famous for his books *Honest to God* (1963), clearly influenced by modern existentialist thinkers, and *Redating the New Testament* (1976), in which he argued that all of the New Testament texts were written before A.D. 70; his book *The Priority of John* was posthumously published (1985)
- Raymond E. Brown (1928–1998) – American Roman Catholic biblical scholar and theologian, especially focused on Johnannine literature, author of *The Gospel According to John (I–XII) & (XIII–XXI)* (1966, 1970), *The Community of the Beloved Disciple* (1979), and *An Introduction to the Gospel of John* (2003, posthumously published)
- Leon Morris (1914–2006) – Australian New Testament scholar and theologian, known for his work on the atonement and the Gospel according to John, author of *The Gospel According to John* (1971, revised 1995)
- R. Alan Culpepper (b. 1946) – American biblical scholar, known for his work on the Gospel of John and narrative criticism, author of *Anatomy of the Fourth Gospel: A Study in Literary Design* (1983), *John, the Son of Zebedee: The Life of a Legend* (1994), and *The Gospel and Letters of John* (1998)

Notably absent are Rudolf Schnackenburg, who wrote one of the most comprehensive commentaries on John (*Das Johannesevangelium*, 3 vols.) and

Juan Mateos, a Spanish Jesuit priest and biblical scholar, whose interpretive approach blended rigorous linguistic analysis with a deep theological sensitivity. For Mateos, John's account was carefully crafted, rich in symbolism, dual meanings, and theological depth. He emphasized how John's language functions theologically, not just descriptively. There are others, of course, which the editors acknowledge in their preface: "We of course realize that there are many other worthy and able scholars who could have been included in this discussion. . . . [T]he list of worthy scholars would far exceed the confines of a single volume such as this one." Porter and Fay selected scholars who represented broad backgrounds and methodologies. Bultmann offered a radically different perspective—source-critical, existentialist, and demythologizing approaches to John. As they state, Bultmann is "a scholar to whom most scholarship still must react, not because his conclusions have necessarily endured, but because the force of his scholarship has cast a long and enduring shadow over all of New Testament studies" (12). His influence is evidenced through the scholarship, embraced and tempered, of his former doctoral students Ernst Käsemann (thesis: *Das wandernde Gottesvolk*, "The Wandering People of God") and Hans Conzelmann, who applied Bultmann's scholarship in his work on Lukan discourse.

The Gospel of John in Modern Interpretation consists of front matter (series introduction, preface, list of contributors [7 total; Porter authored two biographies], chapters on each key thinker, and conclusion. The individual chapters were invited papers delivered at the Evangelical Theological Society annual meeting in the years 2014 and 2015. The series introduction indicates the aim: "The series will produce brief biographies of scholars who have had an impact on the study of a given book, corpus, or major issue in New Testament studies, and thereby established a milestone in the area" (9). Porter and Fay continue: "We have intentionally utilized an extended chronology for chosen scholars, in order to show how their impact is felt by subsequent generations," with unique attention given to "life circumstances, the influences on the person, and how that person impacted the specific area in New Testament studies" (9).

The introduction itself is one of the hallmarks of the book. As students of the New Testament have come to expect with Stanley Porter's surveys of scholarship in many other volumes, he and Fay prepare readers to engage the lives and contributions of these eight scholars of modern Johannine interpretation. The introduction is divided into seven main sections: 1. "The Early Church"; 2. "The Rise of Historical Criticism" (especially Strauss and Baur); 3. "Traditional Reaction" (how scholars [e.g., Tischendorf] responded to arguments that diminished the value of patristic testimony and the historical reliability of the Gospel itself); 4. "The History of Religion Movement" (how 19th- and early 20th-century scholars approached Christianity as a religious and historical phenomenon, rather than solely as divine revelation; e.g., Bultmann and how Jesus' teachings were "shaped . . . according to transmissional pattersn that crossed religious boundaries" [28–29]); 5. "New Source-Critical Problems" (note: this is longest section in the introduction; e.g., the rise of the independence view of the origin of John's account [Gardner-Smith → Dodd → John A. T. Robinson]; John Bailey's argument for dependence on Luke); 6. "Literary and Social-Scientific Theories," which Porter and Fay ponder might have arisen out of "general exhaustion over current debates, [and] led to some new directions over authorship, sources, and history, and introduced new literary interpretive frameworks" (37; Culpepper and Jerome Neyrey fit here); 7. "Conservative Resurgence" (e.g., Leon Morris, D. A. Carson, and Richard Bauckham, "the arguably most significant" [41]; arguments like John was written pre-AD 70). The chapter provides a nice timeline for the material that follows and an opportunity to draw readers' attention to contributors beyond the eight bios in the monograph. Be sure to consult Porter's resources in the footnotes.

The chapters are not uniform, meaning they might begin with a more detailed look at an individual's experiences and background (e.g., Porter on Westcott), while another author might provide a brief bio-introduction but work through a man's life and scholarship diachronically (e.g., Yarbrough on Schlatter) or synchronically (e.g., Stovell on Dodd; Jipp on Brown). Worth mentioning, Porter provides an annotated analysis of Westcott's commentary, which feels and reads like a commentary on the commentary. For example, "1:1–18: Prologue. Westcott takes the length of the Prologue as extending from John 1:1 to 18. Westcott's distinctive regarding the prologue is that he believes John 1:1 stands on its own as a kind of title of the Gospel" (64). Porter does go beyond the scope of the book (Gospel), discussing Westcott's interpretations/contributions to the Johannine letters. Certain details that often go unexplored when reading their scholarship are highlighted in the biographies—how many siblings they had, what kind of faith was evidenced in their household in childhood, friendships they formed, obstacles they faced in life and academic preparation, early publications which laid the foundation for later significant scholarly contributions.

Though Porter, Fay, and the other contributors do not mention Erik Erickson, this book is a reminder that the stages of human development are a helpful theoritical framework for analyzing scholars and their scholarship. The interpretations of scholars are not made from experiences. Interpretations, we might say, are the *foreground* of New Testament philology. But they are not made without a context, a very specific historical and socio-cultural *background. The Gospel of John in Modern Interpretation* practices what every philologist believes about the most important texts in human history. That to understand them, we need to know more than just the words penned. We need to know as much as we possibly can about the historical record left behind, every trace of the world in which the authors lived, studied, and wrote.

The most valuable components of the monograph are: 1. The authors have moved well past summary and synthesis. 2. Each contributor introduces readers to a significant scholar and justifies how they have been a leading voice in the ongoing, evolving scholarly conversation over the past two centuries. Some of these voices might not be as familiar to younger students of the New Testament, and a book like this can help them understand the state of the research.

All learning is scaffolding (Vygotsky). Ideas do not come into existence *ex nihilo* (Kuhn). And to quote Solomon, "There is nothing new under the sun" (Ecclesiastes 1:9). This book will make them better students of John and better students of the New Testament in general.

Thomas W. Hudgins
thomashudgins@hotmail.com

Carlos Gil Arbiol, *Escritos paulinos*. Introducción al estudio de la Biblia, 7 (Estella, España: Verbo Divino, 2024). ISBN: 978-8490739570.

Carlos Gil Arbiol's new monograph on the Pauline corpus, *Escritos paulinos*, replaces Jordi Sánchez Bosch's 1998 book of the same title within the same series of introductions. To be clear, this is no second edition but rather a new composition by an author with decades of experience in Pauline research and publication.

Gil divides his work into three parts: 1) three chapters on introductory themes (pp. 21–249); 2) seven on Paul's undisputed letters (pp. 251–539); and 3) the Deutero-Pauline letters in three chapters, including one on Colossians and Ephesians, another on Second Thessalonians, and a third on the Pastoral Epistles (pp. 541–644). The Letter to the Hebrews, on the margins of this corpus, has been omitted. The ample page count has allowed Gil to delve deeper into his subject than some shorter Pauline textbooks and to provide footnotes that frequently cite not just one source but a whole slew of them. Besides those ample references, Gil has selected key works, mostly in English and Spanish, for commented bibliographies at the end of each chapter. There is a detailed table of contents ("Índice general," pp. 645–650) in addition to the one-page version (p. 9), but no index.

I leave it to others to review this book *qua* textbook and to evaluate its content in general. Instead, I limit myself here to a review of this book's contributions that fall most squarely within the field of New Testament Philology, for the eponymous journal's readers.

Gil has taken the 1998 Spanish Jerusalem Bible as his base translation for citations, which he has sometimes modified according to the exegesis presented (p. 20). He frequently adds key words and phrases in transliterated Greek, within parentheses. Although some less expert readers will gloss over all of these, he has done well to include them in this thick introduction to a subject that hangs so much on the niceties of the original Greek. Gil aids the reader in encountering key terms in their original context. For example, the church is the *ekklēsia*; by avoiding *iglesia* he helps the reader to rethink the term in its Pauline contexts and to set aside later developments so familiar to us. Likewise, *Jesús Mesías* rings fresh and emphasizes the messianic claim and title in way that *Jesucristo* can do only with difficulty as it rolls off the tongue in a single word.

Although the chapters on the undisputed letters hold the greatest philological interest, Gil's treatment of Ἰουδαϊσμός in Chapter 2 (pp. 97–98) deserves mention, especially since the author has recently published research on the term (p. 98, n. 45). The usual translation "Judaism" (*judaísmo*) is ambiguous, for it can refer to the Jewish religion in contrast with Christianity, but it can also refer to a Jewish identity in continuity with the Maccabees and, more generally, violent defenders of Jewish tradition in the mold of Phinehas (Num 25). So, when Paul refers to his previous conduct in Ἰουδαϊσμός (Gal 1:13), one should not conclude that he refers to a religion left behind after his "conversion." Rather, he refers to the exaggerated and violent zeal for his ancestral traditions that led him to persecute Jews not observing those traditions so strictly. Now I turn to points of philological interest within the central part of the book, the chapters on the undisputed letters.

Gil takes up the difficult term σκεῦος in 1 Thes 4:4 (εἰδέναι ἕκαστον ὑμῶν τὸ ἑαυτοῦ σκεῦος κτᾶσθαι ἐν ἁγιασμῷ καὶ τιμῇ), which he interprets as a metaphor for the body of a male or female believer in Jesus, with a sexual connotation (pp. 281–282). He justifies his preference—*pace* those who read it as a reference to a wife—by appealing to another Pauline usage (1 Cor 4:7), a Septuagintal one (1 Sam 21:6), and the context of 1 Thes 4:4.

In phrases like "the word of the cross" (ὁ λόγος γὰρ ὁ τοῦ σταυροῦ; 1 Cor 1:18), Gil draws out the richness implied by ambiguous genitives (pp. 315–317). Most interpreters read the genitive "of the cross" as an objective one: this word proclaims the event of Jesus's death on the cross. Nevertheless, a subjective genitive reading is also possible, in parallel with the δύναμις θεοῦ of the same verse, which defines it. In this reading, Jesus's cross is the subject announcing its word, the kerygma; the cross proclaims God's power. Gil concludes that both readings are "syntactically possible and semantically logical, and they mutually shed light on and enrich one another" (p. 317).

Gil shows how Paul's choice of two verbs at Gal 1:15, ἀφορίζω and καλέω, are the same ones used for calling great Old Testament figures like Abraham, Isaiah, and Jeremiah, all figures related to the mission to the Gentiles (Gen 12:3; 22:8; Isa 49:6; Jer 1:5; pp. 357–358). The same God who called them has taken the initiative to call Paul to proclaim Jesus the Messiah to the Gentiles. Within the same autobiographical pericope, Paul says that he met/interviewed/investigated (ἱστορέω; Gal 1:18) Peter in Jerusalem (pp. 358–359). Although most commentators put the emphasis on a *visit*, the verb in this context implies that Paul also observes and evaluates Peter; he wishes not only to communicate his acceptance by Peter but also his independence.

In Second Corinthians, Gil underscores the centrality of reconciliation (καταλλαγή, καταλλάσσω; pp. 403–405). He draws on his own research and that of others to argue that, for Paul, mercy achieves reconciliation, not sacrifice: "Sacrifices had to be, therefore, a sign or expression of the will to accept the reconciliation, but they did not achieve it, because only mercy achieves it" (p. 404). That is why Paul employs language of "not taking into account people's transgressions" (2 Cor 5:19) instead of sacrificial expiation. Paul makes novel use of καταλλαγή (and καταλλάσσω) to convey the *novum* of the injured party, God, taking the initiative to reconcile, a use opposite to the term's denotation of reconciliation by initiative of the guilty (and repentant) party. Paul employs this new divine paradigm of reconciliation when he seeks to heal the rift with those in Corinth who have wronged him: "Let yourselves be reconciled" (καταλλάγητε, *dejaos reconcilar* in Gil's own translation; 2 Cor 5:20), he implores with an aorist passive imperative (p. 405). In the usual use of the verb, they should repent and take the initiative to reconcile; in its new Pauline sense, theirs is merely to respond to the reconciliation here on offer from God and Paul.

In Philippians, the vocabulary of communion (κοινωνία, συγκοινωνός, κοινωνέω, συγκοινωνέω) rings out more than in any other (pp. 429–430). Gil explains that the Philippians have shared in Paul's suffering and difficulties (Phil 1:7; 4:14), have supported him financially (Phil 4:15), and live a similar lifestyle in a social standing similar to Paul's. He rightly dedicates special attention to the kenotic hymn (Phil 2:6–11), presenting it in his own translation and formatting (pp. 442–448). The hymn, probably pre-Pauline for Gil, culminates in the last phrase of Phil 2:8: "He humbled himself ¦ being obedient unto death ¦ and a cross-death [*y una muerte de cruz*]." The διό ("for this reason") with which the next verse (Phil 2:9) begins is key, for here the poem moves from descent to ascent, and to the explanation for the κένωσις that preceded.

In Romans, another ambiguous genitive, δικαιοσύνη θεοῦ (Rom 1:17), has been a *crux interpretum* (pp. 497–498). Traditionally, most Protestant exegetes opted for a subjective genitive, considering God to have acted to bring about a forensic justice whereby the sinner is declared just. Catholic and Calvinist exegetes, by contrast, have read here an objective genitive, seeing this justice as the result of the believer's interior transformation; by God's grace the believer can attain justice. This duality has in large part been overcome, and a focus on the Pauline use of the term (more than on the respective dogmatic theologies) allows one to go beyond the old Protestant-Catholic divide. Justice is the fruit of revelation (δικαιοσύνη γὰρ θεοῦ ἐν αὐτῷ ἀποκαλύπτεται; Rom 1:17) and must be understood within a covenantal framework: God's plan to choose and save a people was interrupted by Israel's infidelity but has now been reestablished through the Jesus event. This communitarian, social, and historical aspect has often been overlooked in the history of interpretation of Romans. Near the end of this final undisputed letter, κοινωνία (Rom 15:26) can be translated "collection [of money]," just as the Philippians' financial support constituted a sign of communion with Paul (p. 482). By this point in the textbook it is obvious that Gil deals directly with the Greek text, for anyone working from a translation would miss unexpected terms like this one underlying the vernacular translation.

Gil already explained in Chapter 3 why he considers only the seven undisputed letters to be authored by Paul; the rest he considers pseudepigraphal, and these receive a briefer treatment in the book's third and final part. He provides an interesting list of terms underscoring the danger of the Colossians falling into syncretistic practices, from Col 2:8-23 (p. 550): συλαγωγέω ("apprehend"), κενός ("false"), ἀπάτη ("deception"), σκιά ("shadow"), καταβραβεύω ("to cheat"), ἐμβατεύω ("invade"), εἰκῇ ("in vain"), φθορά ("corruption"), ἐθελοθρησκία ("*à la carte* religion"). The Ephesians, likewise, faced the threat of syncretism, which its authors warned about in similar terms, like Μηδεὶς ὑμᾶς ἀπατάτω κενοῖς λόγοις (Eph 5:6; cf. Col 2:8).

In the chapter on the Pastoral Letters, some readers will be drawn to the treatment of "The roles of some noteworthy believers" (pp. 624–634), especially the (eventual) ministerial categories of ἐπίσκοπος, πρεσβύτερος, and διάκονος. Suffice it to say that these letters reflect a stage of development in the leadership of Christian communities that does not yet reflect the clear threefold hierarchy that emerged soon afterwards.

Gil has done a great service for those of us who teach the Pauline corpus in Spanish, by composing such a thorough and learned textbook replete with bibliographical references. Beyond that obvious use, however, New Testament philologists will find in it careful evaluations of key Greek terms and constructions by a well-experienced and well-published Pauline scholar. I expect this book to serve as a reference for students and professors alike.

Kevin Zilverberg
kjzilverbergzi@upsa.es

Travis B. Williams and David G. Horrell, *1 Peter: International Critical Commentary*, 2 volumes (London: T and T Clark, 2003) ISBN: Vol.1: 978-0567030563. Vol 2: 978-0567710604.

The appearance of the new *ICC* on the first letter of Peter is a major publishing event in biblical studies. Williams and Horrell (hereafter W-H) have produced a total of 1,743 pages on the five chapters of the letter. It replaces the first *ICC* on the letter by Charles Bigg (1902) which included 2 Peter and Jude. It provides an up -to- date comprehensive assessment on the scholarship of the letter.

A distinctive feature of the *ICC* is the special attention it gives to text - critical issues. W-H have been fully attentive to these issues, both in the introduction and at the beginning of each section. Notable is the thorough explanation and employment of the Coherence Based Genealogical Method (CBGM), which is the current method followed by contemporary textual critics. Since the Catholic Epistles were the first portion of the New Testament to be subjected to this method, and the *Editio Critica Maior* (ECM) which resulted from that method influenced decisions for the 28th edition of the Nestle Aland text, it is very helpful to have a thorough review of the results in this commentary. W-H have noted nine places where NA28 differs from NA27. Among these the variation at 4:16 is "the most significant, substantial" (1.6) change and calls for close scrutiny.

At 1 Peter 4:16 NA 28 reads μέρει instead of ὀνόματι which was the standard reading in our modern critical editions. The long discussion by W -H

(2.415-417) displays commendable independence from the CBGM/ECM and NA 28. They opt for the reading ὀνόματι , emphasizing that it is the reading of the earliest manuscripts (P72, B etc.). By contrast, the reading μέρει of ECM/NA28 makes its earliest appearance in the ninth century (K, L,P). In addition to questions being raised to the choice of μέρει by several scholars on the basis of the manuscript evidence, there are reasons on internal grounds to prefer the reading ὀνόματι (see *FilNeot* XXX. (2017) 167-174).

Another textual note that raises questions about the adequacy of the CBGM/ECM is at 2:3. The three earliest manuscripts of 1 Peter (P72, P125[vid], and C-S 193 , all late third century) read *χρηστὸς* as Χριστὸς, and abbreviate the word. W-H remark, "It is perhaps unfortunate that ECM does not indicate that the *nomen sacrum* is abbreviated at these points." (1.569). The treatment of this wordplay as a *nomen sacrum* in these three early and independent witnesses points to a very early date for such a procedure, perhaps already current at the time when the letter was written.

The focus of the CBGM/ECM is on the manuscript support for readings. But internal criteria, including the style and theology of an author, are equally important for making textual decisions. That this is recognized by W-H and can be seen in their treatment the variant at 2:5 (including the article with θεῷ). They note the "Petrine author's preference for the article with θεὸς," and they opt for the article and not in brackets against both ECM/NA28 and NA27. (1.597 note e).

Another distinctive feature of the ICC is the attention given to the background and meaning of vocabulary. An important issue in the study of 1 Peter in the last three decades has been the exact meaning of house (οἶκος ,2:5, 4:17) in the letter. Is the word to be understood primarily as a household - that is, a community of people - or as a building.? J.H. Elliott had argued strongly against the temple interpretation, and in favor of the household. W-H point out that the word οἶκος, while not the primary word for temple in the period, was nonetheless used regularly of Solomon's temple and other temples in second temple literature, (1.615. note 73). The "semantic flexibility" (1.616) of the word enabled it to function well with the mixing of metaphors in the passage 2:4-5. Another feature to be borne in mind in answering this question is the wealth of temple images in 1 Peter. Andrew M. Mbuvi, in his *Temple, Exile and Identity in 1 Peter* discovered a number of temple references in the letter beyond 2:5, And the number of temple-associated words in the letter is broader than even those discovered by Mbuvi.

The study of any document produced in the latter half of the first century CE, and especially those works that employ temple imagery, must explore what effect the destruction of the Jerusalem Temple in 70 CE had upon that work. W-H follow the majority view among commentators that 1 Peter is a pseudonymous work produced sometime in that late first century. This was, of course, after the destruction of Jerusalem, a cataclysmic event for both Israel and the church. There is no mention of that event in the letter, and the wording of 4:17 seems to point to a time before the destruction. W-H address this issue in their comment on 4:17 (2.470). This verse is taken by some to be an allusion to Ezek 9:6. W-H place this proposal in the category of "potential (or possible) allusions" (1.47-48). But if an allusion is detected here, as I suspect it is, then it is important to address the question of whether the author is here simply lifting a few words found in Ezekiel (an atomizing approach) or whether the phrase suggests a deeper engagement with the narrative of Ezekiel, which depicts the judgment and then destruction of the temple, and the subsequent restoration of the temple. Is the author echoing Ezekiel's story here? Given the rich use of scripture allusions in 4:12-19, I suspect that the writer has not just plundered words from Ezekiel, but pondered the story of the temple in that prophetic book.

This raises the question as to what other scriptural stories informed the writer and recipients? And how does their use in 1 Peter relate to the use of the same scriptures by other groups within Judaism at the time. In a brief section on 1 Peter's relation to non-scriptural sources (1.52-53) W-H note the strong parallels with Qumran in 2:6-8 and the similarities with 1 Enoch in 3:19-20. Missing from this section, however, is any mention of 4 Maccabees 18:10-19. In common with this document, 1 Peter makes use of Psalm 34, Proverbs 3 and Isaiah 43. These scriptures, among others, appear to have been especially treasured by Jews of the era who were undergoing trial for their faith and steadfastness. Given the striking similarity of scriptures treasured by both documents, it seems reasonable to see 1 Peter, like 4 Maccabees, as a Jewish persecution document intended to encourage God's people in a time of trial.

But to speak of 1 Peter as a Jewish document is to be at odds with W-H who believe the intended audience in the five named provinces in Asia Minor were largely gentile in character. The extensive use of scripture and allusions to scripture stories (Exodus, Abraham and Sarah, Noah etc.) implies that the recipients would have a thorough grounding in the Jewish scripture and story. If they were not Jewish in origin, they would probably be "godfearers" of long standing, who had now made their way from the synagogue to the church.

In line with most contemporary commentators, W-H offer their own case for the pseudepigraphic nature of the letter. But they show thoughtful and respectful attention to the more traditional view. This is especially evident, for example, in the considerable attention they give to Jobes' observations on the stylistic level of the letter (1.155). Their long excursus on "Pseudonymity in Early Christianity and 1 Peter," (1.163-189) provides a thorough review of the issues, and a strong case for 1 Peter as a pseudonymous letter. Among the many strands of evidence they review is 2 Thes 2:2. (1.177). Many consider this Pauline letter to be pseudonymous as well as 1 Peter. Whatever the origin of the letter, the concern, even alarm, concerning letters "as from us" (δι' ἐπιστολῆς ὡς δι' ἡμῶν) was real in the early church.

Nevertheless, the evidence for 1 Peter with a strong connection to the apostle remains viable. With an absence of any doubt about the authenticity of 1 Peter in the early church, with an alertness in the era concerning forgeries, with a reasonable suggestion that Peter collaborated with others (5:12-13), and with the total lack of awareness of the destruction of the temple in 70 CE, the case for Petrine authorship remains viable, even strong. This will not be the majority view in critical scholarship, but it still has much to commend it.

W-H make a considerable effort to define the recipients' social situation and their response to it. Both authors have employed post-colonial perspective, and have produced substantial volumes on the subject (Williams: *Good Works in 1 Peter.* Horrell: *Becoming Christian*). Debate continues as to whether the letter urges conformity (Balch) or resistance (Elliott). W-H posit that the boundaries separating insiders from outsiders was "somewhat porous." (1:722). Perhaps the best characterization of the Petrine author's response remains that of Miroslav Volf, "soft differences."

The lack of any index at the end will impede efficient use of this commentary. Nonetheless, it remains a valuable, indeed indispensable resource, and the most thorough and up to date treatment of 1 Peter. No serious student of the letter can afford to be without it.

Peter R Rodgers
peterrodg@gmail.com

M. Karrer - D. Müller - M. Sigismund - H. Struthwolf - A. Hüffmeier - G. S. Paulson (eds.), *Die Offenbarung: Revelation.* 3 vols. Novum Testamentum Graecum: Editio Critica Maior VI. (Stuttgart, Deutsche Bibelgesellschaft, 2024). ISBN: 978-3438056238.

"The volumes of the Editio Critica Maior (ECM) are not only a milestone in the history of the edition of the text of the Apocalypse, but also in the history of the edition of the New Testament in general. Work on this publication began in 2011 and was published 13 years later. The cover page names six editors (Martin Karrer, Darius Müller, Marcus Sigismund, Holger Strutwolf, Annette Hüffmeier, Gregory S. Paulson) and three contributors (Matthias Geigenfeind, Peter Malik, Oliver Humberg).

The ECM Revelation offers a number of useful innovations over the previous ECM editions (Catholic Epistles, Acts, Mark): Consideration of paratexts such as *kephalaia* numbers, a segmentation apparatus, the identification of *nomina sacra* or *abbreviata*, and the listing of earlier editions.

For the *nomina abbreviata*, the letters that are omitted by the abbreviation are placed in brackets, for example: Ἀποκάλυψις ἰ(ησο)ῦ χ(ριστο)ῦ (1:1). This provides an immediate overview of the words written in this way, which is an excellent feature. In my opinion, this practice (possibly with adaptations) would also make sense for other ECM editions. Concerning the naming of the phenomenon, it is a step in the right direction to move away from the adjective *sacra*, as not all *nomina* are sacred. However, one article explains in detail that there are many words with an overline that are not abbreviated. Therefore, a broader umbrella category seems necessary: One possible option would be *nomina insignia* (marked words), which more neutrally draws attention to the fact that there are certain markings. Words are either abbreviated or marked with an overline or both. It is regrettable, but understandable given the potential workload involved, that the *nomina sacra/abbreviata/insignia* of the Church Fathers have not been documented (1:5*). The cataloging of such words in these patristic writings thus represents a desideratum.

An example of the reference to other editions is "the words of prophecy" (τοὺς λόγους τῆς προφητείας) in 1:3—a formulation that also appears in NA[28]. One can now immediately see in the apparatus that Tischendorf (TIS), however, preferred the reading that is rendered here as b, namely "the word (Sg.) of prophecy" (τον λογον της προφητειας, attested by 01, among others). It is not surprising that the discoverer of Codex Sinaiticus goes for his favorite manuscript here—a decision that in this case was not made in any of the other editions included, as can now be seen quite clearly in the ECM.

The references to conjectures proposed in the editions examined are also worth mentioning. It is emphasized that no conjectures find their way into the main text of the ECM Revelation.

A fundamental change compared to NA[28] is the abandonment of italics in the text since the selected manuscripts from the first millennium contain no significant citation markers (*diples* or textual references *in margine*) (1:14*, 37*). This decision is to be welcomed, as it makes the history of the text and not the editors' assessment the criterion. It turns out that a dozen passages italicized in NA[28] have no citation markers at all in the manuscripts.

The square brackets familiar from NA[28] are not used for uncertainties here. In the ECM Revelation, such square brackets are interpreted as a slightly preferred component of the text by NA[28] (1:46*). This decision makes sense, as the status of the bracketed text is unclear in the Nestle-Aland editions: on the one hand, it is interpreted as an insertion and as such would belong in the apparatus; on the other hand, in the view of the editors, the insertion occurred at such an early stage that they want to make it visible in the initial text, even though it is not part of the initial text. However, the absence of brackets does not mean that there are no more uncertainties in the ECM: instead, there are now many verses in which the editors consider two readings to be equivalent, the "split guiding lines" (106 SGL in total, 1:47*).

In 9 cases, square brackets became SGL (1:51*; if 21,27/20-22 were added, it would be 10). In all other cases (i.e., 97 or 96), these are newly introduced SGL. One gets the impression that the concept of a single initial text is becoming increasingly unstable, as each SGL ultimately stands not for one but for several initial texts. In addition, 19 SGL were controversial in the Main Editorial Board, and there were minority votes against certain SGL (1:60*). The fact that not only the disagreements regarding the SGL but also other differences of opinion are documented transparently is praiseworthy (1:60*-61*). An eye-catching example is the first half of verse 13:7: Here, there was a minority vote to exclude καὶ ἐδόθη αὐτῷ ποιῆσαι πόλεμον μετὰ τῶν ἁγίων καὶ νικῆσαι αὐτούς ("Also, it was allowed to wage war on the saints and to conquer them") from the initial text.

Compared to NA[28], there are 84 "new initial readings" (NIR) and 95 "new initial orthography" (NIO, 1:47*). The most striking change in the text compared to NA[28] is 20:5/1 (1:50*), where an entire sentence is removed from the initial text and moved to the apparatus, namely οἱ λοιποὶ τῶν νεκρῶν οὐκ ἔζησαν ἄχρι τελεσθῇ τὰ χίλια ἔτη ("The rest of the dead did not come to life until the thousand years were ended"). It is not hard to imagine that this major intervention in the text was controversial (1:61*). Most of the other changes concern minor details, such as omitted or inserted articles (e.g., 3:7/38-40) or conjunctions (e.g., 12:2/5). The precise documentation of all SGL, NIR, and NIO is invaluable. It remains to be seen to what extent the changes will influence future editions of existing translations (e.g., NRSVUE, Luther, Einheitsübersetzung, etc.) or new translations.

Of the NIO, the lower-case spelling of people and places is particularly notable. This procedure was already implemented in the ECM Mark and naturally leads to a very different typeface compared to NA[28], for example: τῷ δούλῳ αὐτοῦ Ἰωάννῃ vs. τῷ δούλῳ αὐτοῦ ἰωάννῃ (1:1). In contrast to the ECM Mark, the ECM Revelation uses capitalization at the beginning of paragraphs to imitate the structural features of the manuscripts (3.1: 27).

The segmentation apparatus contains valuable information about the text structure in the manuscripts and reveals the differences between our current editions and the texts of the past. An example: the first line break in NA[28] is between 1.3 and 1.4. A blank line is also inserted here. The reading text in part 3.2 allows a good comparison: here you can see immediately that in the ECM the first line break is placed after 1.2 (without a blank line). Then, in agreement with NA[28], both the line break and a blank line are inserted after 1.3 (3.2: 413-414). If one looks at the segmentation apparatus, one sees that after the last word of 1,2, namely εἶδεν, in Gregory-Aland (GA) 82 there is a major break (¶, here: wide spatium with an additionally highlighted letter of the following word), while in 01 and 2329 there is a break (□, in the case of 01 an ekthesis of the following letter), in 1424 a wide spatium (÷), in 046. 1611. 2351 a high dot (ΣΤ) and in 02 as well as 04 a middle dot (ΣΜ). Important manuscripts use various layout options to mark a caesura, which is reflected in the edition. The manuscripts considered are selected manuscripts from the 1st millennium and are listed in the supplementary material volume (2:391).

The references to the paratexts are highly useful. This can be illustrated with an example from the *kephalaia*: It is clear from the edition that *kephalaion* λ extends from 11:3-10. In the German-Greek edition of NA[28], section 11:3-14 is entitled "Die beiden Zeugen", which is the same title as in GNT UBS[5] "The two witnesses" for 11:1-14. Apart from the different lengths of the pericope, a glance at the supplementary material reveals that the pinax of the Andreas tradition according to GA 2028 chooses the heading "On Enoch and Elijah" (Περὶ Ἐνὼχ καὶ Ἠλία, 2:406), which showcases the directing effect of headings on the reader: the anonymous witnesses in the text become two well-known key figures in the paratext. In addition to such references to the text structure, I would like to particularly emphasize the transcription and translation of supplementary scholia by Anne-Elisabeth Beron (2:403-404). The holistic perception of the manuscripts as artifacts is also evident in David Herbison's compilation of the graphic features of the permanent witnesses (2:419-426).

Overall, the scope and content of the supplementary material are excellent: Not only are the Greek manuscripts listed, quite a few of which were newly discovered or explored as part of the ECM work (2:13-16), but the singular readings are also clearly listed (2:16-66). The latter is particularly helpful if someone wants to analyze the profile of individual manuscripts in more detail. Updated "Text und Textwert" data on the relationship between the manuscripts has also been documented (2:66-93). Additional readings of witnesses that are not part of the ECM selection illustrate the existing diversity of variants (2:95-109). Among the orthographica, abbreviated numerals, accents, spiritus, words with overlines, and other details are explained in a helpful way (2:111-189). For researchers conducting intertextuality studies, the compilation of references to third-party passages is a treasure trove (2:191-192). The patristic quotations show that they are important witnesses, although the editors were unable to find any usable attestation for a number of verses (2:211). The focus is widened to include texts that allow conclusions to be drawn about *Vorlagen*, even if the statement is not considered a quotation (2:211). Allusions are also taken into account (2:225-234). Reference is also made to readings that are patristic, but not from the current selection of manuscripts (2:235). Such a supplementary list will prove helpful, for example, when collating further manuscripts in the future. The significance of the versions for the text of Acts is elaborated in various contributions on the different languages (2:237-389).

The studies on the text (part 3.1) begin with a detailed editorial report by Karrer (I), followed by Müller's remarks on the history of the Greek text. Markus Lembke describes the manuscripts that have subsequently become accessible, as well as the main strands of Byzantine transmission in relation to reconstructed initial texts. The text-historical part is concluded by Berghorn's and Gegenfeind's examination of the special and singular readings of GA 1611 (II). In the text-critical commentary, Karrer and Müller address selected passages (III), after which the controversial verse 2,13 is discussed by Hans Förster and Thomas Paulsen. The latter also deals with the questions of glosses in 13:7 and 20:5 (IV). Jan Krans presents important conjectures from Erasmus to Eberhard Nestle (V). From the field of versions, Skaverelidze discusses the Georgian and Sigismund the Hebrew (VI), which are additions to the notes in the supplementary material (ch. 7). Finally, Siegfried Kreuzer analyzes the biblical references (VII) and Ulrich Huttner city names and minerals (VIII).

In the last volume (3.2), punctuation and text structure are examined in an editorial report and a commentary. There are a total of 710 deviations from NA^{28} with regard to punctuation and paragraph structure. These cases are referred to as "new punctuation", NIP (3.2: 91). Among other supplementary material and appendices, you will find one of the highlights of this volume, namely the reader's edition of Revelation with the Greek structuring. The volume concludes with a list of the people involved in projects related to this ECM and a bibliography.

Overall, it is laudable that German texts are also provided in English translations. However, there are also a number of German chapters that remain untranslated. The fact that the volumes (apart from the apparatus) were not published digitally, but only as print copies, means that it will not be easy for the international audience to have the German texts translated for them using AI, for example.

It is not ideal that you have to look in different places if you are interested in the collations (1:7*). However, given the many years of work and the wealth of material, this is understandable. The comparison lists of the manuscripts should always be compared with the results of the "Coherence-Based Genealogical Method" (CBGM), as the comparison lists are based on a maximum of 123 *Teststellen*, whereas the CBGM compares significantly more instances with each other. An example: The *Teststellen* collation suggests a match of 72% (62/85) between GA 02 and 04 (2:67). In phase 3.1, the CBGM provides an agreement value of 89.5% for these two manuscripts: 2286 of a total of 2553 instances agree with each other.

Texts of the Church Fathers are considered quotations if the wording of a certain passage of the church writer corresponds literally with the surviving text of at least one of the New Testament manuscripts. Ideally speaking, however, these should not be just any manuscripts, but preferably those that are older than the respective Church Father. However, since more recent manuscripts naturally also transmit older texts and dating is often not particularly precise, this approach is pragmatic and reasonable.

With regard to the German texts, it is noticeable that some words are gendered (e.g., "Schreiber*innen", 1:13*.22*; "Leser:innen", 3.1: 32) and others are not ("Korrektor/Korrektoren", 1:12*).

Unfortunately, at the present time, almost none of the abbreviations for the indexing of the paratexts are available online (e.g., G46002 does not yield any hits in the search form https://www.manuscripta-biblica.org/paratexts/ in the PTB inventory under the number G46002 at the time of the review in June 2025). Such links are, however, valuable and useful. This becomes clear from an example that already works: G43016 is listed for 1:13-15. The search form mentioned above takes you directly to the transcription of the corresponding scholia and the link for the images in the New Testament Virtual Manuscript Room. In this case, these are marginal notes in GA 1872 from fol. 209v. Overall, the presentation of the information is very user-friendly. For the paratexts, however, one is not dependent on the online function, as the details of the PTB numbers are listed in the supplementary material volume (2:396-403). G46002, therefore, stands for a zoomorphic sketch in the frontispiece in GA 337 on fol. 332v.

No review can do justice to this four-volume academic achievement, and it will probably take a long time for the plethora of information to be processed by the scholarly discourse.

Zacharias Frey-Shoukry
zacharias.frey-shoukry@uni-rostock.de

Paul L. Danove. *A Case Frame Grammar and Lexicon for the Book of Revelation*. Library of New Testament Studies 666 (London: T&T Clark, 2022). ISBN: 978-0567706027.

Paul Danove continues his exploration of case frame analysis in this volume applied to the New Testament book of Revelation. Danove has been a major proponent of case frame analysis—in fact, to my knowledge, the only New Testament scholar of significance to pursue this line of research. He has used it—or at least a form of it—in all his major monograph publications throughout his career. However, he has gone much further than simply providing such analyses for a variety of predicators. He has extended his work to characterization and to New Testament theology, especially in Mark's Gospel.

This book follows Danove's usual plan of attack, with part one being introductory. The first chapter presents his case frame analysis, which is based upon the construction grammar of the linguists Charles Fillmore and Paul Kay. Danove had the good fortune to study with Fillmore, who was at UC Berkeley, while Danove was doing his PhD at the Graduate Theological Union. The basis of Danove's analysis is what he calls predicators. Predicators are not just verbs but any element that forms phrasal constructions (most are simple but some are themselves phrasal). Verbs certainly fall into this category, but so do other elements that he lists: "participles, adjectives, prepositions, interjections, and conjunctions, as well as those nouns, pronouns, and adverbs that either require or permit the completion of their meaning by other phrasal elements" (p. 3), a variety of which are treated in this volume focusing upon Revelation. The case frame analysis results in identification of arguments that complete the predicator. These are then described with three layers: syntactic function, semantic function, and lexical realization (p. 5). The resultant display is called a valence description. The syntactic analysis involves one-, two-, and three-place predicators (and the two instances in Revelation of zero-place predicators), depending on the number of arguments. The semantic description also involves identification of thematic roles, of which Danove lists twenty-seven (a larger number than most case semanticists). These semantic cases include agent, goal, cause, and condition, among others. The grammar and lexicon to which Danove refers in his title is his analysis of the predicators in the book of Revelation. The two subsequent chapters are devoted to identifying the various features of the grammar and lexicon that are described in the lexicon (which is described in chapter 8 using ποιέω as an example and contained in chapter 9, a chapter of over sixty pages with summaries of the valency descriptions for each of the predicators in Revelation). These features include identifying events and their features (chapter 2), usage features (chapter 3), and further semantic features (chapter 4).

Part two contains three chapters with Danove's case frame analyses of the predicators in Revelation categorized around various types of predicators and what Danove calls their usages. Chapter 5 includes discussion of predicators of transference, motion, location, communication, experience, and capacity (along with some with only one usage) that include the thematic roles of theme, experiencer, and occurrence. This covers a wide range of predicators. Chapter 6 treats usage of other events (and three non-events) according to their thematic roles of benefaction, communion, effect, instrumentality, materiality, modification, partition, and separation. Chapter 7 includes discussion of some grammatical characteristics distinctive of Revelation. As mentioned above, part three includes Danove's lexical example and then the lexicon for predicators in Revelation. The appendix includes three sections, with definitions of thematic roles, the designations of roles, and the 92 usages Danove has identified in Revelation.

Danove's work is rigorous, technical, and clear, even though directly dependent upon his nomenclature. I am not a case frame analyst and have in fact written critically of semantic case (Danove's thematic roles). Nevertheless, I have also been an advocate for his work almost from its outset and believe that there is a place for such analysis, even though I do not follow it. In that sense, the comments that I make below are offered out of respect for Danove's continued work in this area, even if they attempt to raise some questions for further consideration.

Comments on a work such as this may be made on two levels, the first concerning broad questions and the second concerning specific descriptive issues. I will forego the latter to concentrate upon the former.

Concerning larger issues, we can begin with the obvious question: in what sense are all the elements that Danove identifies predicators? For example, are conjunctions predicators? Danove seems to think so, since he includes them in his analysis and his lexicon. However, even he recognizes that there is a difference in the way that he conceives of their description. Even though conjunctions may create relationships between elements, they do so in different ways than do, for example, verbs. However, once the question is raised regarding conjunctions, the entire field of predication is opened. Prepositions are probably not predicators, at least in the same way (or perhaps only metaphorically speaking). One must even raise the question regarding nouns, adjectives, and the like—as does Danove when he admits that there are two nouns in Revelation that do not function as predicators. If nouns are predicators, then why are these not also? This indicates that perhaps predication and its application need to be more tightly defined.

A second major question is: what are meant by thematic roles? The notion of semantic roles or cases (the terminology varies) has long been difficult, in terms of both their number and their conception. Danove at least defines what he means by each of his thematic roles. However, he has a much larger number than do most case theorists—the general thought is that the smaller the number of case roles the better. His definitions, while clear enough in themselves, raise a host of further issues. Besides examples of potential confusion, such as content and topic, there is the larger question of criteria for differentiation. There is also the question of how these thematic roles correlate with traditional syntactical relations. Some appear to be closer (e.g. locative) than others.

A third question concerns levels of explicit description in light of larger contextual considerations. The case frames are focused upon predicators and therefore are limited to the clause as the maximal descriptive unit (some units are smaller, depending on the predicator). This raises two further issues. The first is the explicit role of context and the second is how context plays an implicit role, apparently without theorization. The semantic and even syntactical (depending on the predicator) levels of analysis are dependent upon local contextual considerations (what other linguistic theories might call immediate context or co-text) and even on larger contextual factors. However, case frame analysis does not take context into explicit account, so far as I can tell. To be fair, case frame analysis is not the only linguistic analytic that does not have a robust theory of context. Nevertheless, without one there are contextual factors that play a role in the analysis that perhaps call for further consideration.

The third raises a fourth question concerning the place of text or discourse within case frame analysis. One of the most important trends in recent linguistics has been development of textual or discourse theories, which are directly related to questions of context both narrowly and more broadly conceived. The localized descriptions of case frame analysis do not appear to take textual or discourse considerations into account. Legitimate immediate questions to raise would concern how textual and discourse considerations influence both syntactic and semantic descriptions in light of texts or discourses being considered not just analytic units but semantic units.

The fifth and final question I will ask concerns what exactly a case frame analysis actually does. A case frame analysis provides a means of describing some syntactical and possibly some semantic features of various classes of words and some phrases. Whether all the identified elements should be classified as predicators is a debatable matter, as noted above. There is even some question about the syntactical descriptions because there are, as Danove admits, variations in the valency descriptions due to contextual factors. In light of these issues, one cannot help but wonder about case frame analysis and its valency descriptions—that is, whether and how they are informative, especially in regard to larger linguistic issues, such as clausal syntax and semantics.

This volume by Paul Danove provides a thorough and rigorous treatment of what he identifies as predicators in Revelation. As a result, he provides a lexicon for easy reference. More importantly, he raises questions regarding some fundamental categories in linguistic description.

Stanley E. Porter
porters@mcmaster.ca

LIBROS RECIBIDOS

DE VILLIERS, PIETER G.R. - MERZ, ANNETE B. (eds), *Power in the New Testament.* Contributions to Biblical Exegesis and Theology, 107 (Leuven-Paris-Bristol, Ct: Peeters, 2021) 268 p. 17 x 55 cm. ISBN 978-9042947054.

Influential research by authors like Foucault and Arendt revealed the significant role of power in shaping relationships in society and faith communities. This volume contributes to this research trend by analysing the formative role of power in early Christian documents and communities.

An introductory essay investigates theoretical approaches to power and the nexus between power and religion. It functions as orientation for the exegetical analyses of individual texts in the rest of the volume. Two contributions analyse power dynamics in the Bible generally and nine others investigate its use in specific early Christian texts. They attend to the vocabulary of power as well as the networks and actors involved in the execution of diverse forms of power. They focus on how these dynamics operate specifically in the Gospels, Pauline texts and traditions and the Apocalypse. They show that power can be abusive and dangerous, but it also is a positive, restraining force.

LUTTICK, JANINE E., *Jairus's Daughter and the Female Body in Mark.* Early Christianity and Its Literature Book, 33 (Atlanta: SBL Press 2023). 314 p. 15 x 23 cm. ISBN 978-1628374919.

Jairus's Daughter and the Female Body in Mark challenges modern assumptions that children were disposable and of little interest in the ancient world. Through an analysis of first-century artifacts depicting female children and of the story of Jairus's daughter in Mark 5, Janine E. Luttick reveals how ancient hearers of this story understood the story of the daughter as one of hope and continuity for the newly-formed early Christian 'family' faced with suffering and loss. In this book, the image of Jairus' daugther rises to take place within the greater story of Mark's Gospel as it was heard in the first century CE.

Ma, Yan, *Johannine Portrayal of Jesus.* Mapping "I Am" in the Gospel of John. Linguistic Biblical Studies, vol. 28 (Leiden-Boston: Brill, 2025). 276 p. 16 x 24 cm. ISBN 978-9004715028.

This book introduces a new methodological framework based on the theory of Systemic Functional Linguistics which can examine the linguistic features of the New Testament text.

By applying a two-step discourse analysis model that includes a functional-semantic analysis and a rhetorical-relational analysis, this book argues that the twenty-eight occurrences of "I am" in Jesus's utterances throughout the Gospel of John reinforce John's portrayal of Jesus's divinity. In the light of John's construing of Jesus's divinity, this new analysis of the Johannine "I am" phrases demonstrates how Johannine Christology is expressed through the narrative of John's Gospel with various textual characteristics.

Marchal, Joseph A., *After the Corinthian Women Prophets.* Reimagining Rhetoric and Power. Semeia Studies, 97 (Atlanta: SBL Press 2021). 230 p. 15.5 x 23 cm. ISBN 978-1628374063.

Thirty years after the publication of Antoinette Clark Wire's groundbreaking *The Corinthian Women Prophets*, an interdisciplinary, international, and intergenerational group of scholars reflects upon Wire's impact on New Testament scholarship.

Essays pursue further historical and theoretical possibilities, often in search of marginalized people, including the women of Corinth, using feminist, rhetorical, materialist, decolonizing, queer, and posthumanist approaches to interpret Paul's letters and the history of ancient Mediterranean assemblies.

The contributions from Cavan Concannon, Arminta Fox, Joseph A. Marchal, Shelly Matthews, Anna Miller, Jorunn Økland, and Antoinette Clark Wire reconsider how both the methods and results of Wire's work reveal the possibilities of other people beside Paul who are worth our attention and effort. The essays in this collection introduce students and scholars to the possibilities of interdisciplinary and intersectional approaches for engaging the broader Pauline corpus.

Mathieson, Ruth Christa, *Matthew's Parable of the Royal Wedding Feast: A Sociorhetorical Interpretation.* Emory Studies in Early Christianity, 26 (Atlanta: SBL Press 2023). 410 p. 15 x 23 cm. ISBN 978-1628373301.

Ruth Christa Mathieson's unique reading of Matthew's parable of the royal wedding feast (Matt 22:1-14), which concludes with the king's demand that one of the guests be bound and cast out into the outer darkness, focuses on the means of the underdressed guest's expulsion. Using sociorhetorical interpretation, Mathieson draws the parable into conversation with early Jewish narratives of the angel Raphael binding hands and feet (1 Enoch; Tobit) and the protocol for expelling individuals from the community in Matt 18. She asserts that readers are invited to consider if the person who is bound and cast out is a danger to the little ones of the community of faith unless removed and restrained.

The author offers a strong, well-argued, and creative response to the exegetical and ecclesiological challenges reflected by this text of Matthew 22:1-14 in its canonical form. The strengths of this book are her unflagging commitment to read Mathew against Mathew and the detailed and outstanding intertextual work that she lays out patiently, theme by theme.

Mtukwa, Gift, *Work and Community in the Thessalonian Correspondence* (London: Langham Academic). 226 p. 15 x 22.5 cm. ISBN 978-1839732393.

In this study, Dr. Gift Mtukwa investigates the relationship between work and community in Paul's letters to the Thessalonians. Utilizing an African biblical hermeneutic, he provides a theology of work that takes seriously the communal nature of Paul's context and its parallels with a traditional African worldview. He combines cultural and historical insight with biblical analysis to demonstrate that work has a critical role to play in community formation. It is neither a burden nor an individual pursuit but a purposeful communal activity done to benefit self and neighbor. This fresh look at Paul's work exhortations from a contextualized African perspective offers a powerful reminder that work - like all human endeavors - should have the glory of God and love of others as its goal.

Novenson, Matthew V., *Paul, then and Now* (Grand Rapids, Michigan: William B. Eerdmans Publishing Company). 248 p. 15.5 x 23 cm. ISBN 978-0802881717.

Matthew Novenson has become a leading advocate for the continuing relevance of historical-critical readings of Paul even as some New Testament scholars have turned to purely theological or political approaches. Novenson puts contextual understandings of Paul's letters into conversation with their Christian reception history. After a new, programmatic introductory essay that frames the other eleven essays, Novenson explores topics including the relation between theology and historical criticism, the place of Jews and gentiles in Paul's gospel, Paul's relation to Judaism, the relevance of messianism to Paul's Christology, Paul's eschatology in relation to ancient Jewish eschatologies, the aptness of monotheism as a category for understanding antiquity, the reception of Paul by diverse early Christian writers, the peculiar place of Protestantism in the modern study of Paul, the debate over the recent Paul-within-Judaism movement, anti-Judaism in modern New Testament scholarship, disputes over Romans and Galatians, the meta-question of what it would mean to get Paul right or wrong.

Engaging with numerous schools of thought in Pauline studies, Novenson illuminates the ancient Mediterranean context of Paul's letters, their complicated afterlives in the history of interpretation, and the hermeneutical struggle to make sense of it all.

PARK, SUNG MIN, *The Prestige Language of Christianity in the Book of Acts.* Historical Sociolinguistic Approaches to Multilingualism. Linguistic Biblical Studies, vol. 29 (Leiden Boston: Brill, 2024). 446 p. 16 x 24 cm. ISBN 978-90-04-72708-3.

Researching ancient languages is notoriously difficult in sociolinguistics, due to the scarcity of data. This challenge is addressed by utilizing recent sociolinguistic theories and models to investigate the prestige languages used by early Christians in Acts.

Drawing on historical documents, archaeology, and inscriptions, this study reconstructs the complex multilingual settings of the time. It reveals how Greek, despite the diverse linguistic landscape, became the dominant language in nearly all official contexts of early Christianity. This work breaks new ground in understanding early Christian communities and their linguistic practices, offering historical sociolinguistic approaches to the study of ancient languages and societies.

PORTER, STANLEY E., *The Pastoral Epistles. A Commentary on the Greek Text.* (Grand Rapids, Michigan: Baker Academic, 2023), 970 p. 15.75 x 23.11 cm. ISBN 978-0801027185.

In this book, Stanley E. Porter offers a comprehensive commentary on the Pastoral Epistles that features rigorous biblical scholarship and emphasizes Greek language and linguistics.

This book breaks new ground in its interpretation of the controversial Pastoral Epistles by focusing on the Greek text and utilizing a linguistically informed exegetical method that draws on various elements in contemporary language study.

Porter pays attention to the overall argument of the Pastoral Epistles while also analyzing word meanings and grammatical structures to tease out the textual meaning. Porter addresses major exegetical issues that arise in numerous highly disputed passages and--while attentive to the history of scholarship on First Timothy, Second Timothy, and Titus--often takes untraditional or innovative positions to blaze a new path forward rather than adopt settled answers.

This is not just one commentary among many but a unique commentary on the Greek Text of the Pastoral Letters. It is intensive and detailed (clause by clause, not word for word, explaining the meaning in context); consistent (based on the linguistic method, *Formal Ssystemic Functional Grammar*), thorough and encyclopedic (discussing the opinions of other commentors), and extensible (about 1000 pages). Its language is accesible to the average reader, avoiding technicalities as much as possible. This is a commentary full of original interpretations that presents a new and comprehensive reading of the Pastoral Letters. This commentary will appeal to professors, students, and scholars of the New Testament.

PORTER, STANLEY E, *Linguistic Descriptions of the Greek New Testament*, New Studies in Systemic Funcional Linguistics (London - New York - Oxford

- New Delhi - Sydney: T&T Clark, 2023). 222 p. 17.5 x 25 cm. ISBN 978-0567710055.

Stanley E. Porter provides descriptions of various important topics in Greek linguistics from a *Systemic Functional Linguistics* (SFL) perspective; an approach that has been foundational to Porter's long and influential career in the field of New Testament Greek. Deep insights into Porter's understanding of SFL are displayed throughout, based either upon how he positions SFL in relation to other linguistic models, or how he utilizes it to describe topics within Greek and New Testament studies. Porter reflects on his core approach to the Greek New Testament by exploring subjects such as metaphor, rhetoric, cognition, orality and textuality, as well as studies on linguistic schools of thought and traditional grammar.

PORTER, STANLEY E. - DAWSON, ZACHARY K. - AND WISHART, RYDER A., *The Literary-Linguistic Analysis of the Bible.* The Enduring Legacies of Russian Formalism and the Prague Linguistic Circle. Linguistic Biblical Studies, vol. 27 (Leiden-Boston: Brill, 2024). 488 p. 16 x 24 cm. ISBN 978-9004698956.

This collection of essays explores the rich intellectual heritage of Russian Formalism and the Prague School of Linguistics to illuminate their influence on the field of biblical studies and apply their constructive and creative potential for advancing linguistic theory, discourse analysis, and literary interpretation of the texts of the Old and New Testaments in their original languages.

The contributors to this volume further demonstrate how the ideas of major linguistic and literaty thinkers have been or can be applied by biblical scholars to appropriate them for the analysis of the biblical languages and biblical texts.

This feature is represened in the chapters in various ways. Some contributors focus special attention on contextualizing major figures of the Prague School within their lives, careers, and cultural contexts to illuminate the environments and circumstances in which their contributions were made before showing how they have been developed further and applied within biblical studies. Other chapters focus more on specificic approaches to linguistic analysis often with reference to key scholars, offering detailed descriptions and critiques of their development as they have been apropriated within biblical studies. Still others focus on showing the applicability of theoretical concepts and models that have grown out of Russian Formalism and the Prague School as they bear directly on analyzing Old and New Testament texts. Interpreters of the Bible who have an interest in the historical development of linguistic analysis will appreciate the perspective and creativity offered in this volume. The potential is great for the continuing advancement in linguistic analysis of the Old and New Testament that draws from the linguistic and literary-linguistic approaches that owe much to their Russian-formalist and Prague School roots.

STERLING, GREGORY, E., *Shaping the Past to Define the Present. Luke-Acts and Apologetic Historiography* ((Grand Rapids, Michigan: William B. Eerdmans Publishing Company). 282 p. 15.5 x 23 cm. ISBN 978-0802848734.

Shaping the Past to Define the Present comprises both new and revised essays by New Testament scholar Gregory E. Sterling on Jewish and early Christian historiography. A sequel to his seminal work, *Historiography and Self-Definition,* this volume expands on Sterling's reading of Luke-Acts in the context of contemporary Jewish and Greek historiography. These systematically arranged essays comprise his new and revised contributions to the field of biblical studies, exploring the genre of apologetic historiography exemplified by Josephus and Eusebius, the context of Josephus's work within a larger tradition of Eastern historiography, the initial composition and circulation of Luke and Acts, the relationship of Luke-Acts to the Septuagint, the interpretation of the Diaspora in Luke-Acts, the structure of salvation history as it is manifested in Luke-Acts, the Socratic influences on Luke's portrayal of Jesus's death, the early Jerusalem Christian community as depicted in Acts compared with other Hellenized Eastern traditions such as Egyptian priests and Indian sages and the establishment of Christianity's "socially respectability" as a guiding purpose in Luke-Acts

Engaging with current critical frameworks, Sterling offers readers a comprehensive analysis of early Christian self-definition through Judeo-Christian historiography.